Franks and Saracens

Franks and Saracens is the first and only book to examine the Crusades from the viewpoint of psychoanalysis, studying the hidden emotions and fantasies that drove the Crusaders and the Muslims to undertake their terrible wars.

Using original documents as well as secondary sources, Avner Falk demonstrates that the deepest and most powerful motives for the Crusades were not only religious or territorial – or the quest for lands, wealth, or titles – but also unconscious emotions and fantasies about one's country, one's religion, one's enemies, God and the Devil, Us and Them. The book demonstrates the collective inability to mourn large-group losses, and the collective needs of large groups such as nations and religions to develop a clear identity, to have boundaries, and to have enemies and allies. Falk investigates the unconscious dynamics of the Crusades, both on the individual and on the collective level, to understand why the Crusading fantasies persisted for nearly two centuries, and why the "northern Crusades" went on until the early fifteenth century. This updated edition adds a new chapter on collective trauma both as cause and as consequence of the Crusades and has been fully revised to include literature on trauma and other psychological aspects of the Crusades.

Franks and Saracens will be of great interest to historians, political scientists, medievalists, psychologists, psychiatrists, psychoanalysts, anthropologists, and sociologists interested in questions of conflict, fantasy, and identity, collective psychological processes, and to academics of the Crusades and military history.

Dr Avner Falk (born 1943) is an internationally known Israeli clinical psychologist and independent scholar. His scholarly specialty is applied psychoanalysis, including psychohistory, psychobiography, political psychology, and psychogeography. He has published 11 books and dozens of articles. His most recent book is *Agnon's Story: A Psychoanalytic Biography of S. Y. Agnon*, the winner of the 1966 Nobel Prize in Literature (Brill 2018).

"The Crusades that occurred between 1095 and 1291 are among the most violent and ruthless events in human history. Their religious, historical, political, and economic aspects have been extensively studied. Avner Falk's unusual book, first published in 2010, focuses on the psychodynamic aspects involved in carrying out the Crusades. It illustrates how both individual and large-group fantasies and behaviors, such as perceiving our own large group as 'good' and the Other as 'bad,' the need to establish psychological borders between 'enemy' large groups, the difficulties in collective mourning and the psychology of shared trauma, played roles in the Crusades. This new version of this important book includes an expanded, up-to-date bibliography and a new chapter on the traumatic aspects of the Crusades."

Vamık D. Volkan, M.D., Professor Emeritus of Psychiatry, University of Virginia; Past President, International Society of Political Psychology, American College of Psychoanalysts and International Dialogue Initiative

Franks and Saracens

A Psychoanalytic Study of the Crusades

Revised Edition

Avner Falk

LONDON AND NEW YORK

Designed cover image: Bibliothèque nationale de France

Revised edition published 2025
by Routledge
4 Park Square, Milton Park, Abingdon, Oxon OX14 4RN

and by Routledge
605 Third Avenue, New York, NY 10158

Routledge is an imprint of the Taylor & Francis Group, an informa business

© 2025 Avner Falk

The right of Avner Falk to be identified as author of this work has been asserted in accordance with sections 77 and 78 of the Copyright, Designs and Patents Act 1988.

All rights reserved. No part of this book may be reprinted or reproduced or utilised in any form or by any electronic, mechanical, or other means, now known or hereafter invented, including photocopying and recording, or in any information storage or retrieval system, without permission in writing from the publishers.

Trademark notice: Product or corporate names may be trademarks or registered trademarks, and are used only for identification and explanation without intent to infringe.

First edition published by Routledge 2010

British Library Cataloguing-in-Publication Data
A catalogue record for this book is available from the British Library

Library of Congress Cataloging-in-Publication Data
A catalog record has been requested for this book

ISBN: 978-1-032-86386-3 (hbk)
ISBN: 978-1-032-86385-6 (pbk)
ISBN: 978-1-003-52736-7 (ebk)

DOI: 10.4324/9781003527367

Typeset in Times New Roman
by Taylor & Francis Books

Contents

Acknowledgments vii
Preface viii

1 Us and Them 1
2 Romans, Franks, and Germans 25
3 Myths of Origin 32
4 The Cross and the Crusades 37
5 The Fantasy of the Holy Roman Empire 42
6 A Short History of the "Saracens" 50
7 The First Crusade: Acting Out Rescue Fantasies 56
8 The Latin Kingdom of Jerusalem as a Psychogeographical Fantasy 76
9 The Second Crusade: Persisting Rescue Fantasies 93
10 Templars and Hospitallers: Monastic Knights? 103
11 The "Saracens" Look at the "Franks" 107
12 The Third Crusade: A Lionheart in Search of a Holy Land? 118
13 The Fourth Crusade: "Latin" Christians Kill "Greek" Christians 122
14 The Fifth Crusade: An Invasion of Egypt that Predictably Fails 132
15 The Sixth Crusade: Winning Jerusalem Peacefully 140
16 The Seventh Crusade: The Unhappy War of "Saint Louis" 145
17 The Eighth Crusade: The Tragic Death of "Saint Louis" 150

18	The Ninth Crusade: The End of a Two-Century Fantasy	152
19	Trauma in the Crusades	155
20	Aftermath: The End of a Two-Century Fantasy	166
	Epilogue: "The New Crusaders"	170

Bibliography   172
Index   188

Acknowledgments

I am deeply indebted to Vamık Volkan, a professor emeritus of psychiatry at the University of Virginia who pioneered the psychoanalytic study of large groups such as clans, tribes, nations, ethnic groups, and religious groups, and the in-depth study of inter-group conflict, and to whom I owe much of what I know about the psychoanalytic interpretation of history. I also wish to thank Robert Hinshelwood, who encouraged me at an important stage of my scholarly work many years ago. Thanks are also due to Oliver Rathbone, who published the first edition of this book in 2010. Last but not least, I am deeply indebted to my editor at Routledge, Susan Frearson, for her offer to publish a Revised Edition of this book, whose first edition was inadvertently published with an incomplete bibliography. Without her, this book would not have seen the light of day. I am also indebted to this book's production editor, Alanna Donaldson, for generously accommodating my numerous requests for amendments in the proof stage, which have made this book that much more readable. The responsibility for any errors and omissions is, of course, mine alone.

Avner Falk
Jerusalem, Israel
August 2024

Preface

The reader of this book may be surprised to see many terms that are commonly used by Crusade historians placed in quotation marks: for instance, "Franks," "Saracens," "Latin Kingdom of Jerusalem," "Holy Roman Empire," "True Cross," and even the word "Crusade" itself. The purpose of the quotation marks is to highlight the fact that these terms were often more fantasy than reality. For instance, the people who called themselves "Franks" were actually Normans, Frenchmen, Germans, Flemings, Italians, Englishmen, Spaniards, or members of a dozen other ethnic groups. The "Latin Kingdom of Jerusalem" kept its name even after it lost Jerusalem and most of the "Holy Land" to the Muslims in 1187, and when it only consisted of Acre and a few other coastal towns in what are now Israel and Lebanon. The Muslims who fought the Crusaders never called themselves "Saracens": this was a fantastic "exonym" given them by the medieval Europeans. The word "Crusader" only came to be used centuries after the Crusades were over: the Christian knights and soldiers who "took the cross" and went to fight the "Saracens" in the "Holy Land" during the twelfth and thirteenth centuries called themselves "pilgrims." In that sense, much of what happened during the Crusades, including their extreme violence and extensive trauma, involved collective fantasies that were "acted out" in reality. This book sets out to study the psychological origins of those fantasies and to explain how they came into being and why they were acted out.

The interdisciplinary approach to history is still viewed with reservation and suspicion by some Israeli historians, especially when it involves psychoanalysis, which they dislike and fear. It is better accepted in the U.K., and in other "Western" countries. The psychohistorical approach is especially useful for our understanding of the medieval Crusades, which have not only fascinated novelists like Walter Scott and their readers, or film makers like Ridley Scott and their viewers, but have also been the subject of enormous interest and meticulous study by countless historians, political scientists, geographers, economists, and other scholars. There are thousands of books and tens of thousands of articles about the Crusades, most of them by "Western" scholars. There is a scholarly Society for the Study of the Crusades and the Latin East, which publishes the journal *Crusades*, and other groups for which the Crusades are their primary interest. The derogatory way in which the

"Franks" viewed the "Saracens" – and vice versa – has been thoroughly studied, yet the psychological studies of the Crusades are few and far between.

There are other scholarly journals devoted to the study of the Crusades, multi-volume histories of the Crusades, multi-volume editions of original documents and primary sources of the Crusades, and international conferences on the Crusades. There are books aiming to acquaint "Western" readers with the Arabic and Muslim writings on the Crusades, such as the monumental work of Carole Hillenbrand (born 1943), who, among other things, found that the most important thing learned by the Crusaders who remained in "the Holy Land" was to use soap. Geographers like the late Ronnie Ellenblum (1952–2021) have studied Crusader castles, cities, and villages in Israel to unravel their history (Ellenblum 1998, 2007; Hillenbrand 1999).

One crucial aspect of the Crusades, however, has been largely neglected by scholars: the unconscious psychological motivations of the Crusaders and of the Muslims who fought them. One notable exception was the Scottish psychiatrist William Ireland (1832–1909). During the last decade of his life, Ireland published a two-part article on the psychology of the Crusades, in which he pointed out the "enormous credulity of the Dark Ages" and the "paranoid" nature of the Crusades. Nonetheless, Ireland believed that "the pilgrims [who went to Jerusalem during the Crusades] cannot be said to have acted illogically" (Ireland 1906–1907, Part II, p. 322). A recent psychological study of the Crusades was published by Spencer Ford Rowan, an American late-life scholar who applied Vamık Volkan's theories about large-group psychology (Volkan 2013A) to the Crusaders (Rowan 2023). For an historical subject that cries out for psychological explanations, these studies are like cries in the wilderness.

The incredible fact that one of the Crusades (the fourth) was a "Latin" Christian war on "Greek" Christianity, with no relation to "the Holy Land," and that other Crusades were waged against Basque "Saracens" in Spain and against pagan "Saracens" in the Baltic lands has not seemed odd enough to scholars to warrant a psychological investigation. The Crusader use of the ancient Roman term *franci* (Franks) to designate all European Christians and of the still more ancient Roman term "Saracens" to designate all Arabs, Turks, Muslims, Mamluks, Persians, and even the European "heathen," is only one example of the irrational aspect of the Crusades. The Muslim Arab notion of the Crusaders as totally inferior *ifranji* was equally irrational.

This book sets out to fill the enormous void in the psychological study of the Crusades, to investigate the unconscious meanings of "the Holy Land," "the Holy City," "the Holy Sepulcher," and "the relic of the True Cross" to the Crusaders, and the mutual projections and externalizations of the warring parties. It is a psychoanalytic study of the irrational aspects of religious and ethnic wars.

As this book sets out to offer new explanations rather than to discover new facts, it relies on secondary sources as well as on primary ones. However, wherever possible I have tried to cross-check the facts between the various sources, and to cite only reliable and reputable secondary sources.

Chapter 1

Us and Them

Human evolution scholars, anthropologists, and historians have many theories about how ethnic groups, clans, tribes, and nations came about, but recorded human history is often the story of the wars that they fought. Organized human warfare has existed for the last 10,000 to 15,000 years – a short period of time relative to the hundreds of thousands of years it took for our species to evolve from its African origins. One of the earliest warring civilizations was that of Egypt. The ancient Egyptian pharaohs made war on their neighbors to enlarge their kingdom, yet the earliest archaeological evidence for large-scale organized warfare dates from around 3500 BCE, and a unified Egyptian kingdom was only founded around 3150 BCE by the pharaoh Menes, giving rise to a series of dynasties that ruled Egypt for the next three millennia and, "naturally," made wars on their neighboring peoples to subjugate them.

However, organized human warfare has been with us ever since recorded history and "prehistory," and among its psychological accompaniments have been *ethnocentrism* and racism. Deriving from the Greek word *ethnos* meaning tribe or people (hence "ethnic group" and "ethnic cleansing"), ethnocentrism is the perception of a human "race," tribe, or nation of itself as the center of the world, and racism is its perception of itself as superior to all other "races." Large-group psychology has been developed by the Turkish-Cypriot-born American psychoanalyst Vamık Volkan (born 1932). Among his key concepts are chosen glory, chosen trauma, the depositing of adult images into the child's self-representation, entitlement ideology, large-group narcissism (ethnocentrism), collective mourning, the purification of the group from foreign elements, suitable reservoirs for externalization, time collapse (telescoping), time expansion, and the ethnic tent (Volkan 1997, 2000, 2001, 2004, 2006, 2013, 2013a, 2014, 2017; Volkan et al. 2023).

Understanding ethnocentrism and warfare requires a multidisciplinary approach, involving psychology, political science, sociology, anthropology, and biology (Bizumic 2018). The Italian psychoanalyst Franco Fornari thought that another, deeper cause of human warfare was the collective inability to mourn of large human groups. Those who cannot mourn their losses unconsciously project their guilt feelings on their "enemies," and make

DOI: 10.4324/9781003527367-1

war on them. (Fornari 1975). We shall look into this crucial issue below when discussing the origins of the medieval Crusades.

The American social psychologist James Waller cited psychological experiments, ethnological field studies, and evolutionary theory to argue that human beings are *genetically predisposed* to divide into groups, to value their in-group over other human groups, and to treat those within the group better and more "ethically" than those outside the group. This predisposition has caused or encouraged racism, ethnocentrism, xenophobia, bigotry, hatred, war, and genocide. Our biological heritage also influences our response to authority and our desire to exert authority over others (Waller 2002).

Genocide, the killing of entire ethnic groups by other human groups, has also been with us for millennia (Charny 1999). Waller thought that there are "social forces" that help prepare "ordinary people" to commit genocide. One such "force" is cultural beliefs, like nationalism, racism, or "manifest destiny." Another evil-disposing "social force" is disengaging morality from conduct by displacing responsibility, using euphemisms, seeking moral justification, looking for advantageous comparisons, minimizing, distorting, dehumanizing the other, distancing ourselves from the consequences of our actions (such as not broadcasting the disturbing images of war, concentration camps, or mass killing; calling torture "abuse" and calling the destruction of a village "liberation"). Waller believed that the more highly regarded one's self-interest becomes, the easier it is to justify evil done to others (Waller 2002).

Language is of primary importance in the formation of large groups. Languages developed when human beings communicated with one another by uttering sounds that designated objects. (Locke & Bogin 2006). Ethnic groups formed when people who spoke the same language got together. *Ethnonyms* (Greek for peoples' names) are the *names* that large human groups have given themselves and other groups. They are divided into *endonyms* and *exonyms*, and they are psychologically significant and fascinating. An *endonym* or *autonym* (a self-appellation), is the name that the local people call themselves. An *exonym* is a name for a people or place that is not used within that place by the local inhabitants (neither in the official language of the state nor in local languages), or a name for a people or language that is not used by the people or language to which it refers themselves. For example, the ancient Greeks called themselves *Hellenes*, while the Romans called them *Graeci* and the Jews called them *Ionim* (Ionians), which was later corrupted into *Yevanim* when the Hebrew scriptures were vocalized in the tenth century by Jewish scholars in Tiberias who only spoke Arabic, Hebrew, and Aramaic.

Some endonyms and exonyms may be neutral, while others may be highly prejudicial. *Deutschland,* which comes from *Teutschland* (the people's land), is the Germans' endonym for their own country, while *Germany* is the English exonym for that same country and *l'Allemagne* is the French exonym for it. In the Slavic languages, however, the Germans are called *niemci*, meaning "mute" or "dumb." *Spanish* is the English exonym for the language whose speakers call it *español* or *castellano*. In the Spanish language, *inglés* is the exonym for either an English male person or the English language. The Greeks called their Persian enemies and others who could not speak Greek *barbaroi* (barbarians) because that was how their speech sounded to them.

Endonyms and exonyms are part of human group psychology. Human groups, such as families, clans, tribes, peoples, and nations, have tended to place themselves in the center of the world and to see other groups as inferior or even inhuman. We call this tendency today ethnocentrism or racism. The warring indigenous tribes of North America, who may have come there from Central Asia through *Beringia* (the then land-covered Bering Straits) some twelve thousand years ago, often called their own tribe "the human beings" and all other tribes, their enemies, non-human. The ethnic group's perception of the other, the stranger, the enemy has always been distorted and unrealistic, and it was always given derogatory names. The endonym of the North American "Apache" (a Spanish exonym) is *indeh* meaning the people, or the human beings, and their exonym for other tribes is *indah,* meaning the non-humans or non-people (Ball 1970, 1980; Haley 1981).

Similarly, orthodox Jews have perceived ourselves since ancient times as the Chosen People and our exonym for non-Jews is *goyim* (gentiles), which has become a pejorative term, while some ultra-orthodox Jews also call them *shkotsim* (abominations). Orthodox Jews also call non-Jews "idolaters" or "worshipers of stars and astrological signs." The *Talmud*, the record of rabbinic discussions pertaining to Jewish law, ethics, customs, and history which is second only to the Hebrew Bible in importance, has verses saying that we are human (*adam*) while pagan people are not human: "And ye, my flock, the sheep of my pastures, ye are called *adam*; ye are called *adam*, but the idolaters are not called *adam*" (Epstein 1935–1948, *Yebamoth,* Chapter VI, Folio 61a, and *Nezikin*, Chapter IX, *Baba Mezi'a,* Folio 114b). The English rendering of the Hebrew word *adam* as "men" in this work is erroneous.

The Hebrew word *mashiakh,* rendered in English as "Messiah," means "anointed." It referred to the ancient kings of Judah and Israel, who were crowned by being anointed with the "oil of anointment." The Greek word for "anointed" is *christos*, and in the Greek-language "Septuagint" translation of the Old Testament, made by Alexandrian Jews from the third to the first century BCE., *mashiakh* was always rendered as *christos*. Nonetheless, the Talmudic Hebrew name (as well as the modern Hebrew word) for the Christians is not *meshikhiyim* (messianic) but *notsrim* (people from Nazareth), referring to the fact that Jesus came from Nazareth. The term was designed to deny or mask the fact that Christians believe that Jesus was their Christ or Messiah.

Just as the ancient Greeks called all those who could not speak Greek *barbaroi*, the Russians call the Germans *niemtsi*, meaning "mute people," because they cannot speak Russian. The ancient Persians called themselves *arya*, meaning noble people, and the name Iran comes from the ancient Avesta (old Persian) name *Arya-nam* meaning "land of the noble people."

One of the etymological and historical theories of the origins of the word "Aryan," the so-called "Aryan-invasion theory," is that following an "Aryan" invasion of northwest India (now Pakistan) from Persia (now Iran) in the second millennium BCE, the Avesta Persian word *arya* entered the Indian Sanskrit language to denote the light-skinned people of the north, as opposed to the dark-skinned *dravida* from the south. The so-called Indo-Aryans derived from an earlier Proto-Indo-Iranian stage, usually identified with the Bronze Age Andronovo culture at the Caspian Sea. Their migration to and within Northern India is consequently presumed to have taken place in the Middle to Late Bronze Age, contemporary to the Late Harappan phase in Indian history (1700 to 1300 BCE).

According to this theory, from the Sanskrit language of India, the word *Aryan* passed to the "Indo-European" or "Indo-Aryan" languages, including Greek and Latin. In the twentieth century, Adolf Hitler's German Nazis imagined themselves as *Arier* (Aryans), *Indogermanen* (Indo-Germans) and a *Herrenvolk* (master people or master race), and other people as *Untermenschen* (subhuman). They were convinced that "white Aryans" had reached Persia and India from Northern Europe, and, ironically, the Nazi *Hakenkreuz* or swastika, symbol of murder, massacre, and genocide, was a mirror image of an ancient Hindu religious symbol of peace and harmony. Fervently believing in their superiority fantasies, the German Nazis outlawed marriage between "Aryans" and "non-Aryans."

The Nazi Germans murdered not only six million "subhuman" Jews but also millions of "gypsies" (Roma and Sinti), communists, Catholics, homosexuals, retarded people, mentally-ill people – *all those people whom they considered "subhuman" and who unconsciously represented painful aspects of their own self to them.* The fantasy about the "gypsies" was that they had come from Egypt (hence their exonym), whereas they had actually migrated from India in the Middle Ages. An English writer has published a novel describing in the first person singular, the mass murder of the Jews from the point of view of one of their murderers, an S.S. officer who also has a variety of sexual perversions. (Littell 2006). Why are such groups as tribes and nations – and why were the German Nazis in particular – so susceptible to viewing the "enemy" as inhuman, to dehumanize and demonize him, and then to exterminate him? I have tried to answer some of these questions in my book on antisemitism (Falk 2008).

The American psychoanalyst David M. Terman believed that both ancient pagan and later Christian antisemitism were an unconscious defense mechanism employed by the majority group which feels that its *collective ideology* is threatened:

> The fury which may then be unleashed is proportional to so dire a threat. The narcissistic rage of the group, like that of the individual, by definition precludes empathy: the offender appears not as an individual or group with needs, motivations, and goals which arise from quite separate or

different concerns, but only as a malevolent force whose sole purpose is to destroy one's most precious asset [the majority group's ideology], so the proper response is the obliteration of the danger. All manner of evil is then perceived in the dissenter [the Jew]. Such a phenomenon has often been explained as the projection by the offended party of its own disavowed evil, but in this framework that would be a *secondary* rather than a primary cause. More pertinently, the malevolence attributed to the dissenter has to do with the [collective] narcissistic injury to the group.

(Terman 1984, p. 20; cf. Falk 2008, p. 92)

At first sight, this explanation seems stunning: did the German Nazis murder six million Jews only because their racist ideology was threatened by the "different" Jews, whom they had dehumanized, and whose image they had totally distorted out of all proportion to reality? Or did they develop their racist ideology in response to some other, inner threat that had nothing to do with the Jews themselves? The Nazis hated the Christians, too, replacing God and Jesus Christ with Adolf Hitler or the old Germanic god Wotan as their new gods. Many Roman Catholics were persecuted and murdered by the Nazis, and the S.S. chief Heinrich Himmler built great temples to the old Teutonic gods. Hitler's hatred of the Jews was part of the tragedy of his own life and that of his nation (Waite 1977).

The Japanese, too, have a "national superiority complex." Their name for their own country, *Nihon* or *Nippon*, means "source of the Sun" and Japan's byname is "Land of the Rising Sun." This name supposedly originated in the letters of the Japanese emperor to his Chinese counterpart during the reign of the Sui dynasty in China (581–618) and had to do with Japan lying east of China. However, in the third century of the Christian era, the Japanese had already called their country *Yamato-jidai* or *Hinomoto* (the Source of the Sun), and the sun goddess *Amaterasu* was the most important goddess in their Shinto pantheon. Her name means "she who illuminates Heaven."

The Japanese superiority complex includes an ancient myth that Japan was created by *kami* and *omikami* (gods and goddesses) and that the Japanese themselves were descendants of these superior creatures (De Mente 2003, 2005). The Emperor of Japan was considered divine until the twentieth century. During the Second World War, when the Japanese were allied in an "axis" with the Germans and Italians, they called their suicide bomber pilots *kamikaze* (divine wind), the name they had given to a typhoon that saved them from the Mongol invasions of Japan in 1271 and again in 1284 by blowing away the invading Mongol ships. As the myth of the Biblical hero Samson (whose name derives from that of the Canaanite sun god) has him kill himself along with his Philistine enemies, a British psychologist has studied the "Samson Syndrome" of kamikaze pilots and other suicide bombers (Canter 2006).

Some scholars believed that the Japanese "superiority complex" was a defense against an underlying "inferiority complex." The American journalist

Boyé Lafayette de Mente (1928–2017) thought that this complex began with Japan's inferior relationship to Korea and to China around the third century (exactly the time when the Japanese began to call their country "source of the sun"). De Mente wrote:

> at the start of this period, Japan was divided into numerous competing clans, with primitive life-styles, while China was at the height of one of its greatest dynasties and Korea had long been the cultural beneficiary of its huge neighbor. The impact this cultural disparity had on the Japanese mind is still very much in evidence. The big difference between Japan's relationship with China well over a thousand years ago and with the West today is that the Japanese could at least identify with the Chinese radically and emotionally, thus lessening the trauma resulting from their inferior position.
> (De Mente 2003, 2005)

The *Mongols* who tried to invade Japan (as well as most of the rest of Asia and much of Europe) in the thirteenth century, who were originally nomadic tribes from Central Asia, are another example of ethnocentrism and racism. Who were these Mongols? The name *Mongol* appeared first in the eighth-century Chinese records of the Tang dynasty, but only resurfaced in the eleventh century during the rule of the Khitan. At first it was applied to some small and insignificant nomadic tribes in the area of the Onon River. In the thirteenth century, however, the name Mongol grew into an umbrella term for a large group of Mongolic and Turkic tribes united under the rule of Chinggis Khan. It is not clear what the Mongols called themselves in their own languages. In fact, the specific origin of the Mongolic languages is unclear. Some scholars have proposed a link to languages like Tungusic and Turkic, which are often included alongside Mongolian in a hypothetical language group called "Altaic languages," but the evidence for this is rather weak.

Since ancient times Mongolia was inhabited by nomads who occasionally formed unions, whose leaders were called *Khans*. The first of these, the *Xiongnu*, were united by Modu Shanyu Mete Khan in 209 BCE. Mongolia being China's northern neighbor, and it soon emerged as the greatest threat of the Qin Dynasty of China (221–206 BCE), forcing it to construct the Great Wall of China, itself being guarded by up to 300,000 soldiers during Marshal Meng Tian's tenure, as a mean of defense against the destructive Xiongnu raids. After the decline of the Xiongnu, the *Rouran, Ruanruan,* or *Tantan,* who were close relatives of the Mongols, came to power in Mongolia and ruled it from the late fourth to the late sixth century CE before being defeated by the Turkic *Göktürk, Göktürkler,* or *Köktürkler,* who dominated Mongolia for some time.

During the seventh and eighth centuries CE, the *Göktürk* were displaced by the *Uyghurs* and then by the *Khitans* and *Jurchens* as the rulers of Mongolia. Each of these tribes had its own *khan*. During the tenth and eleventh centuries, Mongolia was divided into numerous warring tribes linked through transient alliances and involved in the old patterns of internal strife. In the late twelfth century, a Mongol tribal ruler named Temüjin Khan (1162–1227), after prolonged warfare, succeeded in uniting the Mongol and Turkic tribes and renamed himself Chinggis Khan, "Fierce Ruler". After founding the Mongol Empire, he began the Mongol invasions of East and Central Asia. The Mongols were fierce and effective warriors. During Chinggis Khan's lifetime, the Mongol Empire occupied most of Asia.

Chinggis Khan died in 1227 after defeating the Tanguts. He was buried in an unmarked grave somewhere in his native Mongolia. Chinggis Khan's descendants went on to stretch the Mongol Empire across most of Eastern Europe and Asia, overrunning the Great Wall of China, and conquering all of China, as well as large portions of modern Russia, southern Asia, Eastern Europe, and the Middle East. By 1294, his successors expanded their kingdom greatly by invasions in all directions, until they made it into the largest contiguous empire in human history, covering most of Asia and much of Europe. The Mongols also invaded Kievan Rus and annexed large parts of it. The Russians called the invaders *Tatari*, a name that had designated the nomadic Turkic tribes in northeast Mongolia, around Lake Baikal, whom the Chinese called Dada, Dadan, Tatan, or Tantan. The Western Europeans, however, believing that the "Tatars" came from Tartarus (the Greco-Roman name for the underworld), called them "Tartars."

The Bulgars were an ethnic group that inhabited the Eurasian steppes, a vast grassland region stretching from Central Asia to what is now Ukraine. Their name came from the Turkic word *bulgha* meaning "mixed," "merged," or "combined," because the Bulgars were a mixed group that included various ethnic elements. In the fifth century they migrated westward and settled in the Danube region, in what is now Bulgaria, merging with the local Slavic population. Like the Mongols, the Bulgars had their own *khans* (rulers), who fought the neighboring kingdoms. Volga Bulgaria, also known as Volga-Kama Bulgaria or the Volga Bulgar Emirate, was a multi-ethnic Bulgar state from the ninth to the thirteenth century that began at the confluence of the Volga and Kama rivers in what is now the European part of Russia. In 922 the polytheistic Bulgars converted to Islam and the Volga Bulgar state was ruled by an emir.

Under Chinggis Khan's successor, Ögedei Khan, the Mongol expansion reached its peak. In the late 1230s, the Mongols under Batu Khan invaded Russia and Volga Bulgaria (where they were called *Tatari*), reducing most of its principalities to vassalage, and pressed on into Europe. In 1241 the Mongols were ready to invade Western Europe as well, having defeated the last Polish-German and Hungarian armies at the Battles of Legnica and of Mohi. The tide turned after Ögedei Khan's death, however, which may have saved Europe, as Batu Khan had to return to Mongolia and deal with the election of the next Mongol *Khagan* (Great Ruler or emperor).

The Arabic word *mamluk* means "one who is owned." While they spoke Arabic, the Egyptian Mamluks were non-Arab, mostly Turkic, Caucasian,

Southeastern European, and Albanian enslaved mercenaries, slave-soldiers, and freed slaves, who held high-ranking military and administrative positions in the Fatimid caliphate. Gradually, the slaves ruled their owners. In 1250 the Mamluks deposed the ruling caliph of Egypt, al-Muazzam Turan-shah, killed him, and took over the Caliphate. The fourth Mamluk sultan was al-Malik az-Zahir Rukn Baybars al-Bunduqdari (c. 1228–1277).

During the 1250s, Chinggis Khan's grandson, Hülegü Khan, operating from the Mongol base in Persia, destroyed the Abbasid Caliphate (750–1258) in Baghdad and killed the Nizari Isma'ili "Assassins," moving through Palestine towards Egypt, which had just been taken over by the Mamluks. In 1256 Hülegü founded the Ilkhanid dynasty. Baghdad, the capital city of the Abbasid caliphate, fell to Hülegü Khan in 1258. Hülegü Khan killed the last Abbasid caliph, al-Mustasim, and ended the Abbasid caliphate.

In 1259, after his brother Möngke Khan died, Hülegü Khan inherited the vast West Asian parts of the Mongol Empire, in what are now Turkmenistan, Iran, Turkey, Armenia, Afghanistan, Pakistan, Georgia, and Azerbaijan. In these territories he founded the Mongol Ilkhanate or Hülegü Ulus (people or state of Hülegü), which comprised the entire southwestern part of the Mongol Empire. The Ilkhanate was also called "the Land of Iran" or simply "Iran," even though it comprised what are today several other countries. The Ilkhanate lasted less than a century, however, disintegrating in the mid-fourteenth century into numerous smaller states ruled by minor tribal chieftains.

Unlike his successors, Hülegü Khan never converted to Islam. The Israeli historian Michal Biran, an expert on Mongol history, pointed out that Hülegü, who destroyed the Abbasid Caliphate that had led the Islamic *ummah* (nation) for over half a millennium, had often been portrayed – mainly outside Iran – as one of the great destroyers of Islam. Yet around the mid-fourteenth century (after the end of the Ilkhanate) both Mongol and Mamluk chroniclers wrote two different Islamic conversion stories relating to Hülegü. Biran analyzed the origins of these stories and their use in the context of the later Ilkhanate period (Biran 2016).

In 1265 Hülegü was succeeded as Ilkhan by his son Abaqa Khan (1234–1282), who ruled the Mongol Ilkhanate until his death. During his reign, Abaqa continued the efforts of his father to consolidate Mongol rule in Iran and expand the territory of the Ilkhanate. He pursued an ambitious foreign policy that included a military alliance with the Mamluks of Egypt against the Crusader states in Syria and Palestine on the one hand, and diplomatic and military overtures to the Christian kingdoms of Europe on the other. Abaqa was known for his tolerance of Christianity and for his patronage of Christian missionaries and scholars in his court, although he also faced resistance from some elements of his Muslim population.

Despite his political success, Abaqa Khan faced several challenges during his reign, including an economic crisis, political turmoil at home, Muslim resistance, and conflicts with the Mongol *Ulug Ulus* (Golden Horde) and with the Mamluks. In 1282 Abaqa Khan died and was succeeded by his brother, Ahmed Tegülder (the perfect one, c. 1246–1284), the third ruler of the Ilkhanate, another son of Hülegü Khan. Tegülder was executed by the family of his half-brother Qonqurtai, the Mongol viceroy of Anatolia, a son of Hülegü Khan by his Khitan concubine Ajuja. Tegülder himself had executed Qonqurtai. Tegülder was succeeded by his nephew, Abaqa's son, Arghun Khan (c. 1258–1291), a grandson of Hülegü Khan, the fourth ruler of the Ilkhanate. This Ilkhan died tragically at a young age, however, after taking opium for a long time and after being given a toxic sulphur-and-mercury concoction by a yogi alchemist quack who had promised Arghun eternal life.

In 1291 Arghun Khan was succeeded as Ilkhan of Iran by the fifth Ilkhan, Gaykhalt (Gaykhatu Khan, c. 1259–1295), a son of Abaqa and grandson of Hülegü, who reigned only four years. Gaykhalt was assassinated by Baydu (died 1295), the son of Taraqai (Tarqun Khan) and another grandson of Hülegü Khan. Baydu was the sixth Ilkhan, and he only reigned for six months in 1295. Baydu was overthrown and executed after a war with his successor, Mahmud Ghazan Khan (1271–1304), the seventh Ilkhan, who converted the Ilkhanate into a Muslim state.

The Ilkhanate Mongols underwent a great religious transformation during their brief rule. From 1258 to 1295 their khans tolerated various religions, including Sunni and Shiite Islam, Buddhism, Nestorian Christianity, Judaism, and "paganism." In 1295, however, the seventh Ilkhanate ruler, Mahmud Ghazan Khan, a great-grandson of Hülegü Khan who had been raised as a Christian but had been educated by a Chinese Buddhist monk, ascended to power in Iran and declared himself a Muslim. His conversion to Islam compelled other important Mongols to follow suit, marking a pivotal moment in the Ilkhanate's brief history.

This shift toward Islam had a profound impact on the Mongol Ilkhanate's political, cultural, and intellectual life. Under Ghazan's patronage Islamic learning flourished, fostering brilliant writers such as Rashid al-Din Fadlullah Hamadani (1247–1318), a Jewish-born physician, statesman, and scholar, who authored *Jami al-Tawarikh* (the "compendium of chronicles" or "universal history"), one of the most famous Persian histories of all time (Kamola 2019). Despite its initial unity, however, the Ilkhanate eventually fragmented among local leaders. Meanwhile, Turkic Muslim powers were gaining strength on both flanks of the Mongol domains.

In 1259, having destroyed Baghdad and the Abbasid caliphate, the Mongol army of Hülegü Khan, led by the Christian Turkish general Kitbuqa (died 1260), moved into Syria, took Damascus and Aleppo, and reached the shores of the Mediterranean Sea. Atrocities were frequent. Kitbuqa's men committed atrocities that traumatized the Muslim population. In 1260, however, the tide of war turned against the Mongols. Kitbuqa had sent an envoy to Cairo to demand the surrender of the Mamluk sultan, al-Muzaffar Sayf al-Din Qutuz, whose reply was the execution of the envoy.

Möngke Khan having died in 1259, Hülegü Khan hastened to Mongolia for the election of the new Khagan (Great Ruler). Hülegü's brother Khubilai Khan (1215–1294) was elected Khagan. In 1260 Kitbuqa's Mongol army was destroyed by the Mamluks at Ayn Jalut (the Spring of Goliath) in the southeastern Galilee (now the Spring of Harod in Israel). By some accounts Kitbuqa was personally executed by the Mamluk general Baybars, who would later depose Sultan Qutuz and take his place. The other Mongol armies pushed into Persia, finished off the Xia and the remnants of the Khwarezmids, and fought China, which then, like now, constituted the majority of the world's economic production, and which the Mongols finally conquered in 1279.

The chief rival and enemy of the Mongol Ilkhanate was the *Ulug Ulus* (Great State, 1227–1502), which the Russians called "the Golden Horde," and which was also known as the Kipchak Khanate. It was a Mongolian political entity created in the thirteenth century by Batu Khan, a grandson of Chinggis Khan. In 1227, after the death of his father, Jochi Khan, the young Batu Khan inherited a sub-khanate of the Mongol Empire. Batu Khan expanded his empire in a series of sweeping military campaigns in Kievan Rus that included the sacking of Kiev in 1240. After the conquest of Kievan Rus, Batu Khan created the *Ulus Juchi* in the northwestern parts of the Mongolian Empire. The ethnic composition of the *Ulus Juchi* was a mix of Turkic and Mongolian people, with the latter comprising the majority of the aristocracy. By the time of Özbeg Khan (1282–1341), the *Ulug Ulus* comprised most of Eastern Europe and Russia, including parts of Siberia, and directly threatened the Mongol Ilkhanate of Iran.

During its brief existence the Mongol Ilkhanate of Iran had several capitals, including Maragheh (1256–1265), Tabriz (1265–1306), and Soltaniyeh (1306–1335). Throughout its short existence, however, the Ilkhanate had to defend its territory against incursions by its neighboring states. Its efforts to form a military alliance with European powers against the Mamluks of Egypt were unsuccessful. It did establish trade agreements with the Italian city-states, like Genoa, Pisa, and Venice.

By the mid-fourteenth century, dynastic disputes had caused the end of the Ilkhanate. Its last ruler, Abu Sa'id Bahadur Khan (1305–1335), died without leaving a son and heir. According to the Persian chronicler Ibn Battuta (Abu Abdallah Muhammad ibn Abdallah al-Lawati, 1304–1369), Abu Sa'id Bahadur Khan was poisoned by his wife Baghdad Khatun due to her jealousy. He might also have been the victim of bubonic plague. Baghdad Khatun was executed by her dead husband's successor, Arpa Ke'un (died 1336), who charged her with having made a secret alliance with the Ilkhanate's arch-enemy, Özbeg Khan (1282–1341), the ruler of the *Ulug Ulus*. In 1336 Arpa Ke'un was defeated and killed by his enemies. After that the Muslim Mongol Ilkhanate of Iran disintegrated into numerous smaller states ruled by petty chieftains and ceased to exist as a political entity.

The Crusaders knew little or nothing of all this. While the Mongol Empire had split into several states, such as the Ilkhanate and the *Ulug Ulus* (Golden

Horde), and while the invaders were a mix of Mongolian and Turkic tribes, to the Europeans all Mongols were one and the same: fierce, cruel, and deadly. The Russians called them *Tatari*, and the French corrupted this designation into *Tartares*, which evoked the ancient Greek *Tartarus* (underworld). During the thirteenth century the Mongols were greatly feared for their reputed savagery, cruelty, and brutality. After they sacked Baghdad in 1258, the Crusader leaders in Acre and the Muslim sultans alike tried to ally themselves with the Mongols against their enemies. In the fourteenth century, however, the Mongols themselves became Muslims. We shall return to this theme when we discuss the last Crusades. The Mughal Empire of India, even though it was created by non-Mongol Turkic tribes, was named after the Mongols.

Like other ethnic groups, the Mongols believed that they were the center of the world, that they were superior to other peoples, and that they had the right to conquer the world. After Chinggis Khan's death in 1227, the Mongol empire was administratively divided into four Khanates, which split up after Möngke Khan's death in 1259. One of these khanates, the so-called Khaganate or Great Khanate, consisting of the Mongol homeland and China, became the Yuan Dynasty of China under Khubilai Khan, a grandson of Chinggis Khan who set up his capital in what is now Beijing. His summer capital was Shangdu, better known to English speakers as Xanadu.

After over a century of power, in 1386, the Yuan Dynasty was replaced by the Chinese Ming Dynasty, with the Mongol court fleeing north, into Mongolia. As the Ming armies pursued the Mongols into their homeland, they sacked and destroyed the Mongol capital, Karakorum or Kharkhorin, wiping out the cultural progress that had been achieved during the imperial period and throwing Mongolia back into anarchy. Modern Mongolia has an equestrian statue of Chinggis Khan in its capital of Ulaanbaatar, but it is nowhere near the power it once was. Part of it, called Inner Mongolia, is the "Mongol autonomous region" of the People's Republic of China, although the majority of its population is Han Chinese, just as Tibet is the "Tibetan autonomous region" of China.

The Biblical name *Canaan* is very old. Excavations in Mesopotamia, the land between the Euphrates and the Tigris rivers (now Syria and Iraq) have found it time and again in various documents. Some scholars see the oldest reference to the Canaanites in the ethnic name *ganana* that appears in the Ebla tablets, dated to the twenty-fourth century BCE. The Hebrew name Canaan or the Akkadian *kinahhu* is also mentioned in a document from the eighteenth century BCE found in the ruins of *Mari*, a former Sumerian outpost on the middle Euphrates river. Canaan at that time was a loose confederation of city-states. A letter from that time complains about certain "thieves and *kinahhu*" causing trouble in the town of Rahisum. Tablets found at Nuzi use the term *kinahhu* as a synonym for the red or purple dye, produced from murex mollusk shells on the Mediterranean coast, which was a renowned Canaanite export commodity. Dyes were named after their place of origin. The Greco-Latin name *Phoenicia* for Canaan is related to the Greek word *phoini* (purple), referring to the same dye. The purple cloth of Tyre (now in Lebanon) was well known far and wide and long associated with royalty.

A reference to the "land of Canaan" is found on the statue of King Idrimi of Alalakh (now in Syria) in the fifteenth century BCE. After a popular uprising against his rule, Idrimi was forced into exile with his mother's relatives to seek refuge in "the land of Canaan," where he prepared an eventual attack to recover his city. References to the Canaanites are also found throughout the letters of the Egyptian pharaoh Amenhotep IV (Ikhnaton or Akhenaten), written around 1350 BCE. Alphabetical cuneiform clay tablets from Ugarit (now the Syrian town of Ras Shamra) dating from the second millennium BCE refer to an individual Canaanite, suggesting that the people of Ugarit, contrary to modern scholarly opinion, may *not* have considered themselves Canaanites, even though their language was akin to Hebrew (Tubb 1998; Killebrew 2003, 2005).

With warfare and conquest a matter of course, the mighty empires of Egypt and Mesopotamia (including Sumer, Assyria, and Babylonia) surrounded the smaller Canaanites and often invaded and subjugated them. Archaeological excavations of several sites later identified as Canaanite show that the prosperity of Canaan reached its peak during the Middle Bronze Age under the leadership of the city-state of Hazor, which paid tribute to Egypt for much of the period, into the Late Bronze Age (Killebrew 2005). In the north, the cities of Yamkhad (an ancient Amorite kingdom in what is now Aleppo, Syria) and Qatna (another Amorite kingdom northeast of Homs, Syria) led important Canaanite confederacies, and the Biblical Hazor led another important coalition in the south.

In the early Late Bronze Age, Canaanite confederacies were centered on the cities of Megiddo and Kadesh, before being annexed to the Egyptian empire. The Hebrew language of the Hebrews, Israelites, and Jews was originally that of the Canaanites. The early Canaanite Hebrew language was written in alphabetic cuneiform, as in Ugarit, which later developed into the early Canaanite Hebrew alphabet, and later still into the square Hebrew-Aramaic script. The authors of the Hebrew Bible, whose early parts were written in Canaanite Hebrew, called the various tribes of their land, such as the Moabites, Edomites, and Ammonites, by the collective name of Canaanites (Genesis 10:15–19). The Biblical land of Canaan covered parts of present-day Israel, the Palestinian Authority, Jordan, Syria, and Lebanon. Its borders shifted continually with each battle between the tribes.

The Canaanites living on the eastern coast of what they called the Great Sea (the Mediterranean) were seafaring people. Their greatest city was Tyre (now in Lebanon). During the first millennium BCE they settled in many places around the Mediterranean basin, including present-day Greece, Sicily, and Tunisia, and gave them Canaanite Hebrew names that were later corrupted by the Greeks and Romans. The Greeks called the seafaring Canaanites *phoiniki* or Phoenicians, a name that derived either from the Greek word *phoini* for the famous purple dye or from *phoinix* (phoenix), which meant palm tree, zither, red dye, and the phoenix bird. Some scholars think that this Greek name, which later became the Roman *Phoeni* and *Puni,* originally derived from the Egyptian name *fnkhw* for the Canaanites (and Syrians). It was these Canaanite "Phoenicians" who founded *Qart Khadat* (New City) in the ninth century BCE, a North African city-empire (now in Tunisia), which the Romans corrupted into *Carthago,* and which was later anglicized into Carthage. The chief god of Qart Khadat was *Melqart* (King of the City), the god of Tyre.

The Romans called the Canaanite "Phoenicians" *Puni* or *Punici* (plural of *Punicus*), from which comes the English word *Punic*. To the Romans, who fought the Puni, the exonym *punicus* was synonymous with barbarian, treacherous and perfidious. They fought the Puni relentlessly, and the three Punic wars between Rome and Carthage lasted 118 years (264–146 BCE). During the Second Punic War (218–216 BCE) the brilliant Carthaginian military leader Hannibal (247–183 BCE) led a mighty army composed of elite archers, horsemen, and elephant riders from all over North Africa, into the Roman empire. The capable Hannibal managed to move his army through Spain and Gaul, cross the Alps, enter Italy, and, even though he had lost half his army, defeat the Roman armies in three major battles at Trebia, Lake Trasimene, and Cannae.

The Romans, however, avoided further battle with Hannibal, waging a war of attrition against him. Hannibal maintained an army in Italy for more than a decade, never losing a major engagement with the Romans, but he could not force the Romans to accept his terms for peace, or to fight him. He did not attempt to move on the city of Rome itself, which was very well defended, and where he would lose his battle.

In 203 BCE a Roman counter-invasion of North Africa forced Hannibal to return to Carthage, where in 202 BCE he was defeated in the Battle of Zama. The Romans could not abide the existence of two empires. The Roman senator Marcus Porcius Cato (234–149 BCE), also known as Cato Censorius, Cato Sapiens, Cato Priscus, Cato Major, and Cato the Elder, ended every speech in the Senate with the phrase, *Praeterea censeo Carthaginem esse delendam,* meaning "I also declare that Carthage must be destroyed." After 20 more years of fighting Rome, Hannibal committed suicide at Libyssa, on the eastern shore of the Sea of Marmara, by taking poison, which, it was said, he had long carried about with him in a ring. If, as the Roman historian Titus Livius (Livy, 59 BCE- 17 CE), seems to imply, this happened in 183 BCE, Hannibal died in the same year as his Roman nemesis, Publius Cornelius Scipio Africanus Major (236–183 BCE), at the age of 64.

The Carthaginians had threatened not only Rome's military power, but also its group identity. The Roman response was furious and ruthless. Cato's death in 149 BCE signaled the beginning of the Third Punic War. The Punic Wars brought the end of Carthaginian power and the complete destruction of the city of Carthage by the Roman general Scipio Aemilianus (185–129 BCE). In

146 BCE the Romans pulled the Phoenician warships out into the harbor and set them afire before the city, and then went from house to house, capturing and enslaving the Carthaginians. Fifty thousand Carthaginians were sold into slavery. The city of Carthage was set ablaze, and was razed to the ground, with only ruins and rubble left. The same thing would happen to Jewish Jerusalem in 70 CE. After the fall of Carthage, Rome annexed most of the Carthaginian colonies, including North African cities like Volubilis, Lixus, Chellah, and Mogador, and made Carthage's former North African empire into the Roman province of *Africa pronsonsularis,* which covered present-day northeastern Algeria, Tunisia, and northwestern Libya.

The Mystery of *Sepharad* and "*al-Andalus*"

Linguists believe that the ancient Sanskrit and Avesta languages of India and Iran were related to the ancient Greek and Latin of southern Europe, and that all of them had developed from a "Proto Indo-European" language. The Lydian language of Western Anatolia was an ancient "Indo-European" language with consonants and vowels. The old Canaanite Hebrew language, on the other hand, was a Semitic language with consonants only. The older texts of the Hebrew Bible were written in Canaanite Hebrew, and the Hebrew text of the Old Testament was not vocalized when it was sealed around 100 CE. It was not vocalized until the tenth century, under Arabic influence, by Aharon ben Moshe ben Asher and Moshe ben Naphtali, the leading Jewish *Masoretes* (tradition bearers) in Tiberias. The name *Israel* was an epithet and a byname of the Canaanite father-god El, and it meant "El shall reign." The apocryphal etymology in Genesis 3:27–28 was meant to make the name Jewish, as it had become the name of the Jewish people.

The old Hebrew name *sfrd*, now the Hebrew name for Spain, appears only once in the Hebrew Bible (Obadiah 20). The original name was pronounced *Sfard*, the Lydians' own name for their capital, known in Greek as Sardis. The vocalization of *Sefarad* for *sfrd* was introduced by the *Masoretic* vocalizers of Tiberias, Moshe Ben-Asher, his son Aharon ben Moshe Ben-Asher, and Moshe Ben-Naphtali, in the ninth and tenth centuries CE, under Islamic Arab rule and the influence of the Arabic language. But how did the Biblical name *Sepharad*, which had nothing to do with Spain, come to designate Spain among the Jews? Ironically, the English name "Spain" comes from the Roman name *Hispania*, itself a corruption of the Canaanite-Hebrew name *i-shfania,* meaning "island of hyraxes," or "island of hares," which the Carthaginians had given to their colony on the southern Iberian coast, which flourished from the eighth to the third centuries BCE. During the early Middle Ages, the Jews identified the Biblical *Sepharad* with *Hispania*, and this was alluded to by the eleventh-century Jewish sage Rabbi Shlomo ben Yitzhak (Rashi, 1040–1105) in his commentary on Obadiah. The Jews, however, ironically called *Hispania* by its Aramaic name, *Espamia* or *Aspamia* (Epstein

1935–1948, Order *Thoroth*, Tractate *Nidah*, Folio 30b, translates this name as "Spain").

Some scholars believed that the Jews of Spain called their country *Sepharad* for two reasons: First, Obadiah 20 refers to "the exile of Jerusalem which is in Sepharad," so that the Jews of "Sepharad" were of the prestigious tribe of Judah, and second, because the exile of the Jews to "Sepharad" preceded Christianity, the Jews of Sepharad were not in Jerusalem at the time of Jesus Christ and could not be accused by the Christians of Christ's "deicide." Such "explanations" however are unconvincing. The same was true of the Jews calling France by the Biblical name of *Zarephath* (a Canaanite town now in Lebanon) and Germany *Ashkenaz* (a great-grandson of Noah). Both names had nothing to with France or Germany. The American-Jewish historian Yosef Hayim Yerushalmi believed that this was a symptom of life in the past "for even the most terrible events are somehow less terrifying when viewed within old patterns" (Yerushalmi 1982, p. 36). I believe that it indicated the collective inability to mourn one's historical losses (Falk 1996).

While the Hebrew-speaking Jews called Spain *Sepharad*, the Arabic-speaking Muslims who conquered Spain in 710–712 called it *al-Andalus*. Coming out of Arabia, in 634 they had conquered all the Middle East and North Africa and force-converted their populations to Islam. There are several theories about the origin of the name *al-Andalus*. The best-known one says that it is an Arabic corruption of *Vandalicia*, the Latin name for the country of the *Vandali*, one of the East Germanic tribes that destroyed Rome in the fifth century and that passed through Spain on its way to North Africa. (Houtsma et al. 1954–2007, vol. 1, p. 486; Esposito 2003, entry on "*al-Andalus*"). Another theory is that *al-Andalus* was the Arabic name for *Atlantis*, the mythical lost continent. (Vallvé 1986). This theory, however, has no evidence to support it.

During the middle ages there were several Muslim caliphates, the best known of which were the Abbasid in Baghdad, the Umayyad in Damascus and Egypt (until 750) and later in Córdoba, and the Fatimid in Cairo. Some of the Arabic chroniclers of the Umayyad caliphate's conquest of the Iberian peninsula, written centuries later, mention an "island of *al-Andalus*" on which landed the first Muslim invaders of Iberia, and which was later renamed *Tarifa* after their "Berber" leader, Tarif Abu-Zora (flourished 700), whose fellow conqueror, Tariq ibn Ziyyad (died 720), gave his name to Gibraltar (a corruption of *jebel al-Tariq*). As with the Carthaginians, the name of an island had become the name of the whole country. Another theory is that the name *al-Andalus* has a Gothic origin, that it comes from the Gothic *Lanahlauts*, the name given to Spain by the Visigoths who ruled it in the early Middle Ages, from which the Latin name *Gothica sors* also came. (Halm 1989).

None of these theories, however, is convincing. It is unlikely that even the Arabic language, which changed *Alexandria* into *al-Iskanderiya*, would corrupt names like *Atlantis* or *Landahlauts* into "*al-Andalus.*" The German scholar Georg Bossong believed that the name "*al-Andalus*" predated the

Roman occupation of Spain. He pointed out that the name *Andaluz* exists in several mountainous places of the Spanish region of Castile. The village of *Andaluz* lies at the foot of the Andaluz Mountain on the Duero River in the Spanish province of Soria, and nearby are the villages of *Torre-Andaluz* and *Centenera de Andaluz*. A brook named *Andaluz* supposedly flows in the Spanish province of Guadalajara out of the cave of La Hoz. The prefix *And-* is common in Spanish place names, and the suffix *-luz* (meaning "light" in Spanish, from the Latin *lux*) also occurs in several place names across Spain (Bossong 2002). This does not explain, however, why the Muslims gave the name of "*al-Andalus*" to the whole country, nor is it quite certain that those names predated the Muslim conquest. To me, the name "*al-Andalus*" seems imaginary, a psychogeographical fantasy, just like the names Paradise Island or El Dorado (Stein & Niederland 1989).

The Romans and the Germans

The Romans considered the Germanic tribes north of the Danube River "barbarians," and in 9 CE they fought a major battle against these "savage" tribes. The Teutoburg forest was the site of that battle between the Roman Empire and an alliance of Germanic tribes. The location of the battle was given by the Roman historian Gaius Cornelius Tacitus (56–117 CE) as *saltus Teutoburgiensis* (Teutoburg forest), a northern extension of the central European uplands, extending eastward toward the Weser River, southward from the town of Osnabrück and southeastwards to Paderborn, Charlemagne's future capital. The battle was therefore called the Battle of the Teutoburg Forest. Recent excavations suggest that the final stages of the battle took place farther north, at Kalkriese, north of Osnabrück.

At this battle, Hermann of the *Cherusci* (18BCE-21CE), the leader of the Germanic tribes, who had lived in Rome in his youth as a hostage, and whom the Romans called Arminius, defeated the three legions of the Roman general Quintilius Varus and became a legend for his victory. Hermann followed it up with a clean sweep of all the Roman forts, garrisons and cities east of the River Rhine. The remaining two Roman legions, commanded by Varus's nephew, Lucius Nonius Asprenas, held Moguntiacum (Mainz) and some forts along the river. The Roman fort of Aliso fended off the Germanic tribes for weeks, perhaps months, before its garrison, which included survivors of the Teutoburg Forest battle, broke out from the siege under their commander, Lucius Caeditius, and reached the Rhine. The Roman historian Gaius Suetonius Tranquillus wrote that the first Roman emperor, Gaius Julius Caesar Octavianus Augustus (63 BCE–14CE), showed signs of near-insanity at the news, banging his head against the walls of his palace and repeatedly shouting *Quintili Vare, legiones redde!* (Quintilius Varus, give me back my legions!) (Suetonius 2003). This was the first major defeat of Roman forces by the "barbarians" tribes who would eventually take over their empire.

During the third century the Roman Empire began to divide. In 285, Emperor Diocletianus declared Maximianus, a military colleague from Illyricum, his co-emperor. Each emperor would have his own court, his own military and administrative faculties, and each would rule with a separate praetorian guard and its own prefect as chief lieutenant. Maximian ruled in the West, from his capitals at Mediolanum (now Milan, Italy) or Augusta Treverorum (now Trier, Germany), while Diocletian ruled in the East, from his capital of Nicomedia (now İzmit, Turkey). This division was supposedly for practical purposes: the Roman Empire was still called "indivisible" in official panegyric and both emperors could move freely throughout the Empire.

In 288, Emperor Maximianus appointed the general Constantius his praetorian prefect in Gallia (Gaul), which the Romans so named after a Celtic word meaning "powerful people". Constantius then abandoned his wife or concubine Helena, the mother of his sixteen-year-old son Flavius Valerius Aurelius Constantinus (the future emperor Constantine the Great, 272–337), whom he had hardly seen, to marry Maximian's stepdaughter Theodora, which would secure his political power. In 293, Emperor Diocletianus divided the Roman Empire again, appointing two Caesars to rule over further subdivisions of East and West. During the fourth century Emperor Constantine the Great began the process that would bring about the division of the Roman empire into two rival empires: the "Western" and "Eastern" Roman empires. This process was accelerated by the success of Christianity.

For many centuries, the people whom the Romans saw as "barbarian" Germanic tribes had repeatedly moved south toward Rome, raiding the villages and towns along their way. At other times the Romans moved north to fight and subdue them. Their Roman exonyms were corruptions of the endonyms that the Germanic tribes called themselves. For instance, the name *Chamavus* may have been a Roman corruption of the Old German word *Hamm* (settlement), *Heim* (home), or *Haimaz* (homeland; modern German *Heimat*). The Roman name *Salius* may have been a corruption of the Dutch name of the Ijssel River in the Netherlands, then called *Isala* or *Sal*, signaling the people's movement and residence in that area of Roman Gaul. This Dutch area was called *Salland*. The name *Salius* may also come from *salus* (salt) because to the Romans the *Salii* were sea-dwelling people and hence "salty."

Just as the North American Apache called themselves *indeh* (the people), the Germanic tribe that the Romans called *Teutones* called themselves *teutsch,* meaning "the people." There are other theories about the etymology of the German words *teutsch* and *deutsch*. Some scholars think that they may have derived from *teuta*, a "Proto-Indo-European" word for "people." Other scholars think that they came from the Dutch word *duyts* (German), which derived either from the Dutch *de oudst* (the oldest) or from the Dutch *duidelijk* (clear, like the German *deutlich*), or that *teutsch* came from the Latin *theodiscus*, which became the Old German word *theodisk*, which referred to a West Germanic tribe and language, and that the word *theodisk* turned into the medieval German words *düdesch, tütsch, teutsch,* and *deutsch* (whence the English word *Dutch*). In any event, to the German "Teutons" themselves, the word *teutsch* meant "the people."

During the late second century BCE, the Germanic *Teutones* and *Cimbri* were recorded by Roman historians as passing west through Roman-occupied Celtic Gaul and attacking Roman Italy. Passing through Celtic Gaul, the Teutons adopted as their god Teutates, Toutatis, or Tuisto, one of the three Celtic gods. Probably originating in the Danish area of Jutland during the second century BCE, many Teutones and Cimbri migrated south and west to the Danube River valley, where they faced the armies of the expanding Roman Republic.

The Cimbri under their King Boiorix and the Teutons under the king Theudobod won the opening battles of this war, defeating Gallic or Celtic tribes allied with the Romans and destroying a huge Roman army at the Battle of Arausio in 105 BCE. In 104 BCE the Cimbri left the Rhône valley to raid Spain, while the Teutons remained in Gaul, still strong but not powerful enough to march on Rome on their own. This gave the Romans time to rebuild their army, and the invading Cimbri and Teutones were defeated in 102 BCE by the Roman general Gaius Marius (156–86 BCE) at Aquae Sextiae (near present-day Aix-en-Provence in France). The Germanic King, Teutobod or Theudobod, was taken in irons to Rome. As Greek legend had it about the women of Troy, German myth has the captured Germanic women kill their own children and commit mass suicide rather than be sexually abused by the victorious Romans. This myth passed into Roman legends of Germanic heroism and was noted by Saint Jerome (347–420), the translator of the Hebrew Bible into the Latin *Vulgata*. One of the fascinating aspects of the name *Teutones* is that *Teuton* and *Teutonic* have been used in reference to all of the Germanic peoples, and that the old Germanic word *teutsch* (people) became *deutsch*, the modern German word for "German."

The "Celts" were an ancient people in central Europe around 1000 BCE who by 400 BCE had migrated all the way to Ireland, Iberia, and Anatolia. In Roman Gallia (Gaul) they became known as *Galli* (Gauls). The origin of the various names used since classical times for the people known today as the Celts is obscure and has been controversial. In particular, there are at least 19 records of the term "Picts" being used in connection with the inhabitants of Ireland and Britain prior to the eighteenth century. According to a text by Julius Caesar, the Latin name *Celtus* (plural *Celti* or *Celtae*), which came from the Greek *Keltes* or *Keltos* (plural *Keltai* or *Keltoi*), was based on a native Celtic ethnic name: "All Gallia is divided into three parts, in one of which the *Belgae* live, another in which the *Aquitani* live, and the third are those who in their own tongue are called *Celtae*, in our language *Galli*" (Julius Caesar, *Commentarii de Bello Gallico*, 1.1).

The Roman name *Galli* for the Celts has an obscure etymology which is still debated among scholars. The first literary reference to the Celtis, as *Keltoi*, is by the Greek historian Hecataeus of Miletus in 517 BCE. He wrote that the Greek town of Massalia (now the French city of Marseille) was near "the place of the Celts" and also mentioned a Celtic town named Nyrex. The Greek historian Herodotus located the *Keltoi* at the source of the Danube River, or in Iberia, but the passage in his writings is unclear. The Greeks seem to have confused the Celts with the Germans, just as the Romans later confused the Goths with the Getae. The name of the Germanic god Teutates, Toutatis, or Tuisto, who was also one of the three major Celtic gods, may also have come from the "Proto-Indo-European" word *teuta* (the tribe or the people), so that his name meant "the god of the people."

The Danube River, which flows west to east, and the River Rhine, which flows south to north, were the natural frontiers in Europe. The Greco-Roman world knew little about the people who lived north of the Danube River before the second century BCE. The Roman exonym for the land of the "savage" tribes north of the Danube River was Germania, while the German endonym for it was *Teutsch-Land* (the land of the people). Germania was inhabited by many different tribes, the vast majority of them Germanic but also including some Celtic, Baltic, Scythian, and proto-Slavic. The tribal and ethnic makeup of Germania changed over the centuries as a result of assimilation and, most importantly, great migrations. The Germanic people spoke many dialects, which some linguists think may have developed from a "Proto-Indo-Germanic" language.

Until the fourth century BCE the Greeks and the Romans often confused the Germans with the Celts. Around 320 BCE the Greek sailor Pytheas of Massalia (ca. 380–310 BCE) sailed from Massalia (now Marseille) around Britain and along the northern coast of Europe. What he found on his journeys was so strange to the Greeks that later writers refused to believe his stories. Pytheas may have been the first Mediterranean sailor to distinguish the Germans from the Celts. The Roman leader Julius Caesar (100–44 BCE) thought that the Galli, though quite warlike, could also be civilized, while the Germanic tribesmen were far more savage, and were a big threat to Roman Gallia, and therefore had to be conquered. His accounts of the "barbaric" northern tribes expressed the feeling of superiority of the Romans, including the Gauls, over the Germans, but also expressed the Roman fear of the savage Germanic tribes. Those fears were realized five centuries later, when the Germanic tribes invaded Italy and destroyed the weakened Roman empire.

The most complete account of Germania from ancient times was that of the Roman historian Cornelius Tacitus (ca. 56–117). At the end of the first century of the Christian Era, Tacitus wrote about the origins of the name *Germania*:

> The Germans themselves I should regard as aboriginal, and not mixed at all with other races through immigration or intercourse. For, in former times it was not by land but on shipboard that those who sought to emigrate would arrive; and the boundless and, so to speak, hostile ocean beyond us, is seldom entered by a sail from our world. And, beside the perils of rough and unknown seas, who would leave Asia, or Africa, or

Italy for Germany, with its wild country, its inclement skies, its sullen manners and aspect, unless indeed it were his home?

(Tacitus 1999, p. i)

Tacitus went on to describe the Germans with a mixture of fear, contempt, superiority, and disdain that betrayed his ambivalence about them:

In their ancient songs, their only way of remembering or recording the past they celebrate an earth-born god Tuisco, and his son Mannus, as the origin of their race, as their founders. To Mannus they assign three sons, from whose names, they say, the coast tribes are called Ingaevones; those of the interior, Herminones; all the rest, Istaevones. Some, with the freedom of conjecture permitted by antiquity, assert that the god had several descendants, and the nation several appellations, as *Marsi, Gambrivii, Suevi, Vandalii*, and that these are nine old names. The name *Germania*, on the other hand, they say is modern and newly introduced, from the fact that the tribes which first crossed the Rhine and drove out the *Galli*, and are now called *Tungri*, were then called *Germani*. Thus what was the name of a tribe, and not of a race [nation], gradually prevailed, till all [of them] called themselves by this self-invented name of *Germani*, which the conquerors had first employed to inspire terror.

(Tacitus 1999, p. i)

Actually, the Germans did not call themselves by that name: their endonym was *teutsch*. The name "German" probably came from the Latin *germanus* meaning "related" (hence the English "germane").

Christianity was introduced into Roman *Hispania* in the first century CE and it became popular in the Iberian cities in the second century. The first Germanic tribes to invade Roman *Hispania* arrived in the third century, when the once-mighty Roman empire began to decline politically and militarily. Some historians believe that these Germanic tribes adopted the Roman exonym for themselves, *Franci*, as their endonym, while others believe that these tribes had other, Germanic, endonyms for themselves. By the seventh century, German historians were referring to their own people as *Franci*. We shall discuss the *Franci* in greater detail below, as their name was borne by the non-Germanic Crusaders.

During the first three centuries of the Christian era, Christianity had gradually spread to other Roman provinces than Spain, then to Rome itself. Byzantion was an ancient Greek city, founded by Greek colonists from Megara in 667 BCE and named after their king Byzas or Byzantas. The Romans latinized the Greek name into Byzantium. In the fourth century of the Christian era, the Roman emperor Constantinus (Constantine the Great) adopted Christianity as the religion of his empire and moved his capital from Rome to Byzantium, whose language was Greek rather than Latin. This was a revolutionary move. He is known in the Greek Orthodox Church as "Saint Constantine" and his mother, Helena, as "Saint Helena." They are usually pictured together as the great saints of Greek Orthodoxy.

Constantine was the Roman Emperor from 306 CE (though he was challenged for his throne), and the undisputed Emperor from 324 to his death. He rebuilt the old city of Byzantium, renamed it *Nova Roma* (New Rome), moved his capital there, and issued special commemorative coins in 330 CE to honor the event. He provided *Nova Roma* with a Senate and civic offices similar to those of old Rome. After his death in 337, Nova Roma was renamed *Constantinopolis* (anglicized into Constantinople), and by the end of the century the Roman empire was partitioned into two parts: the "Latin" Roman empire of the West, whose capital was Rome, and the "Greek" Roman empire of the East, whose capital was Constantinople (now Istanbul, a Turkish corruption of the Greek words *eis tin polin*, meaning "within the city").

The Western Roman Empire was greatly weakened, its emperor was a figurehead after 395, and in the fifth century it was invaded by Germanic tribes. The pope of the Christian Church had his seat in Rome, which was called the Holy See or the throne of Saint Peter, but neither he nor the emperor had political or military power. The First Council of Constantinople (381) suggested strongly that Roman primacy was already asserted; however, it should be noted that, because of the controversy over this claim, the pope did not personally attend this ecumenical council, which was held in the eastern capital of the Roman empire, rather than at Rome. It was not until 440 that Pope Leo I more clearly articulated the extension of papal authority as doctrine, promulgating in edicts and in councils his right to exercise "the full range of apostolic powers that Jesus had first bestowed on the apostle Peter." It was at the ecumenical Council of Chalcedon in 451 that Pope Leo (through his emissaries) stated that he was "speaking with the voice of Peter." At this same council, the Bishop of Constantinople was given a primacy of honour equal to that of the Bishop of Rome, because "Constantinople is the New Rome."

The "Eastern Roman Empire," whose people were mostly Greek, and whose language was Greek, was later called the Byzantine Empire by historians, but it was not so called by its own emperors. The seventh century was disastrous for the "Eastern Roman" Christians: they were invaded by Muslim Arabs, Persians, and Slavs, and lost some of their territories in Asia Minor and in the Middle East, including the "Holy Land." The appellation of "Holy Land" for Palestine, which was conquered from the Byzantines by the invading Muslims, was a fantasy. It was based on the religious belief that the land in which Jesus Christ was born and crucified was holy. This belief unconsciously came from a longing for a Great Good Mother who was holy and unblemished, like the Virgin Mary.

Like many peoples who are unable to mourn their collective losses, the Byzantine Greeks seem to have immersed themselves in their past and sought to recover their losses. The writings of Theophylaktos Simokattes, a seventh-century Byzantine chronicler, "the last historian of Antiquity," and the *Chronographia* of Theophanes the Confessor (eighth and ninth centuries) attest to this phenomenon

(Theophanes the Confessor 1982, 1997; Theophylaktos Simokattes 1986). As the American historian David Olster astutely observed:

> Seventh-century [Byzantine] literature reveals the Christian preoccupation with the collapse of the imperial world-order in the wake of the Arab, Persian, and Slav invasions. But their preoccupation with defeat did not find primary expression through the historical genres. Classical biography disappears entirely. Theophylact Simocatta is not only the sole extant historian from the seventh century, but the sole known historian, and he chose to narrate the victories that closed the sixth century, not the defeats that opened the seventh. From the Paschal Chronicle at the end of the 620s to Theophanes' *Chronicle* at the beginning of the ninth century, there is no extant chronicle, and Theophanes' narrative poverty testifies to the Christians' reluctance to face defeat. *Christians may have been preoccupied with defeat, but they had no interest in recording it. They had far less interest in what had happened than in how the past would be restored.*
> (Olster 1994, p. 180, italics added)

During recorded human history (and prehistory), there were many great migrations of entire ethnic groups in quest of, food, power, or territory. These migrations almost always involved wars, conquest, pillage, and bloodbaths. For the ancient Romans, the Germanic *Gothi*, who made great migrations in the fifth century, were divided into the *Thervingi* (forest people), the *Greuthungi* (steppe dwellers or people of the pebbly coasts), and the *Vesi, Wesi,* or *Wisi* (good or noble people), who were later called Visigoths. The name *Visigothi* was an invention of the Roman writer Cassiodorus, who combined *Visi* and *Gothi* and intended it to mean "West Goths" because they ruled Spain. This is another fascinating case of the changing meaning of peoples' names. The word *Wisi* may have come from the Gothic word *iusiza*, meaning "better." The British historian William Henry Stevenson thought that *Wesi* was the Germanic version of the "Indo-European" *wesus* meaning "good," like the Sanskrit *vásus*, and the Gallic *vesu* (Stevenson 1899). There is no way of knowing with certainty the origin of "Gallia" or "Gallic."

Incredibly, the Romans confused the Germanic *Gothi* with the Thracian *Getae*, the Greek name for several tribes that occupied the regions south of the Lower Danube River (now in Bulgaria), and north of the Lower Danube, in the Muntenian plain (now in Romania). The *Getae* lived in the hinterland of Greek colonies on the Black Sea coast, bringing them into contact with the ancient Greeks from an early date. At the end of the fourth century, however, the Roman poet Claudius Claudianus, in the court of the Roman emperor Honorius and the patrician Stilicho, used the exonym *Getae* for the Visigoths. During the fifth and sixth centuries, Roman and Greek writers, including Marcellinus Comes, Orosius, Johannes Lydus, Isidore of Seville, Procopius of Caesarea, and Jordanes, used the same exonym *Getae* as a collective name for the "barbarian" populations invading the Eastern Roman Empire (Goths, Gepids, Kutrigurs, and Slavs).

The sixth-century Byzantine historian Procopius of Caesarea wrote:

> There were many *Gothic* nations in earlier times, just as also at the present, but the greatest and most important of all are the Goths, Vandals, Visigoths, and Gepaedes. In ancient times, however, they were named Sauromatae and Melanchlaeni; and there were some too who called these nations *Getic*."
> (Procopius of Caesarea 1653; cf. Boia 2001, p. 14)

The *Getae* were called the ancestors of the Goths by the sixth-century Roman historian Jordanes, who was of Germanic Alan origin (his father's name was Alanoviiamuth), in his Latin work *De origine actibusque Getarum* (The Origin and Deeds of the Getae). Jordanes also wrote that a river gave its name to the *Vesi*, but this is a legend, like his story about the *Greuthung* name. Jordanes assumed the earlier testimony of Orosius.

The Germanic Goths (not the Thracian Getae) had begun to attack Rome in the third century. The Gothic Thervingi made one of the first major "barbarian" invasions of the Roman Empire from 262 to 267. A year later, however, they suffered a devastating defeat at the Battle of Naissus and were driven back across the Danube River by 271. The Goths continued their migrations and raids into the Roman empire during and after its division in the fourth century. By the fifth century the "Roman empire of the West" had been invaded by several marauding Germanic tribes – Visigoths, Swabians, Vandals, and Alans – whom the Romans often called *Franci*, and who arrived in Roman Hispania by crossing the Pyrenees from Gallia. From 407 to 409 the Vandals, with the allied tribes of the Alans and Suevi, swept into the Roman Iberian peninsula.

In response to this invasion of Hispania, the Roman emperor of the West, Honorius (384–423), enlisted the aid of the Visigoths, who entered Hispania in 415, and in 418 Emperor Honorius made them *foederati* or allies of Rome. In Gaul and Spain, the Vandals were attacked by Galli allied to the Romans. They crossed the Pillars of Hercules (now the straits of Gibraltar), settled in the North African highlands, west of Carthage (now in Tunisia and Algeria), established a sizable kingdom in North Africa, and finally "sacked" Rome in 455. The word "vandal" has become synonymous with "barbarian," "violent," and "uncivilized." The "Pagan" Visigoths remained in Spain. After their conversion to Roman Catholicism in 589, and after conquering the Swabian territories in the northwest and the Byzantine territories in the southeast, the Visigothic kingdom of Spain comprised a great part of the Iberian Peninsula.

Unconscious Psychological Processes: Splitting and Projection

The derogatory exonyms that each ethnic group gives other groups, especially its "enemies," are not accidental. Psychologically, each human group needs an enemy, a foreign group, against which it can define its own identity and maintain its internal cohesion. In this classical *Us and Them* paradigm, we are the good guys and they are the bad guys. On the individual level, *consciously* seeing oneself as all-good and others as all-bad is the product of two *unconscious* defensive processes that operate in each of us from a very early age: *splitting*, by which the infant defends itself from unbearable ambivalence and anxiety by splitting its world (its mother) into all-good and all-bad parts, and *projection*, by which one's painful feelings are attributed to the other. These processes are supplemented by *externalization* and *internalization*, in which painful aspects of ourselves and our painful relationships are blamed on other people, while the early object of our feelings (the early mother) is internalized. Some "object-relations" psychoanalysts think that externalization and internalization do not bear on aspects of the "object" (of our painful feelings) but rather on the relationships and conflicts that are inherent in the object and that it maintains with other objects (Mijolla 2005).

These unconscious defensive processes begin in our infancy, because of the total dependence on the baby on its mother, who has no way of being good, nourishing, and care-taking all the time. Even the best mother is at times tired, sleeping, depressed, worried, or not totally attentive to her baby. The baby wants absolute attention and endless supplies. It cannot integrate its perception of its mother as a "good object" that supplies all its needs and as a "bad object" that frustrates them. It therefore splits up its image of its mother into two, one all-good, the other all-bad, one a fairy, the other a witch, as if it had two different and separate mothers. This theme is abundant in legends, myths, and fairy tales. In addition, the infant also unconsciously splits its own image of itself into two, so that it harbors a good self-image and a bad self-image at the same time, but the two are not integrated, as in the classic story *The Strange Case of Dr. Jekyll and Mr. Hyde* by the Scottish novelist Robert Louis Balfour Stevenson (1850–1894), who died of a cerebral hemorrhage on his Samoan estate at the age of forty-four. Through splitting, projection, and externalization we attribute to the other, the foreigner, the enemy all the painful aspects of our own self.

Collective splitting and projection were active on a very large scale in the seventh century of the Christian era, when Islam rose as the major religion in Arabia. In great waves of marauding *jihad* (holy warfare), seeing themselves as the righteous people who had seen the light and the non-Muslims as "the infidel" who had to be converted, the Muslims conquered most of the Middle East and North Africa, and, in the early eight century, most of Iberia, which led to almost eight centuries of continual warfare with Christian Europe, primarily with Spain. The Europeans called the invading Muslims "Moors," "Saracens," or "Barbarians," while the Arabic-speaking Muslims called the Europeans *al-ifranji* (the Franks). Let us look at these dramatic events, which a few centuries later, led to the Crusades, and at the incredible fantasies that they involved and that were acted out on a huge scale.

Chapter 2

Romans, Franks, and Germans

As we have seen, *ethnocentrism* is an age-old and universal phenomenon. In a kind of collective group narcissism, each ethnic group prides itself on being superior to all the others, on being elected by its gods or God, and on being good while others are bad. The indigenous North Africans whom we call *Berbers, Kabyles*, or *Chaoui*, called themselves *Imazighen* (singular *Amazigh*), meaning "free men" (presumably, to them, other men were slaves). The ancient Greeks called those who did not speak their language *barbaroi*, meaning "foreign," "strange," or "ignorant," an onomatopoeic word in which the "bar-bar" represented the impression of random "hubbub" the Greeks had from hearing a language they could not understand, such as Persian, similar to "blah blah" or "babble" in modern English. The English word "Barbarian" derives from the Latin *barbarus*, the Latin form of the Greek *barbaros*, and from the Latin name *Barbaria*, meaning "foreign country." Similarly, the name "Berber" was the derogatory name given by the Arabs to the nomadic Imazighen of North Africa and sub-Saharan Africa who invaded Spain as Muslims in the eighth century.

The River Rhine, one of Europe's longest and most important rivers along with the Danube, begins in Switzerland, runs north between France and Germany, then runs north through Germany and turns west in the Netherlands, where it flows into the North Sea. The exonym *Berber* that was given to the Muslim *Imazighen* by the Arabs was a corruption of the Latin word *Barbarus*, which had been given by the Romans to their northern hostile Germanic neighbors from the land they called *Germania*, the Latin exonym for a geographical area east of the Rhine, as well as an area under Roman control on the west bank of the Rhine. The name *Germanus* came into use after Julius Caesar adopted it from a Gallic term for the peoples east of the River Rhine, and it may have meant "neighbor." The Roman name *Barbaria* at first designated the land of the Germanic "Barbarians," but was later applied to the pirate-ridden North African Mediterranean coast, inhabited by the "Berbers." The term first appeared in writing in the fourth century during the schism in the Roman Catholic church between the North-African bishop Saint Augustine of Hippo (354–430) and the "heretical Donatists," the followers of the "Berber" Christian "heretic" Donatus Magnus (ca. 311–355), and the allies of the "Barbarians."

DOI: 10.4324/9781003527367-2

While all humanity originated in Africa, the hundreds of thousands of years of human migrations all over the globe gave rise to all kinds of skins colors, from very dark in sub-Saharan Africa and in other hot and tropical countries to very light in the northern and polar ones. Skin color has to do with pigmentation, which adjusted itself to the intensity of the sun, but it became a psychological symbol of racial superiority. White-skinned people have long felt superior to dark-skinned ones. Light-skinned Europeans felt themselves superior to the dark-skinned "Barbarians" from African and Asia who came to Europe.

When the dark-skinned Arabic-speaking "Berber" Muslim conquerors of Spain arrived from Morocco in 710–712, the Christian Spaniards called these invaders *Moros*, meaning "swarthy ones," "dark ones," or "black ones." The Spanish word *moro* derived from the Roman word *mauro*, which came from the Greek *mauros*, and which had the same meaning, as does the Spanish word *moreno*. The English called these Muslims *Moors*. Ironically, in modern Morocco, Algeria, and Mauritania (the ancient Mauretania), it is the *light-skinned* people who are called *Maures* and *Berbères*. The French word *Maures* referred to the ancient native people of North Africa, and later to the medieval Muslim, Arab, and "Berber" inhabitants of Iberia, Sicily, Malta, and the Maghreb. In Mauritania, the endonym for the dominant political group is *Beidane* (the white ones), and the French exonym for them is *les Maures blancs* (the white Moors). The endonym for the dark-skinned people and former slaves is *Haratine* (the black ones), in French *les Maures noirs*. In modern Spanish the word *Moros* denotes all Muslims, not only those from North Africa but also those in faraway lands such as the Philippines and Granada.

Among the major Turkic tribes of Central Asia were the Oghuz Turks. Other major Turkic tribes were the Seljuks and the Ottomans. The Oghuz are considered the ancestors of the Azeris, the Turks, the Turkish Cypriots, the Balkan Turks, the Turkmens, the Qashqai, the Khorasani, the Gagauz, and the Salar. During the mass westward migrations of the ninth through the twelfth century, the Oghuz Turks were among the indigenous tribes of Central Asia who migrated to western Asia and eastern Europe via Transoxiana (the Asian land beyond the Oxus River, now in Uzbekistan, Tajikistan, Kazakhstan, Turkmenistan and Kyrgyzstan). From the fifth century onward, the Oghuz Turks were the founders and rulers of several important Turkic kingdoms and empires, such as those of the Seljuk Turks and the Ottoman Turks. In later centuries, after the rise of Islam, they adapted and applied their own traditions and institutions to the ends of the Islamic world and emerged as empire-builders with a constructive sense of statecraft.

Just as the Crusaders called all Muslims, Persians, Turks, Mamluks, Arabs, and other Near Easterners "Saracens," the Muslim Arabs lumped their European Christian enemies into the name *ifranj*, or *ifranjiyy*, the Arabic versions of the Latin name *Franci*. The Arabic word *Rum* referred to the Byzantine empire or "Eastern Rome," whom the Muslims met in battle, rather than to the Roman empire, which went out of existence two centuries before Islam came into being, but the word *Rumi* later acquired the wider meaning of "Christian" or "European." In the thirteenth century, a Persian Muslim poet and scholar was named Rumi (Jalal ad-Din Muhammad Rumi, 1207–1273). In 1071, after defeating the Byzantines at Manzikert, the Seljuk Turks, who a century earlier had adopted Islam as their religion, created a sultanate in Anatolia, called the "Sultanate of Rum." To this day, the Arabic words *rumi* and *franji* denote all Europeans, and even all Westerners.

Medieval French had two major dialects, whose names derived from how the French word for "yes" (now *oui*) was pronounced: the *langue d'oïl* and the *langue d'oc*. The latter gave its name to the geographical region of the Languedoc. By the end of the ninth century, the Frankish empire no longer existed. The kingdom of France was still called Francia in Latin, but it was called France in the *langue d'oïl*, from which the modern French language developed.

The twelfth-century French poet Jean Bodel, author of the *Chanson de Saisnes*, famously wrote, *Ne sont que trois matières à nul homme atandant / de France et de Bretaigne, et de Rome la grant* (There are but three matters awaiting every man / of France, and of Britain, and of Rome the great). The late-eleventh and twelfth-century Crusaders who fought the Muslims called themselves in their spoken language *François* (Frenchmen) and *Normands* (Normans), yet they wrote in Latin, and, in their Latin-language documents, such as the letter of Estienne de Blois to his wife Adele from the siege of Antioch in 1098, and the anonymous *Gesta Francorum* (Deeds of the Franks), these Crusaders called themselves *Franci* (Franks). This was a fantasy which was acted out in reality.

In the European languages, the word *Moor, Maure*, or *Moro* denoted swarthy skin as late as the fifteenth century. The Milanese duke Ludovico Sforza (1452–1508) was called *Ludovico il Moro* because of his dark complexion. The Umayyad Muslims, who had conquered Spain in 711–712 and called it *"al-Andalus,"* had met the Franks at "the battle of Tours-Poitiers" in southwest France in 732, where they were forced back into *"al-Andalus"* by Charles Martel (688–741). That battle actually took place at Moussais-la-Bataille, near the border between *Francia* and *Aquitania*. The Frankish and Burgundian armies were led by Charles Martel, while the "Saracen" armies were commanded by Abd ar-Rahman al-Ghafiqi, who was killed in the battle. Charles Martel won without using his cavalry. The surviving "Saracens" escaped southward during the night, crossed the Pyrenees, and returned to *"al-Andalus."*

After the battle of Tours-Poitiers, Francia expanded to southwest France (Aquitania), and Muslim expansion in Europe halted. Modern historians are still arguing about the significance of the battle of Tours-Poitiers, which some see as a minor skirmish, others as a major war. The name Martellus (the Hammer) was given to Charles by ninth-century European Christian historians, who thought that he had delivered to the "Saracens" or "Moors" a divine blow that stopped Islam and saved Christianity, the true religion. The most detailed account of that battle was written in 754 in a Latin book titled *Chronica Byzantia-Arabica* (in

Spanish *Crónica Mozárabe*), written by an anonymous "Mozarab" (from the Arabic word *musta'arib*, meaning Arabized), an Arabic-speaking Christian Spaniard who lived under Muslim rule in Spain (López Pereira 1980). Muslim Arab historians called the battle of Tours-Poitiers *marrakat balat ash-shuhada* (the battle of the court of the martyrs). As always, all was in the eye of the beholder.

Every German schoolchild, when taught the history of his or her country, learns that from the third to the fifth centuries the Germanic tribes gradually conquered the Roman empire and built the largest empire that had ever existed in Europe, covering most of present-day central and western Europe, and that it was called Francia (pronounced *Frankia*). In fact, Frankish history was more complicated. During the third century the Franks lived on the east bank of the lower Rhine but did not invade the Roman Empire. In the fourth century the Franks attempted to invade Roman Gaul and the Roman Empire yielded parts of Belgica Secunda between the Meuse and Scheldt rivers (now in Belgium) to the Franks. In 401–403 the Germanic Visigoths fought "the Gothic War" with the Romans in northern Italy, forcing Emperor Honorius to move from Milan to Ravenna. In 406 the Germanic Vandals invaded Gaul, and the Franks seized the lands west of the middle Rhine and parts of northeastern Gaul. In 480 the Frankish hold on northeastern Gaul resulted in the loss of the Roman province of Germania and parts of the two Roman provinces of Gallia Belgica (Belgica Prima and Belgica Secunda) to the Franks. The Gallo-Roman population in these areas merged with the waves of Germanic immigrants, and Latin was supplanted by early medieval German as the everyday language.

The name "Frank" remains in such German place names as *Frankfurt*, *Franken* (Franconia), and *Frankreich* (France). Medieval France also called itself Francia, but in the twelfth century it was already called France. Along with the *écu* and the *Louis d'Or*, the *franc* was the currency of France for centuries: only in the twenty-first century did it give way to the Euro. The European Christian Crusaders who invaded "the Holy Land" in the late eleventh century did not call themselves "Crusaders": they called themselves *Franci* and *Latini,* even though the Frankish kingdom had disappeared in the mid-ninth century, being replaced by France and Germany, and the "Frankish" Crusaders were mostly Frenchmen and Normans, with some Germans and others among them. The Frankish endonym gave the Crusaders the feeling of being part of a great empire, like that of Charlemagne (748–814), the great *"imperator romanorum."*

The old Latin name *francus,* and the Old English word *franca,* may have derived from the Old German word *frankon* meaning a "lance" or a "javelin." In Latin, however, the word *francus* also meant "a free man," just as the word *sclavus* meant "a slave." The Franks, as the conquering class, had the status of freemen in ancient Rome, while the Slavs were slaves. The Romans gave the name of *Franci* to the Germanic tribes that entered Roman history around 260 CE after crossing the River Rhine southward into the Roman Empire. Over the next century other Frankish tribes appeared in Roman written records. The major sources are the *XII Panegyrici Latini*, a collection of 12 ancient Roman panegyric orations in praise of important people written between 100 and 389 (Mynors 1964), and the Greek and Roman chronicles of Ammianus Marcellinus (1911), Claudius Claudianus (1979), Zosimus (2017), Sidonius Apollinaris (2024), and Gregorius de Turones (Gregory of Tours 1976).

Most historians like to divide history neatly into periods such as Prehistory, Classical Antiquity, the Middle Ages, the Early Modern period, Modern times, and the Post-Modern era. The "Migration Period" or the "Barbarian Invasions" is a name given by historians to the great wave of human migrations in Europe which lasted about seven centuries, from about 300 CE to 1000 CE, marking the transition from Late Antiquity to the Early Middle Ages. During that time, especially in the fifth century, the Western Roman Empire was destroyed by marauding tribes.

The invaders included the Huns, Goths, Vandals, Swabians, Franks, and other Turkic, Germanic, and Slavic tribes. The Huns, led by Attila (died 453), were a confederation of Central Asian equestrian nomads or semi-nomads (like the Mongols), with a Turkic aristocratic core. The migration of the Germanic tribes may have been triggered by the incursions of the Huns, which were connected to the Turkic migrations in Central Asia. Eight centuries later, in the thirteenth century, the Mongols made the vast "migration" which led them to conquer most of Asia and large parts of Europe and create the largest contiguous empire in human history.

The migrations of the "savage" tribes from Central Asia to Eastern Europe continued into the eleventh century, with successive waves of Slavs, Alans, Avars, Bulgars, Magyars, Pechenegs, Cumans, Turks, and Mongols radically changing the ethnic makeup of Eastern Europe, much more than the Muslim and Arab migrants of our own time have changed it. Western European historians, however, tend to emphasize the migrations that were most relevant to Western Europe. Most scholars of the Migration Period agree that the Franks emerged in the third century out of smaller groups, including the "savage" or "barbarian" Germanic tribes whom the Romans called *Salii, Ripuari, Sicambri, Chamavi, Bructeri, Chatti,* and *Chattuarii,* and who inhabited the northwestern coasts of Europe, the lower Rhine valley, and the lands immediately to its east. These names were later rendered into English as "Salian Franks," "Sicambrian Franks," "Chamavian Franks," and so on.

The exonyms the Romans gave the various Germanic tribes were corruptions of German names. For example, the *Salii,* whom we call the "Salian Franks," were a subgroup of the early *Franci* who originally had been living north of the *limes,* the boundary of the Roman empire, in the coastal areas above the River Rhine in the Netherlands, which had a region called "Salland," located west and north of the present Dutch province of Overijssel. The Merovingian Frankish kings who conquered Gaul from the Romans were of Salian stock. From the third century on, the *Salii* appear in Roman historical records as warlike Germanic pirates and as *Laeti*, the Roman exonym for "barbarians" permitted to settle on imperial Roman territory if they provide soldiers for the Roman legions.

The *Salii* were the first Germanic tribe from beyond the Roman *limes* that settled permanently on Roman land. Later the *Salii* were absorbed into the *Franci* and ceased to appear by their original name, especially from the fifth century, when they became the dominant Franks. The *Salii* were mentioned by Roman historians long before the *Ripuari*. The *Lex Salica* (Salic law) was an important body of Frankish law codified for governing the Salian Franks in the early Middle Ages during the reign of the Merovingian Frankish King Clovis in the sixth century. Although the Salic Law reflects ancient usage and practices, the *Lex Salica* was probably enacted between 507 and 511. The *Lex Ripuaria* originated around 630, in the Cologne area, and was a later development of the Frankish laws known from the *Lex Salica*.

To recapitulate, the Romans used the exonyms *Franci* (pronounced *Franki*) and *gens Francorum* (Frankish people) for the "savage" Germanic tribes that lived in the Lower Rhine valley and east of it, who later crossed the Rhine into the Roman province of Gaul, defeated the Celts and the Gauls, fought the Roman rulers, and were first mentioned in Roman writings in the third century. Their land was *Francia*. Scholars of human migrations think that the "Frankish" ethnic identify began to coalesce in the third century through the amalgamation of smaller Germanic tribes, just as the Teutonic identity encompassed several "savage" Germanic tribes worshiping several gods.

One of the ancient Germanic tribes were the *Alamanni*, also called *Allemanni* or *Alemanni* (ancient spellings often varied). Their name in Old German meant "all men," as in the modern German *alle Männer*, but the Romans had no idea of this. The *Allemanni* may have called themselves "all men" because they were originally an alliance of West Germanic tribes located around the upper Main River, one of the largest tributaries of the River Rhine, on land that is today part of Germany. One of the earliest references to the *Alamanni* is the Roman *cognomen* of *Alamannicus* assumed by the Roman emperor Marcus Aurelius Septimius Bassianus Antoninus Augustus Caracalla (186–217), who ruled the Roman Empire from 211–217 and who by that title claimed to be the vanquisher of the *Alamanni*. Eventually, these *Alamanni* merged with the Germanic tribes that the Romans called *Franci*. Nonetheless, the French exonym for Germany is still *l'Allemagne*, after the *Alemanni*.

In 241 CE, the future Roman emperor Aurelian (c. 214–275), then a military tribune, defeated the *Franci* in the neighborhood of Mainz and marched on against Persia. His troops sang, "*Mille Sarmatas, mille Francos, semel et semel occidimus; mille Persas, quaerimus*" ("We kill a thousand Sarmatians, a thousand Franks, once and for all; we want a thousand Persians": Given 2014). The first Roman document to mention the *Franci* was a third-century

Roman road map now known as the *Tabula Peutingeriana*. It is named after Conrad Peutinger (1465–1547), a German humanist, diplomat, politician, economist and antiquarian who brought it to the world's attention. The map had been discovered by the German scholar Conrad Celtes (1459–1508), who handed it over to Peutinger for his antiquities collection. Its thirteenth-century copy in the Austrian national library in Vienna is the only surviving copy of the *cursus publicus*, the road map of the Roman Empire. It covers all of Europe, parts of Asia (Persia and India) and North Africa. The map is a parchment scroll, 34 cm high and 6.75 m long, assembled from eleven horizontal sections. It was first published in 1591 by the Antwerp-based publishing house of Johannes Moretus (Peutinger 2003).

The inscription on the upper left corner of the *Tabula Peutingeriana* called the Franks *Chamavi qui et Pranci* (the Chamavi who are Pranci). The word *Pranci* was either a typo for *Franci*, or for *Phranci*. During the fourth century, the *Franci* appear in Roman manuscripts such as the *Panegyrici Latini* (Mynors 1964). The Germanic tribes whom the Romans called *Franci* were alternately Rome's enemies (*dediticii*) and its allies (*laeti*). Around 250 or 260 a group of Franci invaded a weakened Roman empire in Gaul and went as far as Tarragona in Hispania (now in the Spanish region of Catalunya). They bothered the Romans for about ten years before the Romans succeeded in expelling them.

From around 290 the Franci ruled the area around the River Scheldt (now in the Netherlands and Belgium) and raided the "English Channel" between Gaul and Britain to foil Roman shipping there. The Romans managed to get control of the area, but they did not expel the Franci, who continued their pirate raids until 358, when the Roman emperor Julian the Apostate invited the Salii or "Salian Franks" to settle in his empire as *foederati* (allies) of Rome. Later other Franks did the same. The *foederati* were bound by treaties to defend Rome militarily, while the *laeti* were foreign settlers who were granted land in exchange for military service to Rome.

Gradually, over two or three centuries, the Germanic tribes assumed a collective identity of "Franks" as they conquered the Roman empire from the Romans. They later believed that they were the Romans' successors, and even called themselves Romans. Beginning with Heinrich II in the early eleventh century, the German king had the official title of *rex Romanorum* (King of the Romans) and, after being crowned in Rome by the Pope, of *imperator Romanorum* (Emperor of the Romans). The Franks developed myths of origin showing their descent all the way back to the Trojans in early antiquity. The myth of Dido and Aeneas (the queen of Carthage and the prince of Troy) was created by the Roman poet Publius Vergilius Maro (70–19 BCE), better known as Virgil, even though Carthage (a Roman corruption of the Canaanite Hebrew name for "new city") was only founded by seafaring Canaanites (whom the Greeks called Phoenicians) in the ninth century BCE and Troy had been destroyed centuries earlier.

Chapter 3

Myths of Origin

Let us look at the collective psychology and identity of the Franks as it developed over the centuries. The "Merovingian" Franks were a royal Salian Frankish dynasty who believed that they were descended from a legendary king named Mariwig. His name, which meant "famed warrior" in Old German, was gradually transformed to Merovech, and was then Latinized into Meroveus, hence the Roman name *Merovingi*.

After conquering parts of the Roman empire, especially Gaul, and after defeating the Visigoths and the Burgundians, the Merovingians created a "Frankish" empire that ruled the former Roman Gaul and adjacent lands from the late fifth to the eighth century. Due to the psychologically complicated and at times even dangerous human family structure and sibling rivalry, there was continual strife and civil war between different branches of the Merovingian dynasty.

The "savage" Germanic tribes did not cut their hair, and the Merovingian kings were referred to by their Roman contemporaries as *reges criniti* or "long-haired kings" because their tribal leader wore his hair long, unlike the haircuts of the Romans and of the tonsured clergy. During the final century of Merovingian rule, ending in 751, their dynasty was pushed into a ceremonial role by their rivals, the "Carolingians," who previously were their *major domus* or "Mayors of the Palace."

As part of their myths of origin, some peoples believe that they are descended from the gods, some that they are chosen by God. The Jews have their myth of election as God's chosen people. While the Germanic "Franks" spoke various Germanic dialects, they imitated the "higher" Roman civilization, and wrote their documents, books, and histories in the Latin language of their former allies, the Romans, whom they had conquered, merged with, and displaced. The Latin word *vulgaris* meant "of or pertaining to the common people," from *vulgus* meaning "the common people, multitude, crowd, or throng." Vulgar Latin differed from classical, written Latin. The vulgar Latin brought by Roman soldiers to the provinces was not identical to the Latin of Cicero, and differed from it in vocabulary, and later in syntax and grammar as well. Some time in the mid-seventh century, during Merovingian Frankish rule, the history of the Franci in Gallia from 584 to 641 was written in a seventh-century Latin-language manuscript entitled *Fredegarii chronicon* (the Chronicle of Fredegarius), whose authorship is uncertain. It is written in Vulgar Latin, the popular spoken dialects of the Latin language in the Roman empire, which diverged from each other in the early Middle Ages, evolving into the Romance languages by the ninth century.

The intriguing question of who wrote the *Fredegarii chronicon* has been hotly debated by scholars. Fredegar is an unusual Frankish name. The Vulgar Latin language in which this work is written is pre-French, suggesting that it was written in Gaul. There are several theories about the authorship of this work: that this chronicle was written by one person, Fredegar, (suggested mainly by French historians), that this chronicle was written by *three authors* (a theory embraced by several prominent historians), and that this chronicle was the work of *two authors* (Fredegar et al. 1960). Fredegar himself is presumed to have been a Burgundian from the region of Avenches who spoke the *Langue d'oïl* and knew the alternate German name of Wifflisburg for this locality, a name just coming into usage. He also had access to the annals of many Burgundian churches and to court documents and interviewed Lombard, Visigoth, and Slavic ambassadors. His awareness of events in the Byzantine world is usually explained by the proximity of Burgundy to Byzantine Italy. Even though Fredegar was alive around 660, he did not continue the chronicle past the year 642.

The fascinating *psychological* aspect of the *Fredegarii chronicon,* however, is its myth of origin. Fredegar's chronicle related that the Franks were descended from the ancient Trojans, and that their name of *Franci* derived from a mythical ancient Trojan king named "Francio." In its "continuations," in 727 a Latin Frankish book titled *Liber Historiae Francorum* (Book of the History of the Franks) claimed that after the fall of Troy (some two thousand years earlier) 12,000 Trojans, led by their king Priamus and their sage Antenor, migrated to the Tanais River (now the Don River) and settled in Pannonia (now in Hungary, Austria, Croatia, Slovenia, and Bosnia), near the Sea of Azov (the northern part of the Black Sea), where they founded a town named *Sicambria*, whence came the tribe that the Romans called *Sicambri*.

Why did the Franks need to imagine themselves as descendants of the ancients Trojans? The Trojan prince Aeneas, according to Virgil's myth, went to Carthage and thence to Italy, to found Rome. If Rome was created by Aeneas, could the Franks have wished to see themselves as greater than Rome? If they had been founded by his father, Priam, they had preceded the Romans, and the Roman empire was theirs by right of ancestry, not only conquest. As the Franks became the major European power in the seventh and eighth centuries, they needed myths of origin to match their greatness. This was part of their ethnocentrism and group narcissism. On the other hand, they may have felt inferior to the Romans, whose language and culture they eagerly adopted.

The Merovingian Franks expanded from central Europe in all directions. In the eighth century, the Frankish empire comprised *Neustria* in the northwest, *Aquitania* in the southwest, *Austrasia* in the northeast, *Burgundia* in the south, *Lombardia* in northern Italy, and several other kingdoms. *Francia* comprised large parts of the territory of present-day Italy, France, Germany, Belgium, Luxembourg, and the Netherlands.

The original Frankish capital was Turniacum, now Tournai in Belgium. The *major domus* (superior of the house or "Mayor of the Palace") was an early medieval office, also called *majordomo*. It was used in the Frankish kingdoms in the seventh and eighth centuries. The *major domus* was the most powerful courtier after the king. As we have seen, in 732 the Franks under Charles Martel won a battle over the invading "Saracens" or "Moors" from Spain between Tours and Poitiers in Aquitaine. The "Saracens," who were Arabized "Berbers," called it in Arabic *ma'arakat bala ash-Shuhada* (Battle of Court of The Martyrs). The battle of 732 was fought near the village of Moussais-la-Bataille (modern Vouneuil-sur-Vienne) north of Poitiers. The location of the battle was close to the border between Francia and the "independent" Aquitaine, which had not effectively resisted the "Moors" (another exonym for the "Saracens").

The Muslims who invaded Spain were formally ruled from Damascus by their Umayyad Caliph, Al-Walid ibn al-Malik (668–715). The word "caliph" is an anglicized form of the Arabic word *khalifa*, which means "the successor," "replacement," or "representative" of the Prophet Muhammad (died 632 CE). The word "caliphate" is the anglicized form of the Arabic word *khilafa*, meaning the realm and reign of the *khalifa* and it is the Islamic conception of government representing the political unity and religious leadership of the Muslim world. Muhammad was called *rasul Allah* (messenger of Allah), and the early caliphs of "the Muslim nation" following his death were called *khalifat rasul Allah*, meaning "the successors to the messenger of Allah." Not that the Muslim *ummah* (nation), a word that comes from *umm* (mother), was ever unified. There were several rival caliphates at the same time in Muslim history, which we shall discuss below. However, the Muslims took their caliphs and caliphates very seriously, and those living in a given caliphate saw their caliph as their supreme lord, leader, king, and master, above all the *emirs* (princes) and *sultans* (rulers).

As we have seen, the battle of Tours-Poitiers in 732 pitted Frankish and Burgundian forces under the Austrasian *major domus* Charles Martel against the army of the Umayyad caliphate led by Abdul Rahman al-Ghafiqi, the governor-general of *"al-Andalus."* The Franks won, Abdul Rahman al-Ghafiqi was killed, and Charles extended his authority into Aquitaine in the south. Ninth-century chroniclers, who interpreted the outcome of the battle as a divine judgment in his favor, gave Charles the nickname of *Martellus* (The Hammer), recalling Judas Maccabeus (The Hammer) of the Jewish revolt against the Syrian Greeks in the second century BCE. Details of the battle, including its exact location and the exact number of combatants, cannot be determined from the accounts that have survived; although the Frankish troops seem to have won the battle without cavalry.

The Merovingian Frankish leader Charles Martel was a brilliant military leader. He helped found the Carolingian Frankish empire, which succeeded the Merovingian one. In fact, Merovingian rule ended in 751 with a palace coup by Pepin the Short (714–768), the *major domus* of the Merovingian king Childeric III (died 753). Pepin deposed his king and took his place, beginning a new dynasty that later became known as the Carolingian Frankish monarchy, after Charles Martel. Its most famous king was Charlemagne, who became "Roman emperor" in 800. Indeed, the newly constituted "Franks" gradually took over the Roman empire. In fact, despite the fact that they spoke German dialects, they adopted Latin as their official language and considered themselves the successors of the Roman empire. Later, in 962, after the German king Otto was crowned *Imperator Romanorum*, this became known as the *translatio imperii* or transfer of the empire. This was a fascinating notion, based on the fantasy that the Roman empire was "translated" or "transferred" from the Romans to the Franks.

The most famous king of the Franks was Charlemagne (748–814), whose Latin name (*Carolus Magnus*) and German name (*Karl der Grosse*) both meant Charles the Great, and who was King of the Franks with his younger brother Carloman (751–771) from 768 to his death. Later Frankish historians "continued" Fredegar's Chronicle to the coronation of Charlemagne (and of his brother Carloman) as *Rex Francorum* (Kings of the Franks). Beginning with Heinrich II, in 1002–1003, the German kings were also elected and crowned *Rex Romanorum* (King of the Romans) rather than *Rex Germanorum* (King of the Germans) and even *Imperator Romanorum* (Emperor of the Romans). This was based on the fantasy that the Franks and later the Germans were the direct successors to the Romans. In the late Middle Ages, this fantasy led to the notion of the "Holy Roman Empire of the German Nation." The title of *Rex Romanorum* meant that its holder was not only King of Germany but also of Italy and of all the other "Holy Roman" territories. Even though Charlemagne suffered some defeats, such as at the one at Roncevaux Pass in 778, he called himself on his coinage *Karolus Imperator Augustus*.

The Byzantine Empire often encroached on Rome's eastern territories. The eighth and ninth centuries were dominated by the religious controversy over *Iconoclasm* (the breaking of religious icons). Icons had been banned as pagan idolatry by the Byzantine emperors Leo III and Constantine V, leading to revolts by the "iconodules" throughout the empire. The efforts of the Byzantine Empress Irene Serantapechaina (died 803) led to the Second Council of Nicaea in 787, which affirmed that icons could be *venerated* but not *worshiped as idols or gods*. Empress Irene endeavored to negotiate a marriage between herself and Charlemagne, but, according to Theophanes the Confessor, the scheme was frustrated by Aetios, one of her favorites (Theophanes the Confessor 1982, 1997).

In 800 CE, after protracted negotiations, Charlemagne was crowned *Imperator Augustus* in Rome by Pope Leo III, who wanted the German king as his ally against his rival, the Byzantine empire. In 962 Pope John XII crowned the "King of the Romans" (the German king) Otto (912–973) "Holy Roman Emperor" and a new political entity called *Sanctum Romanum Imperium* (Holy Roman Empire) was born, a fantastic psychogeographical entity that later became the "Holy Roman Empire of the German Nation." As the great French writer Voltaire (François-Marie Arouet, 1694–1778), wittily observed, this "body" was neither holy, nor Roman, nor an empire, and not even German. Nonetheless, it was considered a real political entity, with its own coats of arms, army, and all the trappings of a real empire.

The Frankish empire, which became the "Holy Roman Empire," had begun with small Germanic tribes. During the fifth century the Germanic people whom the Romans called *Salii* and whom we now call the "Salian Franks," had crossed the Rhine into Roman Gaul and Spain. They later extended their hold on the Roman empire to northwestern Europe, including the Low Countries south of the River Rhine, Belgium, and northern France, absorbing other "Frankish" tribes, such as the Salians of Lorraine, the Ripuarians of Franconia, the Saxons, the Bavarians, and the Swabians. The German name *Franken* refers to the geographical region of Franconia, as well as to a medieval duchy, one of the five "tribal duchies" or "young duchies" that arose within the "Holy Roman Empire of the German Nation" during the late ninth and early tenth centuries (Saxony, Franconia, Bavaria, Swabia, and Lorraine), and which comprised the "Frankish" territories east of the River Rhine, in what is now Germany.

Chapter 4

The Cross and the Crusades

In a collective psychohistorical process that characterizes many ethnic groups, the Romanized Germanic tribes that migrated and conquered most of Western Europe from the Romans adopted the Roman exonym *Franci* for themselves and developed a steadily growing kingdom in Central and Western Europe that later became the Frankish empire. As was common in medieval Europe, kingdoms were ruled by dynasties, which were established amid much bloodshed and later divided amid fratricidal wars among the successors. The "Merovingian" Frankish dynasty was named after the mythical *Meroveus*, and the "Carolingian" after the actual *Carolus*, the Latinized name of Charles Martel, the hero of the battle of Tours-Poitiers against the invading Muslims in 732. Some scholars, however, believe that the medieval Latin name *carolingi* for this dynasty was an altered form of an Old High German name *karling* or *kerling* meaning "descendant of Charles," similar to the Middle High German *kerlinc*.

With the fall of the Roman empire in the fifth century, the Germanic "Merovingian Franks" set up their kingdom in Italy in its place. In 493 the first "Merovingian" Frankish king, Clovis (466–511), who united the various Germanic "Frankish" tribes, married a Burgundian Christian queen named Clotilde (475–545). The name Clovis was a Latinized form of the German name Chlodovech, which became the Latin Chlodovechus, from which came the Latin name Ludovicus, and also into the French name *Louis*. By that time the Roman language, Latin, was evolving as the common language of literate Europe. The "Franks" adopted it as their own. Centuries later, the Vulgar Latin dialects that were spoken in various parts of the Roman empire evolved into different languages such as Portuguese, Spanish, Catalan, Provençal, French, Italian, and Romanian. Church Latin was as used in documents of the Roman Catholic Church and in its Latin liturgies. Though its pronunciation differed somewhat from that of Classical Roman Latin, Church Latin was not a distinct language but rather Latin used for ecclesiastical purposes: the same language was also used for many other purposes.

From 382 to 405, the *Vulgata* Latin version of the Hebrew Bible was largely the work of Eusebius Sophronius Hieronymus (347–420), also known as

DOI: 10.4324/9781003527367-4

Hieronymus Stridonensis, but better known as Saint Jerome, a Confessor and Doctor of the Church who was commissioned by Pope Damasus I (died 384) to make a revision of older Latin translations. The *Vulgata* accelerated the spread of Christianity, which Constantine had made into the religion of the Roman empire. In 496, after marrying the 21-year-old Queen Clotilde of Burgundy, the 30-year-old King Clovis of *Francia* became Christian, as did his "Frankish" subjects. Myth has it that this dramatic act followed his victory in battle over the *Alamanni* at Tolbiacum (now the German town of Zülpich), between Aachen and Bonn, but Clovis had fought an earlier battle at Soissons in 486, a later battle near Strassbourg in 506, ten years after his conversion. It is more likely that Clovis was following the Roman empire in his conversion.

The Frankish kingdom that Clovis created gradually expanded, but with each generation, the king needed to divide it among his rival sons, and he also feared coups d'état by the *major domus* or Mayor of the Palace. With many splits, divisions, and battles, the Merovingian Frankish empire lasted some three centuries, with several kings named Clovis. At the same time, the "Carolingian" Franks slowly gained the ascendancy. Charles Martel defeated the Muslims at Tours-Poitiers in 732, forcing them back into Iberia. The Carolingian Frankish empire, which supplanted the Merovingian one in 751, lasted two centuries. During the eighth century it covered much of Western Europe, including most of present-day France and Germany. In the ninth it split into several kingdoms. Nonetheless, the name *Francia* remained that of France until at least the twelfth century.

The "Moorish" Conquest of "al-Andalus"

At the beginning of the eighth century, after the Muslim conquests of the Middle East and North Africa, the Muslim *emir* Musa bin Nusair (640–716) governed the province of *Ifriqiya* (now Tunisia and eastern Algeria) for the sixth Umayyad caliph, Al-Walid ibn al-Malik (668–715), who ruled from Damascus. Musa's father Nusair was an Arab from Syria who had been captured during the first Muslim expansion and enslaved. After regaining his freedom, he returned to his hometown, where Musa was born. In 711 CE Musa sent the "Berber" Muslim conqueror Tariq ibn Ziyad (died 720) to the place now called Gibraltar (from the Arabic *jebel al-Tariq*, or Mount Tariq), where the Muslim expedition discovered that a large Gothic army was marching nearby. The seventeenth-century Muslim historian Abu-l-Abbas Ahmad ibn Mohammed al-Maqqari, who was born in the North African town of Tlemcen (now in Algeria), wrote that Tariq ibn Ziyad burned his own ships and told his men that they had no choice but to fight, and that they would be glorious. On July 19, 711 Tariq ibn Ziyad won the Battle of Guadalete River and the Gothic king Roderic was lost or killed. The name *Guadalete* is a corruption and misnomer of the Arabic *Wadi al-lakko*. The battle actually took place near the former La Janda lagoon, between Algeciras and Jerez de la Frontera.

Envious of his subordinate Tariq, Musa bin Nusair decided to land his army in "*al-Andalus*" to lead the Muslim army instead of Tariq, and he was apparently successful in his battles. After taking Iberia in 712, he crossed the Pyrenees into France, but then, according to some Muslim historians (see below), he was summoned to his caliph in Damascus. According to an anonymous medieval Muslim Arab historian, the caliph asked Musa, "Now tell me, who are these *franj* and what is their nature?" Musa answered, "They are a great people, brave and tempestuous in attack, but cowardly when defeated." The caliph then asked Musa, "How did the battle turn out between you and them? For you or the reverse?" Musa answered, "The reverse? No, by Allah and His Prophet! Not a company of my army was defeated in battle. Never did the Muslims hesitate to follow me when I led them, even though they were half the number of the *franj*."

Musa bin Nusair had not fought the "Franks." He was probably speaking about his battles against the Goths in Spain, but to the Muslims, all European Christian were "*franj*." In contrast to Musa's poor opinion of the *franj*, the twelfth-century Kurdish Muslim *sultan* of Egypt and Syria, Salah ed-din Yusuf ibn Ayyub (1138–1193), whom the Franks called "Saladin," and who defeated the "Franks" at the Battle of Hattin in 1187 and took Jerusalem from them, reportedly told his troops: "See the *franj!* See with what tenacity they fight for their religion, while we, the Muslims, show no zest for holy war!" "Saladin" was probably trying to exhort his men to fight more tenaciously.

There are many legends about Musa bin Nusair. According to some Muslim historians, such as Al-Hakim, Musa bin Nusair had been sailing in the "Dark Sea" where he came upon cage-like bottles floating and a great voice screaming "No Prophet of God, Not again!" Musa brought one of these bottles on deck and, to his surprise, a man (or genie) appeared on the ship, who took him for Suleyman (Solomon), and said in astonishment "By God, You are them! If it wasn't for a favor you (meaning Solomon) have done to me, I would have drowned your ships!" Then the man disappeared. The report continues to state that Musa said to his crew that the man was a *jinn* (demon) who had been enslaved by King Sulayman (a prophet in Islam) and was given a favor-release by Solomon. The report continues to state that Musa's campaign was so extraordinarily successful that the *jinn* of Solomon might have had a hand in it.

In 712 Musa bin Nusair joined his army to that of Tariq ibn Ziyad to conquer Iberia, then led the Muslim armies into Septimania, in southern Francia, where he annexed some land. Musa, however, cast his rival Tariq ibn Ziyad into prison, and was planning an invasion of the rest of Europe, when he was recalled to Damascus by his Umayyad caliph, Al-Walid: Tariq had smuggled a letter out of his prison informing the caliph of what had happened, and Al-Walid was displeased by Musa's behavior. Both leaders were therefore summoned by the caliph to Damascus. Tariq arrived first. Al-Walid took ill, however, and his brother, Sulayman ibn Abd al-Malik, asked Musa, who arrived in great pomp with a cavalcade of soldiers and war spoils, to delay his entry into the city until Al-Walid had died and Sulayman became the new caliph.

Tragically for himself, Musa ignored Sulayman's request, entered Damascus triumphantly, and brought his case before the ailing Caliph Al-Walid. After hearing from both Musa and Tariq, the caliph concluded that Musa, as *emir*, had wronged his subordinate general, Tariq, by taking all the credit for the victory. Al-Walid died a few days later, and was succeeded by his brother Sulayman, who demanded that Musa deliver all his spoils to him. When Musa complained, Sulayman stripped him of his rank and confiscated all the booty, including a table which had reputedly once belonged to King Solomon. He ordered Musa (a very old man by then) to stand in the sun all day long as a punishment and Musa reportedly said, "O, Caliph, I deserve a better rewarding than this." He was seen begging at a mosque door in the last days of his life.

Regardless of the personal fortunes of Musa and Tariq, the Muslims had conquered Spain, which they called "*al-Andalus*." The battle of Tours-Poitiers in 732 was a turning point, their first defeat after their succession of victories in the Middle East, North Africa, and Spain. Henceforth the Muslims remained in "*al-Andalus*," their imaginary name for Iberia, and no longer ventured into *Francia*. They did not know the Europeans well, and were not interested in the political, social, or cultural changes in Europe. Keeping a fixed mental image of the *franj*, they did not seem to know that Francia had split up in the ninth century, and that new kingdoms such as Germany, France, and Normandy had come into being. If the Crusaders themselves called themselves *Franci*, no wonder the Muslims called them *franji* as well. Perhaps they did not want to know too much about the *franj*. They preferred to live in a fantasy world, divided into *Dar al-Islam* and *Dar al-Harb*. The modern Moroccan Arab scholar Abdallah Laroui argued that the Arabs live in a society that ignored history, that they lived in a kind of ahistorical bubble, just as the Jews had done for almost 15 centuries (Laroui 1976, Yerusahlemi 1982, Falk 1996).

The Disintegration of Francia

In the ninth century the Carolingian Frankish empire fell apart. The Frankish king Carolus Magnus (Charlemagne) was crowned emperor by the pope in Rome in 800 and died in 814. Following bloody fratricidal wars among his sons, the Treaty of Verdun in 843 divided the Frankish empire into three kingdoms: *Francia occidentalis* (West Francia), *Francia Media (Central Francia)*, and *Francia orientalis* (East Francia). Central Francia, the kingdom of Lothair, soon disappeared politically. The realm of Lothair, which included the kingdom of Italy, Burgundy, Provence, and the west of Austrasia, was an unnatural creation, with no historical or ethnic identity to bind its varied peoples. The kingdom was split on Lothair's death into Lotharingia (Lorraine), Provence (with Burgundy divided between it and Lotharingia), and Italy.

Count Welf or Hwelf of Metz was the son of the ninth-century Frankish count Rothard of Metz. He founded the medieval Frankish dynasty called the

Elder House of Welf. In historical chronicles, Welf is mentioned on the occasion of the wedding of his daughter Judith with Emperor Louis the Pious in 819. Welf began the Elder House of Welf, a dynasty of European rulers in the ninth through the eleventh centuries. It consisted of a Burgundian group and a Swabian group. Historians disagree on whether the two groups formed one dynasty or whether they only shared the same name.

In 869 the Frankish "Roman" Emperor Louis II allied himself with the eastern Roman Emperor Basil I against the "Saracens," while Charles the Bald of West Francia tried to take Francia Media after the death of Lothair II, but was resisted by Louis the German. The Central Frankish kingdom was once again divided into Lorraine, Burgundy, and northern Italy. East Francia, essentially Germany and Austria, was divided into four "young" duchies: Alamannia, Franconia, Saxony, and Bavaria, which at that time included Moravia and Carinthia. The dukes elected their king, who was the King of the Germans. Henceforth there was no more Frankish Empire. West Francia became France, East Francia became Germany, and the Normans set up a large duchy as well. Yet, when the French and Norman Christians left on their First Crusade in 1096, they called themselves and wrote of themselves in Latin as *Franci*. We shall try to explain this fantasy below.

By 884 the West Frankish king Charles *le gros* (839–888) had briefly reunited all the Frankish kingdoms under his rule. The fat king was deposed in 887 and died in 888. In 887 Odo (Eudes), the count of Paris, was elected King of West Francia, and he assumed the crown upon the death of Charles the Fat. The Frankish empire split up again. The nobles and leading clergy of Upper Burgundy assembled at Saint Maurice and elected Rudolph, count of Auxerre, from the Elder House of Welf, as King of the Franks. Rudolph of Burgundy tried to reunite Burgundy with Francia Media, but opposition by Arnulf of Carinthia (850–899), the Slovenian King of East Francia (and the future "Holy Roman Emperor"), forced him to focus on Burgundy. Eventually, Francia Media split up, and the other two parts (East and West Francia) vied for the title of "Francia." The rulers of Francia Orientalis, or Germany, who claimed the Roman imperial title and wanted to reunify the Frankish Empire under their rule, renamed their kingdom the "Holy Roman Empire."

The kings of Francia Occidentalis, however, successfully opposed the German claim, and managed to preserve their country as an independent kingdom, distinct from the "Holy Roman Empire", called France. Its capital was Paris. From 888 to 1180 Francia Occidentalis grew steadily and became the kingdom of France, one of the largest and most powerful in Europe. The short-lived Central Francia included parts of northern Italy, Burgundy, Provence and Austrasia, the northeastern portion of the Frankish kingdom, comprising parts of present-day France, Germany, Belgium, Luxembourg, and the Netherlands. These parts were gradually divided among the various kingdoms, chiefly France, Burgundy, and Germany.

Chapter 5

The Fantasy of the Holy Roman Empire

One of the fascinating things about medieval Germany is how East Francia, the eastern part of the former Frankish empire, gradually "revived" the defunct Roman empire and became its successor. This psychohistorical and psychogeographical fantasy was maintained for many centuries. The "Holy Roman Empire" or (as it was called by the Germans from the fifteenth century), "the Holy Roman Empire of the German Nation," came into being after King Otto "the Great" of Germany (912–973) was crowned *imperator Romanorum* by Pope Johannes II in 962. The pope needed Otto to protect him militarily from an Italian nobleman named Berengar of Ivrea (died 966), who had declared himself king of Italy and occupied the Papal States. Ten days after the coronation, the pope and emperor ratified the *Diploma Ottonianum*, under which the emperor became the guarantor of the independence and integrity of all the papal states in Italy, which were the territorial possession of the Pope and a symbol of his temporal power.

The "Translation of the Empire"

Like beauty, history is in the eye of the beholder. In contemporary and later Latin writings, the crowning of the German king Otto I by Pope Johannes XII in 962 was referred to as the *translatio imperii* or "the transfer of the empire." Medieval historians, however, interpreted this *translatio imperii* in different ways, depending on their nationality and loyalty. For example, the twelfth-century *German* historian Otto von Freising saw the *translatio imperii* as the transfer of the empire by stages from Rome to Byzantium to the Franks to the Lombards *to the Germans*. His *French* contemporary Chrestien de Troyes saw it as the transfer of the empire by stages from Greece to Rome *to France*, and the fourteenth-century *English* historian Richard de Bury saw it as the transfer of the empire from Athens to Rome to Paris *to England*. It was all in the eye of the beholder.

Christianity took many centuries to take hold in "pagan" Europe. After King Clovis of the Merovingian Franks married Queen Clotilde of Burgundy and adopted Christianity in 496, the "Salian Franks" had spread Christianity in Europe. Just as the Frankish empire had split up in the ninth century, the

Roman Catholic Christian Church split up in the eleventh, in what is known as the Great Schism of 1054. This East-West Schism divided medieval Christendom into the Western or "Latin" part in Rome and the Eastern or "Greek" part in Constantinople, which later became the Roman Catholic Church and the Greek Orthodox Church.

The causes of the Great Schism were personal, political, theological, linguistic, and, above all, psychological. *One wonders how secure people are in their religious belief when they try to impose it on others.* Pope Leo IX of Rome and Patriarch Michaelis Cerularius of Constantinople heightened the conflict by suppressing the Greek and Latin languages in their respective domains. In 1054, Roman Catholic legates traveled to Constantinople to deny Cerularius the title of Ecumenical Patriarch and to insist that he recognize Rome's claim to be the head and mother of the Church. Cerularius refused. The leader of the Roman legation angrily excommunicated Cerularius, while he furiously excommunicated the Roman legates.

By the eleventh century, the Frankish empire had ceased to exist as a political, geographical, or ethnic entity. The kingdoms that replaced it, such as France and Germany, continued to expand and flourish. In a striking psychohistorical fantasy, the German kings thought of themselves as direct successors of the old Roman emperors. Despite being Kings of Germany, they bore titles such as *Rex romanorum* and *imperator Augustus*. While the Germans spoke many different German dialects, the official language of the medieval German kingdom, like that of the Frankish one, was Latin, and its documents and histories were written in Latin.

Unlike France, which was an absolute and hereditary monarchy, Germany, which became the "Holy Roman Empire," consisted of duchies or principalities, which were ruled by *Fürsten* (princes). The seven most powerful of these were called *Curfüsten* (elector princes, or simply Electors). These *Curfüsten* elected the German king, and were therefore very powerful. The dignity of *Curfürst* was extremely prestigious and second only to the King or Emperor, exceeding such titles as count, duke, and archduke. Formally, however, they elected a *Rex Romanorum* or "King of the Romans," who was crowned in Aachen but only became "Holy Roman Emperor" after being crowned by the pope in Rome, which, at times, took many years, due to the perennial rivalry and power struggles between the older pope and the younger "Holy Roman Emperor."

The Ottonian dynasty (919–1024) was a dynasty of Germanic Kings, named after its first emperor, Otto, but also known as the Saxon dynasty after the family's origin in Saxony. Under the reign of the Ottonian emperors, the German duchies of Lorraine, Saxony, Franconia, Swabia, Thuringia, and Bavaria were consolidated, and the German king Otto was crowned Emperor of these regions in 962. In the eleventh century, the German kings formally assumed the title of *imperator Romanorum* or Roman Emperor. Why had they not done so earlier? Some historians believe that they had tried to avoid conflict with the Byzantine Emperor in Constantinople, which was now no longer a threat to them. The term *imperator Romanorum* became official when the last Ottonian German king, Conrad II (990–1039), who was elected King of Germany in 1024, was crowned *imperator Romanorum* by Pope Johannes XIX (died 1032) in 1027. Under the reign of the Salian emperors (1024–1125), the "Holy Roman Empire" annexed northern Italy and Burgundy.

In the meantime, France had become an absolute monarchy, where the King was not elected by the dukes, as in Germany, but dynastically inherited his throne from his father. The Carolingians Franks ruled France for a while, but lost it when Hugues Capet (938–996), Duke of France and Count of Paris, was crowned King of France in 987, succeeding the last Carolingian king, Louis V or Louis *le fainéant* (the idle). Louis had died that year at about the age of twenty, either accidentally or of poisoning by his mother, Queen Emma of Italy, the widow of Lothair who had married a descendant of Otto. Hugues Capet was the son of *Hugues le Grand*, Duke of the Franks, and a grandson of the German king *Heinrich der Finkler* (876–936), also known as *Heinrich der Vogler, Henricius Auceps*, or, Henry the Fowler. The descendants of Hugues Capet, known as the "Capetians," progressively unified France through a series of wars and dynastic inheritance.

By the eleventh century, West Francia or France was a powerful kingdom, totally separate from the now-defunct Frankish empire. Its language, which scholars call "Old French," was the Vulgar Latin dialect spoken in territories which span roughly the northern half of modern France and parts of modern Belgium and Switzerland. It was known as the *langue d'oïl*, to distinguish it from the *langue d'oc* from which developed the Occitan and Provençal languages, spoken south of the *langue d'oïl*. In the *langue d'oïl* the word for yes was *oïl*, while in the *langue d'oc* it was *oc*. In modern French, both are *oui*. The *langue d'oc* gave its name to the whole southern region of France, called Languedoc. The name of the country, in the *langue d'oïl*, was *France*, not Francia, and its inhabitants were called *François*. Nevertheless, when the Crusades began at the end of the eleventh century, the Frenchmen and Normans who led them wrote Latin letters and documents still calling themselves *Franci*. The Arabs and Muslims, for their part, called *everyone* who came from Europe *al-franj*, the Arabic name for the Franks.

Burgundy and Normandy, which later became parts of France, were not so in the eleventh century. They were separate kingdoms which often warred with France or joined her allies. Burgundy had a complex history. It became a kingdom after the dissolution of the Frankish Empire in the ninth century. After the dynastic succession was settled in the 880s, there were four different geographical regions called *Burgundia* or *Bourgogne*: the Kingdom of Upper Burgundy around Lake Geneva, the Kingdom of Lower Burgundy in Provence, the Duchy of Burgundy west of the Saône River, and the County of Burgundy east of the Saône. In 937 the two kingdoms of Upper and Lower Burgundy were united, while Magdeburg became an important city of the

"Holy Roman Empire," after a Diet held there by Otto I, "Holy Roman Emperor." In 1032 the Kingdom of Burgundy was absorbed into the "Holy Roman Empire" under Emperor Conrad II as the "Kingdom of Arles," which however, existed more *de jure* than *de facto*, its territory slowly dwindling, until its remnants finally passed to France. The duchy and county of Burgundy, however, remained separate from France.

Normandy, as its name implies, was a duchy created by the Normans or "Norsemen," the invaders from Northern Europe who settled in northwestern France, on the English Channel. From there, however, the Normans spread far and wide, attacking Paris and other parts of France and taking lands as far south as Naples and Sicily. Normandy had a long history. In Roman times, Normandy had been Romanized by the building of Roman roads and by a policy of urbanization. The Belgian Celts, known to the Romans as *Galli*, invaded Normandy in successive waves in the fourth and third centuries BCE. When Julius Caesar invaded *Gallia* there were nine different Gallic tribes in Normandy. Classicists have knowledge of many Gallo-Roman villas in Normandy. In the late third century, "Barbarian" raids devastated Normandy. Coastal settlements risked raids by Saxon pirates. Christianity began to enter the area during this period. In 406, Germanic tribes began invading from the West, while the Saxons subjugated the Norman coast. The Roman Emperor withdrew from most of Normandy.

By 486, the area between the Somme and the Loire rivers had come under the control of the Frankish lord Clovis. It remained under "Frankish" rule, but from the eighth to the eleventh century, Roman Normandy was invaded by the Scandinavian "Norsemen." Under the medieval feudal system, the "fiefdom" of Normandy was created in 911 for the Norseman leader Rollo or Roluo (860–932), who later became Duke Robert of Normandy, his baptismal name. The name "Rollo" was probably a Frankish Latin version of the Scandinavian name Hrólf, as we may gather from the Latinization of the name Hrólf Kraki into Roluo in the *Gesta Danorum* (Deeds of the Danes) by the twelfth century Danish historian Saxo Grammaticus.

Frenchmen and Normans

The city of Paris, the capital of *Francia occidentalis*, that is, France, was a frequent target of attacks by the Normans. As we have seen, in 887 the young Odo or Eudes (860–898), Count of Paris, was elected "King of the Franks" in place of the older incumbent, Charles the Fat (839–888), thanks to the fame that Odo had gained in his defense of Paris during the long Viking siege of Paris in 885–886. The young Norseman Rollo, Roull or Hrólf had been one of the lesser leaders of the Viking fleet that besieged Paris, but he became the major leader of the Normans. In 911, in the Treaty of Saint-Clair-sur-Epte, Rollo became a duke and vassal to the king of the West Franks, Charles the Simple (879–929). Rollo was baptized, and took the name of *Robert de Normandie*. In exchange for his homage and fealty, Rollo legally gained the territory that he and his Viking allies had previously conquered. The descendants of Rollo and his followers adopted the local Gallo-Roman language, intermarried with the area's inhabitants, and the Normans became a mixture of Scandinavians, Hiberno-Norse, Orcadians, Anglo-Danish, Franks, and Gauls.

The Normans adopted a dialect of the French language. Rollo's descendant *Guillaume le conquérant* (William the Conqueror, 1027–1087), Duke of Normandy, crossed *La Manche* (the English Channel) with his army, and conquered England in 1066 at the Battle of Hastings, delivering a collective trauma not only to the Angles and Saxons but also to the entire European continent, while retaining the fiefdom of Normandy for himself and his descendants. The Normans were warlike, and they raided and invaded far and wide. Normandy became a great power with territories in England, Wales, Italy, Byzantium, and elsewhere. After conquering England, the Norman language entered Old English, and the Normans spoke an "Anglo-French" or "Anglo-Norman" language, a beautiful example of which can be found in the famous *Estoire de la Guerre Sainte* by the Norman historian-poet Ambroise, written after the end of the Third Crusade, around 1195 (Ambroise 1897, 1941, 2003).

By the eleventh century, the medieval Christian realms of Normandy, France, Spain west of the Rhine and Germany or the "Holy Roman Empire" east of the Rhine were firmly established. It is fascinating to note that the Germans still call France by the Name of *Frankreich*, but when they refer to the empire of *Karl der Grosse* (Charlemagne), they call it *Frankenreich*. Did this exonym mean that the Germans, who regarded themselves as the successors to the Roman Empire, had ceded the succession of their Frankish empire to the French? After *Francia Orientalis* became the "Holy Roman Empire of the German Nation," its name disappeared, and *Francia Occidentalis* became simply *Francia*, from which the word *France* is derived. It is still called *Francia* in Spanish, Italian, and other languages.

No nation is a "pure race." All nations are mixtures of tribes and peoples of different origins. The Franks had been a mixture of Germanic tribes, and the "French" were not Franks but a mixture of Gallic tribes with West Frankish Germanic tribes and Celtic tribes (Braudel 1989–1990). When French children are taught to say *"nos ancêtres les Gaulois"* (our ancestor the Gauls) they are being taught a *myth of origin*. The phrase sounds weird or funny when it is uttered by French people from Martinique, Vietnam, or Mali.

While the "Latin" *François* spoke a language derived from Vulgar Latin, the Germanic "East Franks" spoke various Germanic languages and dialects and called themselves *Teutsche*, meaning "the people," from which comes the modern German word *deutsch*. The Germans of the former East Francia, which later became the "Holy Roman Empire," did not easily give up their Frankish identity. They called their old country *Frankenland* and one of their major duchies was called *Franken*.

The Germans could not as a group mourn their loss of the western part of their empire, and wanted it back. The German kings at first tried to revive the Frankish empire by conquering and annexing the kingdom of France. It was not until the thirteenth century that they were forced to give up that wish at the Battle of Bouvines (1214), in which King Philippe Auguste of France roundly defeated King Otto IV of Germany and Count Ferrand of Flanders (Fernando of Portugal). Otto was deposed and replaced by Friedrich von Hohenstaufen (Friedrich Staufer, or Federico Ruggero di Svevia, 1194–1250), a future "Holy Roman Emperor" who conducted one of the major Crusades. Count Ferrand was captured and imprisoned by the French.

While the Germans call the French *Franzosen*, and not *Franken*, they called the Kingdom of France *Frankreich* (empire of the Frank), rather than *Frankenreich* (empire of the Franks). The French, for their part, in their new *langue d'oïl*, called themselves *françois*, but they called the Germans *allemands*, after the *Allemanni*, one of the old Germanic tribes that the Romans had known, whose name meant "all men." As this tribe had fused with the Franks and with the Germans, and no longer had any separate existence, this appellation is fascinating. As we have seen, the name *Alamanni* was a Latinized corruption of an old German name. Why did the French call the Germans *allemands* after a single ancient tribe that did not exist? Did they wish to deny the Germans' Frankish identity and make it their own? (Braudel 1989–1990).

The Latin phrase *lingua franca* means "the language of the Franks" but later, in the seventeenth century, this phrase came to mean a *common language* spoken in many Mediterranean ports that consisted of Italian mixed with French, Spanish, Greek, and Arabic (Maltese is a hybrid language of that kind). Today, *lingua franca* simply means common language. Classical Latin was the *lingua franca* of the Medieval European Christian world. Between the fifth and tenth centuries, the *dialects* of spoken Vulgar Latin diverged in various parts of their domain, becoming distinct *languages*, while the literary language, Medieval Latin, remained close to Classical Latin. The official language of the Franks had been Classical Latin, and their spoken languages were Germanic, but the new languages of the eleventh and twelfth centuries in Western Europe were French, Spanish, Provençal, Catalan, Portuguese, and Anglo-Norman.

During the tenth and eleventh centuries, some local spoken Vulgar Latin vernaculars developed a written form and began to supplant formal Classical Latin in many of its roles in Italy, Spain, France, Portugal, and other Latin-speaking countries. In Portugal, which was a county of the Spanish Christian kingdom of Leon and Castile, the transition from Latin to Portuguese was expedited by law, whereas in Italy, poets and writers used the Italian vernacular of their own accord. By the time of the First Crusade at the end of the eleventh century, many of the new "Romance languages" were being written, including the *Langue d'oïl*, the basis of modern French, the *langue d'oc*, Occitan or Provençal and the "Anglo-Norman" French vernacular. Nevertheless, at the end of the eleventh century, when the Crusaders, who called themselves *Franci*, wrote letters or documents, they wrote them in Classical Latin. Later, during or after the Third Crusade, the Norman poet Ambroise wrote the *Estoire de la Guerre Sainte* in his own Anglo-Norman French language. Why did the Frenchmen and Normans call themselves "Franks" when the Franks had ceased to exist for at least two centuries? (Braudel 1989–1990).

One of the psychological causes of the Crusades was the need of people who had doubts about their own faith to lessen their anxiety by forcing others to accept their faith. And one of the psychological reasons for the Crusading Frenchmen and Normans, let alone the Germans, English and other peoples who came on the later Crusades, calling themselves *Franci* and setting up a "Kingdom of Jerusalem" was *their inability to mourn their historical losses*, to let go of the past, and to live in the present. If we accept Franco Fornari's theory of war as the "paranoid elaboration of mourning" (Fornari 1975), then that same inability was also the cause of their waging so many wars, through an unconscious externalization of their own failings onto the "Saracens." The breakup of *Francia* in the ninth century into several entities was an historical loss. It led to the creation of *West Francia*, which later became France, and *East Francia*, which later became Germany. *Francia Occidentalis* eventually dropped the whole second part of its name, calling itself simply *Francia*, and later *France*. Its inhabitants, however, as we have seen, were not Franks. They were a mixture of Gauls, Celts, Franks, Basques, Normans, and many other-ethnic groups.

The disintegration of *Francia* in the ninth century was not the only loss of the European Christian Franks. The European Christians had never accepted their loss of Spain to the "Moors," their exonyms for the Arabs and Muslims. For almost eight centuries, they waged a war of *reconquista* to capture "their" land back from the "Saracens." In 778 the young Frankish king Charlemagne invaded Spain, but his plans to conquer it failed, and he had to retreat and head back home, suffering a humiliating defeat by the Basques at the battle of Roncevaux Pass. Centuries later, the *Chanson de Roland* celebrated this defeat as a great heroic battle for the Franks, calling the Basques "Saracens." The pain of the loss and defeat was too great. Unable to mourn their losses, they waged war to recover them. *In the Middle Ages, Christians were preoccupied with Sin, the Devil, and Hell. They externalized the evil they felt within them onto the "evil Moors."* During the Crusades, most of Iberia was still under "Saracen" rule. Indeed, the Christian Spaniards spent almost eight centuries, including those of the Crusades, in their endless *reconquista*, fighting the "Moors," until they drove them out of Spain (along with the Jews) in 1492.

The Muslims could not accept their own defeat in 732 at Tours-Poitiers, and they still wanted to defeat the Franks. But they kept themselves within Iberia, and to them the Spanish Christians were the "Franks." Spain was "*al-*

Andalus," and for centuries thereafter the Spaniards remained *al-franj*, even though the Franks had in the meantime disappeared as a people, nation, and empire. When the French and Norman Crusaders arrived in "the Holy Land" in 1099, they were still *al-franj*, the more so as they called themselves *Franci*. Neither group could mourn its historical losses, and each group waged a "holy war" against the other (Partner 1997; Cole 2002; Hindley 2003).

The inability to mourn historical losses collectively is a universal phenomenon which characterizes large human groups (Mitscherlich & Mitscherlich 1975).The Jews were unable to mourn their great collective losses of the first century, those of the Second Temple, their holy city of Jerusalem, their land and their language, and did not write their own chronological history for fifteen centuries, living in an ahistorical bubble (Patai 1976, Yerushalmi 1982, Falk 1996). As we have seen, the Jews gave Biblical Hebrew names to European countries like Spain, France, and Germany that had nothing to do with those countries. Jewish historians of the First Crusade, writing in the twelfth century, called the River Rhine "the Jordan River" and the massacre of the Jews by Crusader mobs "the binding of Isaac." The Jewish Zionists, rather than mourn their losses, turned back the clock of history and recreated a Jewish state in "the Land of Israel" (Palestine). This was achieved at the cost of enduring Arab hostility, which has caused tens of thousands of Israeli lives, let alone Arab lives. The Serbs are unable to mourn their loss of Kosovo, which they consider a sacred Serbian place, even though they lost their battle of Kosovo against the Ottoman Turks there in 1389, even though it was under Ottoman rule for nearly five centuries, and even though it is formally a separate country ruled by Albanians. Serbian leaders are still waging an international political war to regain Kosovo and withhold recognition from it.

This inability to mourn may have been one of the psychological causes of the Crusades. We shall examine it along with the Crusader notion of the "Saracens."

Chapter 6

A Short History of the "Saracens"

The Latin word *saraceni* has a very interesting history. Over the centuries, it gradually came to refer not only to Arabs or Muslims, but also to all non-Christian or non-European "foreigners." Despite their fantasy of themselves as "the children of Ismail" (Ishmael), the Arabs are an old people which is mentioned in the Hebrew Bible without any connection to Abraham's son by Hagar (*Ezekiel* 27:21, *II Chronicles* 9:14, *Jeremiah* 25:24, *Isaiah* 21:13, *Nehemiah* 4:1). Their life and culture were far removed from those of Europe, and, like all people of antiquity, they were polytheistic. The ancient Romans called all the "savage" and "barbarian" tribes that lived east of the lines of their empire, *Saraceni*. The Arabist scholar Bernard Lewis pointed out that the Greek word *sarakenos* had appeared in old Greek inscriptions (Lewis 1950). It was the exonym that the Greeks gave to a desert tribe in the northern Sinai. Some scholars thought that the Greek name *Sarakenos* derived from the Arabic word *sharqiyyin*, meaning "easterners," but this etymology is disputed by other scholars.

The *Talmud* is the Hebrew-Aramaic record of rabbinic discussions pertaining to Jewish law, ethics, customs, and history, which is second only to the Hebrew Bible in importance. In old Greek, Latin, and Talmudic literature, the word *Saraceni* came to designate Arabs and nomads in general. The Byzantines used it to denote all Arabs and Muslims, including Turks and Persians. In the early centuries of the Roman Empire, the *Saracens* were a nomadic tribe from the Sinai Peninsula, but later the name acquired a much larger meaning, and the Greek-speaking subjects of the Byzantine Empire applied it to all Arabs. After the rise of Islam, and especially at the time of the Crusades, its usage was extended to refer to all Muslims, including non-Arab Muslims, particularly those in Sicily and southern Italy, and even to non-Muslim "heathen" like the "pagan" tribes around the Baltic Sea.

The Arabs as "Ishmaelites"

Just as the Hebrew bible has fantastic genealogies purporting to explain the origins of the various tribes and peoples of its time (cf. *Genesis* 10), so has the seventh-century Arabic *Qur'an*. Medieval Arab genealogists divided the Arabs into three different ethnic groups:

1. The "Ancient Arabs," tribes that had vanished or been destroyed, such as the Ad and Thamud, mentioned in the *Qur'an* as examples of Allah's power to destroy wicked peoples.
2. The "Pure Arabs" of South Arabia, descending from *Qahtan*, the *al-Aribah*, or the Semites who inhabited Yemen. The *Qahtanites* are said to have migrated from the land of Yemen following the destruction of the Ma'rib Dam (sadd Ma'rib) around 570 CE.
3. The "Ishmaleite Arabs" of central and northern Arabia, descending from the Biblical Isma'il (Ishmael), son of Abraham. However, despite the fact that some of the people called "Ishamelites" in the Hebrew Bible (Genesis 25:13–15) may have been Arab, *the Hebrew Bible itself says nothing about any connection between the Arabs and the "Ishmaelites."*

The first connection between the Arabs and Ishmael dates back to the *Book of Jubilees*, also called the *Lesser Genesis* or *Leptogenesis*, an ancient Jewish religious text in Greek, considered part of the *Pseudepigrapha* by Protestants, Roman Catholics, and Eastern Orthodox Christians. It was originally written in Hebrew, but its original Hebrew manuscript has not been found. The lost Hebrew original is thought to have used an otherwise unrecorded text for Genesis and the early chapters of Exodus, one that was independent of either the Masoretic text or the earlier Hebrew text that was the basis for the *Septuagint* Greek translation of the Hebrew Bible. Among other things, the *Book of Jubilees* claimed that the sons of Ishmael had intermingled with the six sons of Keturah by Abraham and were called both Arabs and Ishmaelites:

> And Ishmael and his sons, and the sons of Keturah and their sons, went together and dwelt from Paran to the entering in of Babylon in all the land which is towards the East facing the desert. And these mingled with each other, and their name was called Arabs, and Ishmaelites.
>
> (*Jubilees* 20:12–13)

This "myth of origin" of the Arabs as descendants of the Biblical Ishmael took hold both among Jews and among Muslims, entered the *Qur'an*, and is accepted as truth by believers of both faiths. As the Biblical Ishmael was the son of Abraham's young concubine Hagar, while his half-brother Isaac was Abraham's son by his old wife Sarah, one fascinating interpretation of the name "Saracen" occurred in European Christian writing, where the name came to mean "empty of Sarah" or "not from Sarah." In this fantastic interpretation, the Arabs were called both "Ishmaelites" and "Hagarenes." The "Church fathers" Dionysus and Eusebius, who wrote in Greek, called all non-Greek-speaking "Barbarians" by the name of "Saracens". The word "Barbarians" was a derogatory Greek name for all those who could not speak Greek, just as the medieval Jews called the Christians *Notsrim* or "Nazarenes" to deny their key belief that Jesus of Nazareth had been the Messiah or Christ.

The Fathers of the Church were the early and influential theologians of the Christian Church, particularly those of the first five centuries of Christian history, most of whom wrote in Greek. The term is used for writers and teachers of the Church, not necessarily saints. It is generally not meant to include the New Testament authors, though in the early Church some writings of Church Fathers were considered canonical. Saint Hippolytus, another Church father who lived in the second and third centuries, used the word "Saracens" to denote a nomadic desert tribe in Arabia. Gradually, after the creation of Islam in Arabia in the seventh century, and after the great Muslim conquests of the Middle East, North Africa, and Iberia, the term "Saracen" lumped together all Muslims, Arabs, Turks, Persians, and all other "strange" or "exotic" non-Europeans and non-Christians. By the eleventh and twelfth centuries, the term "Saracen" had spread into Western Europe through the Byzantines and the Crusaders. The "Saracens" were the Muslim enemy of Christian Europe. The "Moors" of Spain were identified as "Saracens." By the early Middle Ages, European Christians equated "Saracen" with Arab, Muslim, Turk, Persian, and their other enemies. The word "Saracen" included all the "savage" tribes in the East that the Romans had fought against.

The unconscious processes of splitting and externalization operated on a large scale. The European Christians, who themselves had committed massacres of Jews and other "children of the Devil," thought of the "Saracens" as evil, violent, savage people who attacked monasteries and churches and murdered people. In the early eighth century, Damascus was still the capital of the Umayyad caliphate. After the "Saracens" had taken Spain, a Christian Arab theologian named Johannes Damaskenos (John of Damascus, born Yuhana ibn Mansur ibn Sarjun, died 749), whom some call "the last father of the church," wrote that the "Saracens" were "Ishmaelites" or "Hagarenes," that they worshiped the morning star and the goddess Aphrodite, whom they called "Akbar" (the greatest), and that after the arrival of the "false prophet Muhammad" the "Saracens" had become Muslims. He called Islam "the heresy of the Ishmaelites." By "Aphrodite" Johannes Damaskenos may have meant Alat, one of Allah's daughters worshiped in Mecca before Muhammad (John of Damascus 1958).

The "false prophet" Muhammad had almost single-handedly created Islam in the seventh century of the Christian era, uniting the warring tribes of Arabia into a single Muslim Arab entity, and the rapid expansion of the Muslims through the Middle East, North Africa, and Iberia posed a new threat to Christian Europe. The Muslims, for their part, believed that all history prior to Islam was ignorance and darkness (*al-jahiliyya*) and divided their world in their own imagination into *Dar- al-Islam* or *Dar al-Salaam* (the abode of peace), where they lived in peace and freedom, and *Dar al-Harb* (the abode of war), where they had to fight the "infidel." In addition, they imagined a *Dar al-Kufr* (abode of the infidel), *Dar al-Hudna* (abode of the truce), *Dar al-Ahad* or *Dar al-Sulh* (abode of reconciliation), *Dar al-Dawa* (abode of the invitation), and *Dar al-Aman* (abode of security). *Dar al-Islam* had many different caliphates: the Abbasids in Baghdad, the Umayyads in Damascus, the Fatimids in Cairo, and later the Umayyads in Córdoba, the capital of *"al-Andalus."* These caliphates fought among themselves over territories, power, and wealth. After 1031 there were also small Muslim states in *"Al-Andalus"* called *tawa'if* (the Arabic plural of *ta'ifa*). A *ta'ifa* in the history of Iberia was an independent Muslim-ruled state, principality, emirate, or petty kingdom, of which a number formed in *"al-Andalus"* after the final collapse of the Umayyad Caliphate of Córdoba in 1031.

In the eighth century, the Abbasids drove the Umayyads, who had conquered Spain, from Damascus. In 750 CE (18 years after the battle of Tours-Poitiers) the Abbasids set up their caliphate in Harran, now in southeastern Turkey. They then conquered Damascus from the Umayyads, massacring the entire Umayyad clan, except for Abd ar-Rahman, who escaped to Córdoba in Spain and became its *emir*. The Arabic title of *emir* meant "commander," "general" or "prince." It was a high title of nobility or office, used until this day in some of the Arab nations of the Middle East and North Africa, and historically, in some Turkic states. The Umayyad emirate of Córdoba lasted until 929, when it became the new Umayyad caliphate, which ruled most of Iberia until it broke in 1031. The last Caliph of Córdoba was Hisham III (1027–1031). At his death, the territories he controlled, which had shrunk to possessions on the Iberian Peninsula, fractured into a number of small independent *taifas*. The Umayyad caliphate had ended.

In 762–764 CE the second Abbasid caliph, Abu-Ja'afar Muhammad Abdallah al-Mansur, moved his caliphate from Harran to Baghdad, an old Persian city on the Tigris River, in what the Greeks called "Mesopotamia" (Between the Rivers) and the Arabs *Iraq*. Baghdad's Persian name means "God-Given." Al-Mansur renamed it *madinat as-salaam* (city of peace), an Arabic term for paradise. Al-Mansur believed that Baghdad was the perfect city to be the capital of the Islamic caliphate under the Abbasids (though this "empire" did not include the entire Muslim world). Al-Mansur loved the site so much he reportedly said, "This is indeed the city that I am to found, where I am to live, and where my descendants will reign afterward."

The choice of Baghdad as the capital city of the Abbasid caliphate gave it security and facilitated its development of a political and economic capital, because its location gave it control over strategic and commercial routes. It was on a trade route where caravans met and traded. During the reign of the illustrious caliph Harun al-Rashid (763–809), Baghdad's streets were paved and monthly trade fairs were held in this area. Baghdad also provided an excellent location for the capital due to the abundance of water and its healthy climate. The Tigris River was wide and unpolluted. Water existed on both north and south ends of the city gates, allowing all Baghdad households to have a plentiful supply of water, which was very uncommon at that time.

The Western Roman Empire had disintegrated two centuries before Islam. The Arabs considered the "Eastern Roman Empire" of Byzantium as Rome, so they called it *Rum*. A few centuries later, the Islamized Seljuk Turks, who had conquered eastern Anatolia from the Byzantines, called their realm the "Sultanate of Rum." The Abbasid caliphate ruled from Baghdad for five centuries, with the support of Arabs, Persians, Turks, and other non-Arab Muslims, until it was destroyed by the marauding Mongols in 1258. Meanwhile, the Umayyads ruled in Córdoba, and the Fatimids in Cairo. The latter were briefly preceded by the Persian Ikhshidid dynasty of Egypt, which ruled from 935 to 969. The Ikhshidids were founded by Muhammad bin Tughj (882–946), who began as governor of Egypt, and was later given the Persian title of *Ikhshid* or Prince by the Caliph of Baghdad. In 935 he founded his own caliphate, but after the reign of five caliphs it came to an end when the Fatimid army conquered Cairo in 969.

The Fatimids had their origins in what the Arabs called *Ifriqiya* (now Tunisia and eastern Algeria). Their dynasty was founded in 909 CE by Abdullah al-Mahdi Billah, who claimed descent from the Prophet Muhammad by way of his daughter Fatima az-Zahra, hence the name "Fatimid." Unlike the Sunni Abbasid and Umayyad caliphates, the Fatimids were Shiite Muslims, and their caliphate was founded in 969 by the *emir* Gawhar as-Siqilli also called Jauhar ar-Rumi, a Sicilian Mamluk of Greek origin who displaced the last Ikhshidid caliph, Abu el-Fawaris Ahmed ibn Ali ibn el-Ikhshid.

The Fatimids entered Egypt in the 900s, defeating the short-lived Ikhshidid dynasty from Persia and founding a new capital at *al-Qāhirat* (Cairo) in 969. The Arabic name referred to the planet Mars, "the subduer," or "the victorious," which was reportedly prominent in the sky at the moment that city construction started. Cairo was intended as a royal enclosure for the Fatimid caliph and his army, though the actual administrative and economic capital of Egypt was in Fustat. From 970 onward the Fatimids continued to conquer the surrounding areas until they ruled the whole area from Tunisia to Syria including Palestine, and even crossed over into Sicily and southern Italy. The Umayyads ruled "*al-Andalus*," which included much of Iberia, from Córdoba, whence they threatened the southwestern parts of "Francia."

For the European Christians, however, there was no difference between Umayyads, Fatimids and Abbasids, Arabs and Muslims, Shi'ites and Sunnis, Persians and Turks. All were lumped under the name "Saracens," which enabled the Christians to unconsciously split up their world into us and them, black and white. They thought of themselves as good people of the true faith, and of the "Saracens" as the evil race or bad people of the false faith. By the time the Crusades began, in the late eleventh century, in the minds of European Christians, the "Saracens" were the embodiment of Evil, while for the Arabs and Muslims, all European Christians were the "infidel" *franj*. The Muslims' military encounters with *al-franj* began when they conquered Iberia in 711–712, through their defeat at Tours-Poitiers in 732, and continued in Iberia for centuries, where the Christian Spaniards and Portuguese attempted to "reconquer" their country from the "Moors."

The Kurdish Muslim historian Abu al-Hassan Ali ibn Muhammad ibn Muhammad, also known as Ali 'izz al-Din ibn al-Athir al-Jazari (1160–1233) or simply Ibn al-Athir, often referred to the *franj* in his works. He distinguished between the Greek Orthodox and Roman Catholic Christians as "those from *ar-Rum* (Byzantium) and those from *al-Franj* (Francia)." The word *al-franj* entered the Arabic language in the eighth century, at first meaning Franks, later, Frenchmen, and later Europeans in general. In Arabic the verb *tafarnaja* means to become Europeanized, the adjective *mutafarnij* means Europeanized, *al-ifranj* means the Europeans, *Firanja* and *bilad al-Firanj* (country of the Franks) mean Europe.

With both the European Christians and the Muslims splitting their worlds into good and bad parts, each seeing themselves as the good people and the other as the evil ones, the stage was set for a great conflict between them, should they ever encounter one another on the battlefield. While the fighting in Spain or "*al-Andalus*" never ceased, the Middle East, including the "Holy Land," was free of such conflict from the seventh to the eleventh century, being under Muslim rule.

The name "Seljuk" was that of the mythical hero of the tribe bearing his name. He was the son of Dukak Timuryaligh (of the iron bow) and was either the chief or an eminent member of a tribe of Oghuz Turks. In the eleventh century, the Seljuk Turks, who came from central Asia, conquered parts of western Asia, and established the "Great Seljuk Empire," a medieval Sunni Muslim empire established by the branch of Oghuz Turks. At its zenith, it controlled a vast area stretching from Central Asia to the Persian Gulf and Eastern Anatolia. From their homelands near the Aral Sea, the Seljuks advanced first into Khorasan and then into mainland Persia before conquering eastern Anatolia. The Seljuks set up sultanates in Hamadan and Kerman (Persia), Syria, and "Rum" (Anatolia). Their advance marked the beginning of Turkic power in the Middle East and led to the Ottoman Turkish empire and to modern Turkey. The Seljuks, however, were Muslim. The great conflict between Christians and Muslims began in the late eleventh century. Let us examine how the great conflict came about.

Chapter 7

The First Crusade
Acting Out Rescue Fantasies

Human beings can believe in anything. Logic or rationality do not play a part in religious belief (Stein 1999). Christians believe that the Church of the "Holy Sepulcher" in Jerusalem houses the real tomb of Jesus Christ, even though no evidence exists to that fact: in fact, while a Jewish preacher named Yeshua of Nazareth may well have existed, there is no historical evidence for the existence of Jesus as described in the New Testament gospels (Cohen 1936, Wells 1975, Ehrman 2012, Zindler & Price 2013, Callahan 2014, Latin 2023). There are contradictions among the gospels themselves, and other than his baptism by John the Baptist and his crucifixion by Pilate, all else about Jesus may be myths that developed after his crucifixion (Fredriksen 1988). This, however, did not prevent the European Christians from fervently believing in his divinity. Being Christians, they also believed he was the Christ, the Messiah, the Redeemer, and the Savior.

Christian religious fervor was powerful. The myths of the Virgin Mary, God the Father, the Holy Spirit, the Immaculate Conception, and Jesus Christ as God the Son involved all the deepest emotions in the human family: the wish of the son for his mother not to be "violated" sexually by his father, the Oedipal struggle of the son against the father, the infantile longing for the Great Good Mother in the person of Mary. Believing that Jesus Christ bore all the sins of the world was a great relief to people who believed in Sin, the Devil, and Hell as matters of course. The "Holy Land," the "Holy City" of Jerusalem, Jesus Christ and his Holy Sepulcher stood for the idealized images of the parents that every infant and child has and that are carried over into adulthood.

Logic and rationality are not the chief characteristics of religious belief. In the Catholic Mass, which Bach, Mozart and other great composers set to divine music, Jesus Christ is said to be in Heaven, seated on the right of God the Father (*qui sedes ad dexteram Patris*), yet he was believed to be buried in the "Holy Sepulcher" in Jerusalem. It is also fascinating to note that the people whom we call the first Crusaders and who set out for "the Holy Land" in 1096 to "liberate the Holy Sepulcher from the evil Saracens" did not call themselves "Crusaders" at all: they called themselves in writing *Franci* (Franks), even though the Frankish empire had ceased to exist for over two centuries, and the people of the kingdoms that replaced it, France and Germany, were not "Franks." These Crusaders also called themselves *fideles Sancti Petri* (the faithful of Saint Peter) and *milites Christi* (soldiers of Christ), their Messiah being Jesus Christ. They saw themselves as carrying out an *iter* (voyage) or a *peregrinatio* (pilgrimage), not a holy war, yet they carried arms, despite the fact that Christian *pilgrims* were not allowed to do so. All in all, the beliefs of the Crusaders were fraught with contradictions.

The Latin-language book *Gesta Francorum* was written around 1100–1101, right after the capture of Jerusalem by the Crusaders. It told "the Deeds of the Franks" in what we call the First Crusade without ever mentioning the word Crusade. Every "Frank" who went on the Crusade took a vow to reach Jerusalem and received a fabric cross which he sewed onto his garment. This act was called "taking the cross." In Latin the word for the cross was *crux* and in the new French language, *croix*. Much later, the French word *croisés* designated the pilgrims. In 1174, in a biography of "Saint Thomas the Martyr" (Thomas à Becket, 1118–1170), Guernes de Pont de Saint-Maxence, a twelfth-century Anglo-Norman historian, used the expression *soi cruisier* (in modern French *se croiser*), to make the sign of the cross. The Spanish word *cruzada* first appeared in 1212, and the French word *croisade* only first appeared in 1460 in the *Chroniques de Chastellain* by the Burgundian historian Georges Chastellain (died 1475).

There are many theories on the religious, political, economic, social, and other causes of the First Crusade. Some scholars still think that it originated in the events that happened at the beginning of the eleventh century under the "mad" Fatimid caliph Abu-Ali al-Mansur al-Hakim bi-Amr Allah (985–1021). This "mad" caliph ascended the throne in 996 CE, at age eleven. He reportedly ordered all the dogs in his realm killed because he could not stand their barking. He began to persecute the Christians, whom the Arabs called "the people of the book" along with the Jews, in his lands, and in 1009 he destroyed the Church of the Holy Sepulcher in Jerusalem, which was under his rule. This "mad" caliph reportedly forced the Jews and the Christians to wear black hats, and then forced the Christians to wear a wooden cross some 20 by 20 inches large, and the Jews to wear a wooden calf, to remind them of their sin of the Golden Calf as depicted in their Bible (Exodus 32:4). However, the Church of the Holy Sepulcher was repaired by al-Hakim's successor, with the help of the Byzantines, and most scholars discount his "crimes" against the Christians as a real cause of the Crusades.

The migrations of Muslim tribes from Central Asia into west Asia and Europe, especially the Seljuk Turkish migrations, in the second half of the eleventh century, and their conquests of eastern Anatolia, posed a big threat to the Byzantine Empire, the major Christian power in the "Orient" (meaning the Middle East), whose capital was Constantinople. As we have seen, the Seljuk Turks were named after their mythical or eponymous leader, Selçuk, the son of Dukak Timuryaligh, an eminent member of a major tribe of Oghuz Turks. The Seljuks split off from the bulk of the

Tokuz-Oghuz group, a confederacy of clans between the Aral and Caspian Seas, and set up camp on the right bank of the lower Syr Darya River, in the direction of Jend, near Kzyl Orda in present day Kazakhstan, where they were converted to Islam.

The city of Baghdad, the capital of the Abbasid caliphate, had undergone stagnation and invasions. By the tenth century, Baghdad's population was several hundred thousand souls. Baghdad's meteoric growth, however, had slowed due to troubles within the Caliphate, including the temporary losses of Baghdad to the Egyptian Fatimids, the relocations of the capital to Samarra (808–819 and 836–892), the loss of the western and easternmost provinces, and periods of political domination by the Persian Buwayhids (945–1055) and by the Seljuk Turks (1055–1135). The latter first became allies of the Abbasids and then dominated them.

Medieval Khorasan was a large Asian region that included parts of what are now Afghanistan, Iran, Tajikistan, Turkmenistan, and Uzbekistan. The Ghaznavid Empire was a Turkic-Persian Muslim state in Khorasan, founded by a Turkic Mamluk dynasty. It lasted from 975 to 1187. It was named after its capital of Ghazni (now in Afghanistan), and ruled much of Persia, Transoxania, and northern India. Due to the linguistic, political, and cultural influence of their Persian predecessors, the Turkic Ghaznavids were Persianized. The Ghaznavid dynasty was founded by Sebuktigin upon his succession to the rule of the territories around the city of Ghazni from his father-in-law, Alp Tigin, a former general of the Persian Samanis. Sebuktigin's son, Mahmoud Shah, expanded the empire to India, from the Oxus river to the Indus Valley and the Indian Ocean, and in the west to the Persian cities of Ray (Rhagae) and Hamadan.

The European Christians knew little about what was happening in Asia, except when migrations of "savage" tribes or "Saracens" threatened their own lives. In the eleventh century, under the reign of Mas'ud Shah, the Ghaznavids suffered great territorial losses. The founder of the Seljuk Turks died around 1038 but, under his sons, the Seljuks marauded into the Ghaznavid province of Khorasan. In 1040 the Ghaznavids' attempts to stop the Seljuks from raiding the local Muslim populace led to the Battle of Dandanaqan, which they lost to the Seljuks. The defeated Ghaznavids were left with Afghanistan, Baluchistan, and the Punjab. In 1151, the Ghaznavid sultan Bahram Shah lost his capital of Ghazni to Ala'uddin Hussain of Ghor, and the Ghaznavid capital was moved to Lahore, until its subsequent capture by the Ghurids in 1186.

The Seljuk Turks would soon threaten Byzantium. Having defeated the Ghaznavids in 1140, the victorious Seljuks became masters of Khorasan, expanding their power into Transoxiana and across all of Persia. The Seljuk Turkish chief Toğrül also expanded his control all the way to Baghdad, allying himself with the Abbasid caliph of Baghdad, Al-Qa'im (died 1075), who was fighting the Fatimids of Cairo. By 1054 – the year of the Great Schism in the Christian Church – Toğrül's Seljuk forces were fighting the Byzantines in

Anatolia. In 1055 Toğrül was commissioned by Caliph Al-Qa'im to recapture Baghdad from the Fatimids. This began a Seljuk rule in Baghdad. A revolt by Toğrül's foster brother in 1058 enabled the Fatimids to recapture Baghdad, but in 1060 a furious Toğrül crushed the rebellion, personally strangled his foster brother with his bowstring, and entered Baghdad again. He then married the daughter of the Abbasid Caliph, who honored him with the title of *sultan*, yet Toğrül died childless in Ray in 1063.

In 1071 the Seljuk Turks, led by Arp-Arslan (1029–1072), fought a battle with the Byzantines at Manzikert in eastern Anatolia (now Malazgirt in Turkey), defeating the "Eastern Roman Emperor" Romanos Diogenes, whom they captured, blinded, and exiled to an island in the Sea of Marmara, where he soon died. This battle was an important milestone in the Turkish settlement of Asia Minor. The warlike Seljuks went on to capture Egypt and Syria, including Palestine, which the Christians called the "Holy Land." Some historians consider the Battle of Manzikert a major cause or origin of the Crusades. A few years later, the Seljuks created their "Sultanate of Rum," the sultanate that ruled most of Anatolia in direct lineage from 1077 to 1307, with capitals at Iznik and Konya, and, at times, at Kayseri and Sivas. At its height the sultanate of Rum stretched across central Turkey from the Mediterranean coast to the Black Sea. In the east, the sultanate absorbed other Turkish states and reached to Lake Van. Its westernmost limit was near Denizli and the gates of the Aegean basin.

The Crusades were born out of internal struggles among the European Christians, and out of their externalization of this struggle onto the "Saracens." After the battle of Manzikert in 1071, the new "Roman Emperor of the East" in Constantinople was Alexios Komnenos (1048–1118), who had served with distinction in the battles against the Turks. Alexios had to defend his Byzantine empire against constant incursions by the Normans from Italy and by the Seljuks from the east. The Byzantines, who were pushed westward by the Seljuks, called them "Saracens." Emperor Alexios would play an indirect role in the first Crusade, when he sent an appeal for military help to Pope Urbanus II in 1095.

In the "Holy Roman Empire," there were two powers: one was the Pope, the other was the "Holy Roman Emperor," who was also the king of Germany. Both were elected: the pope by the college of cardinals, the German king by his elector princes. The German king only became Roman Emperor after being crowned by the pope. Some historians tell us that already in 1072, after he became Emperor, Alexios Komnenos of Byzantium asked the "Holy Roman Emperor" Heinrich IV for military assistance. By some theories, it was this appeal for help by Alexios which brought about the first Crusade. In fact, it took another twenty-three years before that Crusade was called and the German king Heinrich IV (1050–1106), whose Latin name was Henricus, and who is known in English as Henry IV, had not been crowned by the pope, Alexander II (died 1073), and would not be crowned by his successor, Gregorius VII (died 1085), who was his sworn rival and who excommunicated Heinrich – twice. Heinrich was only crowned by Anti-Pope Clement III in 1084.

Heinrich IV was crowned German king at the age of six (1056) and took this office when he was aged 16 (1066, the year the Normans conquered England). Perhaps due to his battles with his mother, Agnes de Poitou (died 1077), Heinrich IV of Germany was strong-willed and impetuous. In 1066 he married Bertha of Maurienne, a daughter of Count Otto of Savoy, to whom he had been betrothed since the age of five. In the same year, at the request of Pope Alexander II, he assembled an army to fight the Normans of southern Italy. Heinrich's troops had reached Augsburg when he received news that his ally Godfrey of Tuscany (died 1076), husband of the powerful Great Countess Matilda of Tuscany (1046–1115), had already attacked the Normans. Heinrich halted the expedition. In 1068, in love with another woman, Heinrich attempted to divorce Bertha, which contravened the rules of the Roman Catholic Church. His speech on this subject at a church council in Mainz was rejected by the Papal legate, Pietro Damiani, who threatened that any further attempt at divorce would lead the pope to deny his coronation. Heinrich obeyed, and his wife returned to Court, but from now on he was convinced that the Papal opposition aimed to overthrow lay power within the Holy Roman Empire, creating an ecclesiastical hierarchy.

In 1073 Gregorius VII (Hildebrand of Sovana) took over the Throne of Saint Peter, and soon a bitter power struggle erupted between the young king and the old pope. The issue for the pope was his supremacy over the emperor. The ostensible issue was that of investiture: which of them had the power to invest bishops, archbishops, cardinals, and other major officials of the Roman Catholic Church. The pope-emperor struggle took on the character of a life-and-death, father-son conflict. Pope Gregorius VII issued a *Dictatus Papae* by which he alone held "the divine right" of investiture. Gregory's "papal dictate" was a radical departure from the previous balance of power between Pope and Emperor, because it eliminated the "divinely-appointed" king's right to invest a prelate with the symbols of temporal power. In early 1076 a furious Heinrich IV reacted to this "paternal dictate" by sending Gregorius a very aggressive and humiliating letter in which he rescinded his imperial support of Gregory as pope. The letter was headed "Henry, king not through usurpation but through the holy ordination of God, to Hildebrand, at present not pope but false monk." It called for the resignation of the pope and for the election of a new pope. His letter ended: "I, Henry, king by the grace of God, with all of my Bishops, say to you, come down, come down, and be damned throughout the ages."

This unprecedented letter was written amid a revolt of the German princes against their young king, Heinrich IV, which became known as "The Great Saxon Revolt." It was actually a civil war in Germany that began either with Gregory VII's accession in 1073 and ended in 1088. The revolt was led by a group of opportunistic Saxon, Bavarian, and Carinthian German *Fürsten* who elected as their "anti-king" Rudolf von Rheinfelden, the Duke of

Swabia, a brother-in-law of King Heinrich. In 1057 Rudolf had kidnaped and married Matilda, Heinrich's sister, who died three years later. In 1075 Gregory excommunicated some members of Heinrich's Imperial Court, and threatened to do the same with Heinrich himself. In a church synod held in February of that year, Pope Gregory clearly established the supreme power of the Catholic Church, with the Empire subjected to it. Heinrich replied with a counter-synod of his own.

The beginning of the Investiture Controversy can be traced to Christmas 1075, when Pope Gregory was kidnaped and imprisoned by Cencio Frangipane, a Roman nobleman, while officiating at the Roman church of Santa Maria Maggiore. Later freed by Roman people, Gregory accused Heinrich of having been behind the attempt to remove him. Having defeated a rebellion of Saxons in the First Battle of Langensalza, Heinrich felt free to accept the pope's challenge. At Worms, on January 24, 1076, a synod of German bishops and princes summoned by Heinrich formally declared Gregory VII deposed and Heinrich sent his furious letter to Gregory. Heinrich IV also installed his own chaplain as Bishop of Milan, when another candidate had already been chosen by Pope Gregorius VII. On February 22 a furious Gregorius replied by excommunicating the emperor and all the bishops named by him as "anathema," formally removing him from the Church and deposing him as German king.

This was the first time since the fourth century that a king of this stature had been so deposed. The pope and the king each claimed to have removed the other from office. However, in early 1077, to be able to put down "The Great Saxon Revolt," Heinrich pretended to come to his senses. He asked the old pope to forgive him for his "folly," accepted all his demands, and traveled to the castle of the Great Countess Matilda of Tuscany, an ally of Pope Gregorius VII, in Canossa, in northern Italy, where the pope was staying. Heinrich wore a hair shirt, knelt in the snow, and did penance before Gregorius. The phrase "Going to Canossa" became synonymous with capitulation and humiliation. Within less than a decade, however, Heinrich would take vengeance on "Hildebrand" for thus humiliating him.

The pope's ally, Matilda of Tuscany, was a very manipulative lady. Both her mother and her husband had died in 1076, leaving her the sole ruler of her great Italian patrimony, as well as lands in Lorraine. In 1080 Heinrich was excommunicated again by Pope Gregorius. Heinrich crossed the Alps, aiming to get the pope to lift the excommunication and crown him emperor, or to depose the pope. Matilda controlled the western passages over the Apennines, forcing Heinrich to approach Rome via Ravenna. Even with this route open, he had trouble besieging Rome with a hostile territory at his back. Some of his allies defeated Matilda at the battle of Volta Mantovana, and the citizens of Lucca, the capital of Tuscany, had revolted and driven out her ally, Bishop Anselm. Matilda commissioned the construction of the Ponte della Maddalena north of Lucca. In 1081, Matilda suffered further losses, and Heinrich formally deposed her as Countess of Tuscany. Matilda remained Pope Gregory's intermediary for communication with northern Europe when he lost

Rome to Heinrich and took refuge in the Castel Sant'Angelo. After Heinrich had obtained the Anti-Pope's seal in 1084, Matilda wrote to her supporters in Germany only to trust papal messages that came though her. She contrived to have Heinrich's son, Conrad (1074–1101), rebel against his father and declare himself King of Germany.

After Heinrich did penance at Canossa, Pope Gregorius VII lifted his excommunication, but the German lords of the "Great Saxon Revolt" continued their insurrection. Heinrich's mother, Agnes de Poitou, died in late 1077. Rather than mourn his loss of her, Heinrich continued to make war on Pope Gregorius and on his rebellious princes. In 1080, Guibert, the Archbishop of Ravenna (died 1100), an ally of Heinrich, was elected "Anti-Pope" Clement III by his fellow cardinals. An antipope was a person who made a widely-accepted claim to be the lawful pope, in opposition to the pope recognized by the Roman Catholic Church. Anti-popes were supported by a fairly significant faction of the cardinals.

As a sworn rival and enemy of King Heinrich IV of Germany, Pope Gregory VII supported the "Great Saxon Revolt" against Heinrich and again excommunicated Heinrich. This humiliation resolved the angry Heinrich to take revenge on Gregorius. Heinrich IV captured and killed Rudolf von Rheinfelden at the Battle of the Elster River. After that Heinrich was the sole king of Germany, and he now planned an expedition to Italy, to consolidate his power as "Holy Roman Emperor," remove Gregory, install a new pope, and be crowned by him.

From 1070 to 1085, the Normans of southern Italy, led by Guiscard of Apulia, had a long-running feud with the Byzantines, who had conquered parts of their lands. Guiscard was successful. Bari was reduced in 1071 and the Byzantine forces were ousted from southern Italy. The territory of Salerno was already Guiscard's. In 1076 he took the city, expelling its Lombard prince, Gisulf, whose sister Guiscard had married. The Norman attacks on the papal fief of Benevento greatly upset Pope Gregorius VII, but pressed hard by the German emperor, Heinrich IV, he turned again to the Normans, and in 1080, at Ceprano, reinvested Guiscard, securing him also in the southern Abruzzi, but reserving Salerno for himself. From 1080 to 1085, when Guiscard died, the Normans of southern Italy raided the southern parts of the Byzantine empire.

From 1080 to 1084 Heinrich IV led several attacks on the Lombards, the Normans, Rome, and Matilda of Tuscany, who had supported Pope Gregorius against him. Heinrich's new ally was Emperor Alexios Komnenos of Byzantium. Alexios enhanced his ability to strike back at the Normans and Seljuks by bribing Heinrich with 360,000 gold soilidi to attack the Normans in southern Italy. This forced the Normans to concentrate on their defenses at home in 1083–1084. Alexios sought to thwart the Normans' aims against his empire, as the Italian Normans often attempted to invade Byzantine territories. Heinrich left Rome, which he had already taken, and marched south against the Normans. The Romans abrogated their allegiance to the pope. Heinrich entered Rome in March 1084, after which Gregory was deposed and the anti-pope Clement III was recognized by the Romans as their new pope.

On 31 March 1084 Heinrich was crowned emperor by Clement, and received the patrician authority. His next step was to attack the fortresses of Castel Sant'Angelo, which was still in the hands of Gregory. The pope was saved by the Norman lord Robert Guiscard of Apulia, who left the siege of Durazzo and marched on Rome. Unwilling to fight the Normans, Heinrich left Rome and Gregory was freed. The Normans sacked Rome, however. The citizens of Rome rose up against Gregorius, and he was forced to flee south to Salerno with the Normans, where Gregorius died in 1085 (as did Guiscard). His last act was to write a letter exhorting the whole of Christianity to fight their emperor. In 1089 Matilda of Tuscany married Welf II of Bavaria, but she secretly gave her lands to the Church. Heinrich continued as "German king and Holy Roman Emperor" to his death in 1106 after the First Crusade.

Did We "Invent" the Crusades?

In 1086 Pope Gregorius VII was succeeded by Victorius III (died 1087), who was succeeded by Urbanus II (died 1099), who preached the First Crusade. The Investiture Controversy continued for decades: each succeeding pope tried to regain the investiture powers by stirring up revolt in Germany. The "Great Saxon Revolt" ended in 1088, but the civil unrest and war went on. At issue was not only who would be king of Germany, but whether the pope or the emperor was supreme. These struggles were in full force when the First Crusade "erupted" in 1095.

The great power struggle between Pope Gregorius VII and the German king and "Holy Roman Emperor" Heinrich IV, which ended with the pope's removal in 1084, may have been a psychological prelude to the papal call for the "First Crusade" by Urbanus II. In fact, as we have seen, while the Crusades as we know them took place, they were not known by that name for a long time, and those who wrote their early histories did not call them that. Do we perceive the Crusades as the Crusaders themselves saw them? Do we romanticize the Crusades, do we distort their meaning? Can we have an accurate perception of their very complex history?

The British historian Christopher Tyerman thought that modern historians invented the Crusades to fit their view of current conflicts between the West and Islam (Tyerman 1998, 2004, 2005, 2006). Tyerman thought that modern historians viewed the Crusades anachronistically, through their own perspective, rather than through that of the Middle Ages. In order to truly understand the Crusades, Tyerman thought, we need to grasp the medieval mind. Our most egregious mistake is to see the Crusades as a medieval precursor of modern conflicts in the Near East. Tyerman considered the idea that the Crusades were a barbaric assault on a superior, sophisticated, and peaceful Islamic civilization "nonsense," but deemed the idea that Islam was a superior, beneficent force for good, wrecked by these evil Westerners, also "nonsense" (Tyerman 2005a). Tyerman thought that far from being the homogenous "movement" that many modern historians have assumed it to be, "Crusading" was never a movement at all, in our modern sense, with all of the self-sustaining features now implied by the term.

By examining how participants, observers, and historians imposed their own attitudes, aspirations, and interpretations on this particular form of Christian "holy war," Tyerman challenged modern historians' commonly-held assumptions about the nature and coherence of the Crusades. In his studies of the ideas, language, practice, and reception of Crusading, and its historiography, he suggested that the Crusades *reflected* the religious and political habits and ambitions of their time, rather than molding them. Crusading was a malleable phenomenon within medieval western society even since 1095, provoking widely divergent views amongst its participants, witnesses, and commentators. Tyerman thought that Crusader literature and historiography often say more about the authors themselves than about what they claim to have seen. The British historian Elizabeth Siberry examined the British historiography of the Crusades in the nineteenth and twentieth centuries and reached similar conclusions (Siberry 2000).

In an online interview with the U.S. National Public Radio in 2005, Tyerman stated his views:

> There was no strategic reason for Western knights and soldiers to be laboring about in the Judean hills in the 11th, 12th and 13th centuries. They were there for essentially ideological religious reasons. The Holy Land and Jerusalem were regarded as part of Christendom, as a relic, and the Crusaders went there, in a sense, to establish a protective garrison to restore, as they saw it, their holy city to Christian control. But the prime motive of Crusading in the Holy Land, unlike Crusading in Spain or in Baltic, was not initially that of settlement. If you wanted to make a profit, you did not go on Crusade. "Crusades habitually made thumping losses."
>
> (Tyerman 2005a)

Tyerman believed that the chief motive for the Crusades was not economic or political but religious: the idea of a "holy war."

In a similar vein, conventional historical wisdom about the Crusades was challenged by the Israeli geographer Ronnie Ellenblum (1952–2021) in his books on the Crusades (Ellenblum 1998, 2007). Ellenblum studied the spatial distribution of the "Frankish" *rural* settlement in the Latin Kingdom of Jerusalem at the time of the Crusades, basing it on an unprecedented field study of more than 200 Frankish rural sites in Israel, and on a close re-examination of the historical documentary sources (Ellenblum 1998). Ellenblum re-examined the basic assumptions of historical scholarship and advocated a new model of the nature of Frankish settlement, as a society of European

Christian migrants who settled in the Levant, had close relations with Eastern Christians, and were also influenced culturally by the Muslim society that lived elsewhere in the country.

Like Tyerman, Ellenblum sought to revise the entire historiography of the Crusades. In his second book, Ellenblum studied the economic, cultural, geographical, architectural, and even family ties between the "Franks" and the "Saracens" in the Crusader castles. Ellenblum studied the location of Crusader castles in Israel and found that there were "architectural" relations between the "Franks" and the local Christians, as well as among them and the local Arabs, Muslims, and Turks, and that dialogue and mutual influences always existed. He argued that, during the past 150 years, historiography had been unduly influenced by the national and colonial discourse, both in Europe and in the Middle East, which tended to introduce an anachronistic reading of nationalism and colonialism into the Crusades. This was why many historians have described the Crusades as a black-and-white "Franks"-versus-"Saracens" story. By studying the location and distribution of the Crusader castles, the tactics of the siege, and the strategies of their defense, Ellenblum found connections between Crusader settlement choices and "Saracen" surroundings, and a mutual inter-cultural influence. Crusader fortifications were built for economic and geographic reasons more than for strategic ones, or to defend imaginary frontiers. Crusader castles are thus live evidence of an "East-West dialogue."

In my view, *the Crusaders were the acting out on a mass scale of a psychogeographical fantasy.* They fulfilled several psychological needs at the same time. After all, the European Christians could have gone on a Crusade to liberate the "Holy Land" centuries earlier. The religious fervor which took hold of Christian Europe in 1095 to wage a "holy war" against the "evil Saracens" was a way of resolving its inner conflicts, as well as a fantasy of rescuing the Good Mother in the shape of "the Holy Land" from the Evil Father in the shape of the "Saracens." Through splitting and externalization, the Christians could imagine themselves as the good people and the "Saracens" as the evil ones. By "liberating the Holy Sepulcher" they imagined setting free their Christ, the son of God. They also imagined themselves absolved of all their sins, avoiding the Devil and Hell.

In March 1095, during the civil war that still went on in the "Holy Roman Empire" of Germany, the French-born Pope Urbanus II (Otho de Lagery, 1042–1099), who opposed Emperor Heinrich IV, held a church council at Placentia (now Piacenza), in northern Italy. With the Seljuk Turks attacking the Byzantines, Urbanus received ambassadors from the Byzantine Emperor, Alexios Komnenos, asking to help him in his war against the "Saracens" who were "destroying the Roman Empire." As the head of a Greek Orthodox empire, the Byzantine emperor was a rival of the pope. Nonetheless, the pope heeded his call. The Council of Piacenza was attended by tens of thousands of European Christian princes, cardinals, and bishops from Italy, France, and Burgundy, so many that it had to be held outdoors.

In November 1095 the French-born pope Urbanus II held another church council in the French town of Clermont, where he "preached" the First Crusade. The word Crusade was never used in his sermon. Here is part of what the pope's sermon said:

> I [the Pope], or rather the Lord [God], beseech you as Christ's heralds to publish this everywhere and to persuade all people of whatever rank, foot-soldiers and knights, poor and rich, to carry aid promptly to those Christians [in Byzantium] and to destroy that vile race [the Saracens] from the lands of our friends. I say this to those who are present, it is meant also for those who are absent. Moreover, Christ commands it [at this point the crowd chanted "God wills it!"].
> (Robert de Rheims 1866; Fulcher of Chartres 1998; Baudric de Dol 2014)

Significantly, the sixty-year-old pope exhorted his listeners to set out for "the Holy Land" by citing the internal wars and problems of Christian Europe. He dangled before his people the prospects of new land, as well as the remission of their sins:

> This land which you inhabit, shut in on all sides by the seas and surrounded by the mountain peaks, is too narrow for your large population; nor does it abound in wealth; and it furnishes scarcely food enough for its cultivators. Hence it is that you murder one another, that you wage war, and that frequently you perish by mutual wounds. Let therefore hatred depart from among you, let your quarrels end, let wars cease, and let all dissensions and controversies slumber. Enter upon the road to the Holy Sepulcher; wrest that land from the wicked race and subject it to yourselves ... God has conferred upon you above all nations great glory in arms. Accordingly undertake this journey for the remission of your sins, with the assurance of the imperishable glory of the kingdom of heaven.
> (Robert de Rheims 1866; Fulcher of Chartres 1998; Baudric de Dol 2014)

Pope Urbanus promised every Christian going on the Crusade that he would receive an "indulgence" (the formal Church forgiveness of sins), namely that "taking the cross" and going to Jerusalem will constitute a full repentance for his sins, and that his home would be protected by the Mother Church, so that he would get it back upon his return. The battle cry of the Crusading Christians would be *Deus vult* (God wills it). Urbanus also gave away fabric crosses to the masses.

"Indulgences," for medieval Christians, who believed in Sin, the Devil, and punishment in Hell, were a very serious matter. An indulgence, in the Roman Catholic church, was the full or partial remission of sins which had already been forgiven. The indulgence was granted by the Church after the sinner had confessed and received absolution. Medieval Christians believed that indulgences drew on the storehouse of merit acquired by Jesus' sacrifice of himself on the Cross, and the virtues and penances of their saints. The indulgences were granted for specific good works and prayers. *Indulgences replaced the severe penances of the early church*, or shortened those penances at the intercession of those imprisoned and those awaiting martyrdom for the faith. Indulgences, and the abuses that accompanied them, including their selling, would become a major bone of contention when Martin Luther initiated the Protestant Reformation in 1517.

"Holy Roman Emperor" Heinrich IV of Germany ignored the Pope's call for a holy war. He was too busy with his internal problems in Germany and in Italy. In 1090 Heinrich had launched his third punitive expedition against his enemies in Italy, Matilda of Tuscany, the Lombards, and the Normans. After some initial successes against the Great Countess Matilda of Canossa, his defeat in 1092 had caused the rebellion of the Lombard communes. The revolt intensified after Matilda had managed to turn Heinrich's elder son, Conrad (1074–1101), against him. Conrad joined the Papal opposition and was crowned King of Italy at Monza in 1093. Heinrich found himself cut off from Germany. He returned there only in 1097: in Germany his power was still at its height. Great Countess Matilda of Tuscany had secretly transferred her lands to the Church in 1089, before her marriage to Welf II of Bavaria (1072–1120). In 1095, when he found this out, the furious Welf left her and, together with his father, switched his allegiance to Heinrich IV, possibly in exchange for a promise of succeeding his father as duke of Bavaria. Heinrich deposed Conrad at the diet of Mainz in April 1098, and named his younger son Heinrich (future Heinrich V) as successor, under the oath sworn that he would never follow his brother's example.

The princes, counts, and barons who led the first Crusade were Frenchmen and Normans, not "Franks." Yet, they thought and wrote of themselves as "Franks." We can see that from the letter that Count Estienne de Blois (1045–1102) wrote to his wife Adele in 1098 from the Crusader siege of Antioch, as well as from the *Gesta Francorum* and other documents. We shall discuss these documents below. Each of the crusaders had temporal ambitions for territories, titles, and wealth, as well as religious fervor. The Normans of southern Italy had been raiding the Byzantine empire for a long time. The French-born pope Urbanus II appointed a French bishop, Adhemar de Monteuil (died 1098), also known as Adhemar du Puy (he had been the bishop of Le Puy-en-Velay), as his personal legate and as the spiritual leader of the "pilgrimage." The word Crusade was never used. There were several military leaders of the "pilgrimage." Notable among them was Count Raymond Saint-Gilles de Toulouse, the first nobleman who "took the cross."

Other European Christians joined the "pilgrimage" for many different reasons, religious, social, economic, familial, personal, and psychological. The stated aim of the Crusade was to liberate the "Holy Sepulcher" from the grip of "that vile race," the "Saracens," but also to strengthen the "Eastern Roman Empire" against those "Saracens" and to win lands, titles, and wealth, to change their whole lives. But why did the Crusaders write in Church Latin, rather than in their vernaculars, and why did they call themselves *Franci*? Did they see themselves as the heirs of Charlemagne's Franks? There were other words, in the *langue d'oïl* and in Anglo-Norman, by that time, that they could have used for themselves, such as *françois* and *normands*. The story of the battle of Tours-Poitiers in 732, where the Franks had defeated the "Saracens," was known to every European Christian from his childhood: it was the victory of the "good race of the Franks" over the "vile race of the Saracens." In their fantasy, the "pilgrims" also wanted to repeat the victory of Charles Martel: to defeat the "Saracens" and drive them out of "the Holy Land" where Jesus Christ, their Messiah and God, had been crucified and buried.

Conventional historians attribute the wide popular response to Pope Urban's call for the Crusade to a variety of rational reasons: the feudal system of medieval Europe, the increase of the population and the economic growth of western Europe, the strengthening of religious fervor among Christians, hopes for territorial expansion and wealth among noblemen, hopes for freedom among vassals and serfs, the colonial ambitions of the Normans in the "Saracen" lands and in Byzantium, the wish of the Italian cities to expand their trade with the cities of the East, and a general attraction of voyages and adventures. Beyond all these rational causes, however, there were also conscious and unconscious psychological reasons. Among the conscious ones were the fear of Sin, the Devil, and Hell: medieval Christians believed in Satan no less than in God, and feared that their sins would take them to Hell after their death, where they would suffer infernally and eternally. Taking the cross and going to "the Holy Land" could save them from this horrible fate.

"Sacred space" is a geographical or physical location which religious people hold to be sacred, such as holy sepulchers, holy shrines, or holy cities. It is a *psychogeographical fantasy* that often leads to "holy wars" (Cole 2002; Spicer & Hamilton 2005). In the unconscious mind of the Crusaders, the "holy city" of Jerusalem and "the Holy Land" of Palestine where their Christ was born and crucified may have symbolized the Great Good Mother of their infancy, captured by the "evil Saracens," like a good wife and mother abused by her cruel husband, whose son wants to save her from him and made her his (Falk 1987). The Virgin Mary, mother of Jesus, unconsciously symbolized the Great Good Mother, as she does in many places. According to the Roman Catholic catechism, the Virgin Mary, "having completed the course of her earthly life, was assumed body and soul into heavenly glory." Mary was "assumed" into Heaven with her body and soul united. If a "pilgrim" came to Jerusalem and supplicated Mary, she would give him grace and pardon all his sins. The "Holy Sepulcher" itself also had a symbolic meaning, as the Crusaders believed that it bore the body of Jesus Christ, Son of God the Father, and it was violated by the "Saracens."

The First Crusade – as it much later came to be called – began in 1096 with riots and massacres by lower-class "pilgrims" throughout Europe. A murderous mob of "pilgrims" massacred thousands of Jews, especially in towns along the River Rhine. The medieval term "pauper" indicated a man's status as impoverished or mendicant wards of the Church. Most paupers were sick in body or mind, as they would otherwise have been able to make a living. The Crusader mob consisted of bands of poor and desperate peasants and "paupers" from both sides of the Rhine, led by disturbed charismatic and violent "cult leader" types like Gautier sans-avoir (Walter the Penniless, died 1096) and Pierre l'hermite (Peter the Hermit, died 1115).

The Crusaders Fight the Kingdom of Hungary

In early 1096 Gautier sans-avoir and Pierre l'hermite led their pilgrims and paupers in the so-called "People's Crusade." Full of religious frenzy, they left with their "people's army" well before the main army of nobles, knights, and their followers could organize their expedition, and without adequate preparation. Gautier and Pierre led their band of paupers through the "Holy Roman Empire" of Germany and Italy, massacring the Jews along the way, then through Hungary, where the new king, Könyves Kálmán (died 1116), had tough choices to make. In May 1096 he let the armies led by Gautier sans-avoir pass peacefully through Hungary, but the next hordes, led by Pierre l'hermite, occupied the Hungarian fortress of Zimony and withdrew only when Kálmán's armies were approaching them.

In the summer of 1096 the troops of a German knight called Folkmar pillaged the territories of the Hungarian county of Nyitra, while the hordes of a German priest named Gottschalk ravaged the Transdanubian region of the kingdom. The able Kálmán managed to rout both of these armies and denied the entrance of new armies led by the German nobleman Emich von Leiningen and the Frenchman Guillaume de Melun. The audacious Crusaders laid siege to Kálmán's fortress of Moson in northwestern Hungary. It took Kálmán six weeks to break the siege and defeat the Crusaders. On 20 September 1096, Kálmán made a pact with Godefroy de Bouillon, the leader of the next Crusader army. Under their agreement, Kálmán took hostages, and mustered his own army to guard the progress; the Crusader armies passed through the kingdom peacefully.

After their traumatic battles in Hungary, the surviving pilgrims and paupers of the "People's Crusade" reached the Bulgarian province of the Christian "Eastern Roman Empire." Bulgaria had been an empire itself, but at the end of the tenth century it had been conquered by the Byzantines. Gautier sans-avoir's hungry and desperate followers plundered the Belgrade area, drawing the wrath of the Serbs. They continued to Constantinople under Byzantine escort, which was meant more to watch over them than to protect them. Gautier sans-avoir and Pierre l'hermite joined their forces at Constantinople, where Emperor Alexios Komnenos provided them with sea transport across the Bosporus to Anatolia. Here the "people's army" finally engaged the "Saracens" – and were massacred by them. Gautier died with his followers in late 1096.

Pierre l'hermite was the other leader of what later came to be known as the "People's Crusade," as opposed to the crusades of the noblemen. He was one of the preachers of the Crusade in France, and soon became famous as a charismatic emotional preacher who carried the masses. Thousands of peasants and "paupers" eagerly took the cross at his bidding, *including women*. Like a charismatic cult leader of our own time, Pierre l'hermite told the "paupers" that they were "spiritually purified and holy" pilgrims who would be protected by the Heavenly Host, the army of angels in Heaven (Luke 2:13; Revelation 19:19). They believed him and followed him to their destruction. Pierre l'hermite led part of the "People's Crusade" from 1096 to 1099, all the way to the destination of their pilgrimage, the Church of the "Holy Sepulcher" in Jerusalem.

The German city of Cologne or Cölln on the Rhine was an important Christian town. The Archbishop of Cologne was one of the seven prince-electors who elected the King of Germany and one of the three ecclesiastical electors. The archbishop also ruled large temporal domains. Pierre l'hermite therefore chose Cologne as his point of departure for the Crusade.

Pierre l'hermite started out from Cologne in April 1096 with some 40,000 men and women, traveled with them for three months, lost some 10,000 on the way, and arrived with some 30,000 men and women at Constantinople in July, after massacring the Jews along the way. Most of the paupers did not make it out of Europe's Roman Catholic jurisdiction. The majority could not be provided for by the various temporal lordships and church dioceses along the way. They either starved to death, returned home, or were put into servitude, which was almost like slavery, while a substantial number were captured and sold into slavery by Slavic robber barons in the Balkans. Western Europeans viewed the Balkan Slavs as evil, vile, unredeemed robbers and villains. The "Eastern Roman Emperor" Alexios Komnenos was unhappy with the arrival of 30,000 pilgrims at his doorstep: as head of the Eastern Orthodox Church, and as the sovereign who had requested aid against the "Saracens" from the Pope, he was required to provide for the care and sustenance of the vast host of pilgrims and paupers for the remainder of their journey.

The "People's Crusade" or "Paupers' Crusade" was just the beginning of the psychohistorical fantasy that we know as the Crusades. It was followed by the "Princes' Crusade" or "Barons' Crusade," which was led by some of the great noblemen of Europe, almost all of them Frenchmen or Normans. By late 1096 and early 1097 four major Crusader armies had reached "the Roman Empire of the East," the name given by the western Europeans to Byzantium. The first one was French, the army of Hugues de Vermandois (died 1102), a brother of King Philippe of France. He bore the Papal Banner and was called Hugues le Grand even though he was not a great leader or soldier. King Philippe himself could not take part in the campaign as he had been excommunicated by the pope for repudiating his wife and taking another woman.

Hugues de Vermandois' army was joined by three Anglo-Norman armies – those of the three sons of the Norman nobleman Count Eustache II of

Boulogne – Baudouin de Boulogne, Godefroy de Bouillon, and Eustache de Boulogne – as well as the army of one of their cousins. The other "Frankish" armies were led by Count Raymond de Saint-Gilles of Toulouse (1041–1105), who represented the knights of Provence, and who was accompanied by the papal legate, Adhemar du Puy; the Norman Prince Bohemond of Taranto (1058–1111), a son of Robert Guiscard of Apulia, representing the Normans of southern Italy, with his nephew Tancred (1072–1112), who would play a major role in the First Crusade; and the "Northern French" armies, led by Count Robert II of Flanders (died 1111), Robert Courtheuse or Robert of Normandy (died 1134), the eldest son of William the Conqueror and brother of King William II of England, and Estienne, Count of Blois. The entire Crusader armies consisted of about 35,000 to 40,000 "Franks," including 5,000 cavalry. Raymond de Saint-Gilles of Toulouse had the largest contingent.

Unlike the "People's Crusade," the princely French and Norman armies crossed the Kingdom of Hungary without being challenged by its king, Kálmán, and reached Constantinople in April 1097, numbering some 4,000 cavalrymen and 25,000 infantry. The "Eastern Roman Emperor" Alexios Komnenos, who had requested military assistance from the pope, was apprehensive: the Normans had already raided his empire, and the "Frankish" princes could try to take his kingdom from him. In 1080–1085 Prince Bohemond had served under his father Guiscard in the Norman attack on the Byzantine Empire, and he had commanded the Normans during Guiscard's absence, penetrating into Thessaly as far as Larissa, but had been repulsed by the Byzantine armies. This time Bohemond publicly paid homage to Alexios. He may have eyed the principality of Antioch (now the Turkish town of Antakya), a major Byzantine city occupied since 1084 by the "Saracens". From Constantinople to Antioch, across Anatolia, Bohemond led the First Crusade. Thanks to his leadership, the First Crusade succeeded in crossing Asia Minor despite the "Saracens," which the following Crusades failed to do.

Before letting the "Franks" cross the Straits of Bosporus and leave Constantinople for Antioch and the "Holy Land", however, the "Roman Emperor of the East," Alexios Komnenos, demanded that the Crusader princes swear allegiance to him and vow to return to him every piece of land they would take from the "Saracens" in his empire. All but two of them – Raymond de Saint-Gilles de Toulouse and the young Tancred of Taranto – who had other ambitions, did so. Alexios exacted a pledge from Raymond not to harm his empire and Bohemond made his tempestuous nephew Tancred pay homage to Alexios. But even those princes who did take the oath had no intention of keeping it: they wanted to set up their own kingdoms, principalities, or counties in the "East."

In October 1097, when the "Frankish" princes reached Antioch, which was occupied by the Seljuk Turks, they laid siege to it with great determination. Since 1088, Antioch's Seljuk governor had been the *emir* Yaghi-Siyan (died

1098). Yaghi-Siyan was well aware of the Crusader army as it marched through the "Sultanate of Rum" in 1097, and he appealed for help from neighboring Muslim states, but to no avail. To prepare for their arrival, he imprisoned the Orthodox Patriarch of Antioch, John VII the Oxite, and exiled most of the Christian population from Antioch, although the Syrian Orthodox citizens were permitted to stay.

The Siege of Antioch by the "Franks" lasted nine months (October 1097 to June 1098), during which both the besieged and the besiegers endured terrible traumas. Antioch contained a large Christian population, and it might have withstood the siege, but it was betrayed by the Islamic allies of Bohemond, prince of Taranto. When the city fell on June 28, 1098, the *emir* Yaghi-Siyan fled with his bodyguard, while his son stayed behind to defend the citadel. During his escape, however, Yaghi-Siyan fell from his horse and was seriously injured. His guards found it impossible to bring the injured governor with them. They left him on the ground and rode away without him. He was found by an Armenian, perhaps one whom Yaghi-Sian had exiled, who cut off his head and sent it as a gift to Prince Bohemund. Antioch became the capital of the "Latin Principality of Antioch" for nearly two centuries.

In July 1098 Bohemond of Taranto became Prince of Antioch, and on August 1 the papal legate Adhemar du Puy died there. At the Council of Clermont in 1095, Adhemar had shown great zeal for the Crusade, perhaps at Pope Urban's prior urging, and had been named the apostolic legate and appointed to lead the Crusade. He had accompanied Raymond de Saint-Gilles de Toulouse to the "East." Whilst Raymond and the other leaders quarreled with each other over the military leadership of the Crusade, Adhemar was always recognized as its spiritual leader. On behalf of Pope Urban, Adhemar had negotiated with "Roman Emperor of the East" Alexios Komnenos at Constantinople, reestablished discipline among the Crusaders, fought a crucial role at the Battle of Dorylaeum, and sustained morale during the siege of Antioch through various religious rites including fasting and special observances of holy days.

Human beings can believe in anything (Saroglou 2021). During the siege of Antioch, the "sacred lance" with which Jesus Christ's side was pierced on the Cross according to the Christian gospels was "discovered" following a vision of the Provençal priest Pierre Barthelemy. This "discovery" was fervently espoused by Raymond d'Aguilers, a chronicler and canon of Le Puy-en-Velay who accompanied Count Raymond de Saint-Gilles de Toulouse on the First Crusade as chaplain to Adhemar, the Bishop of Le Puy and the legate of Pope Urban II. Adhemar himself had been skeptical of the "holy lance." With Pons de Balazuc, Raymond d'Aguilers undertook to write a history of the expedition. However, Pons having been killed, Raymond had to carry out this undertaking alone.

At a sortie of the Crusaders during the siege, Raymond d'Aguilers went before the column, bearing in his hands the "Sacred Lance" which had been "discovered" by Pierre Barthelemy. He later took part in the entry into Jerusalem, accompanied the Count of Toulouse on his pilgrimage to the Jordan, and was at the battle of Ascalon. His major work was the *Historia Francorum qui ceperunt Hierusalem*, eyewitness accounts of most of the events of the First Crusade. The narrative was largely devoted to the visions of Pierre Barthélemy, and to the authenticity of the "Holy Lance" he had found. Modern historians do not take his work seriously. The French historian Auguste Molinier (1851–1904) wrote that Raymond d'Aguilers is partial, credulous, ignorant, and prejudiced. "He may be utilized, but on condition of close criticism" (Molinier 1902).

After the capture of Antioch in June 1098, and its subsequent siege by the Seljuk Turkish leader Qiwam al-Dawla Kerbogha, the *atabeg* of Mosul, which scared the "Franks" to death, Adhemar had organized a procession through the streets of Antioch, and had the gates of the city locked so that the Crusaders, many of whom had begun to panic, could not flee the city. He was skeptical of Pierre Barthelemy's "discovery" of the "Holy Lance," especially as he knew that such a relic existed in Constantinople, but he was willing to let the Crusader army believe it was real if it raised their morale.

Three weeks later, when Kerbogha was defeated, and the Saracen siege of Antioch was lifted, Adhemar organized a council in an attempt to settle the leadership disputes among the Crusader princes, but he died on August 1, 1098, probably of typhus. The territorial and power disputes among the higher nobles remained unresolved, and the march to Jerusalem was delayed for months. However, the foot soldiers continued to think of the dead Adhemar as their leader; some of them even claimed to have been visited by his ghost during the siege of Jerusalem and reported that Adhemar instructed them to hold another procession around its walls. The visions may have been a reaction to the severe trauma of mortal warfare.

There were great personal rivalries among the "Frankish" princes. In 1097 Raymond de Saint-Gilles de Toulouse had sent his army ahead to occupy Antioch, offending Bohemond of Taranto, who wanted the city for himself. The city was, however, still occupied by the "Saracens," and was taken by the Crusaders only after a very traumatic nine-month siege in 1098. Raymond took the *Palatium Cassiani* (the Latin corruption of the name Yaghi-Siyan) and the tower over the Bridge Gate. With typhoid fever and other diseases rampant, Raymond was ill during the siege of Antioch by the "Saracen" Kerbogha, which culminated in the "discovery of the Holy Lance" by Pierre Barthelemy.

The "miracle of the holy lance" raised the morale of the Crusaders, and to their own surprise they were able to rout Kerbogha's Seljuks outside Antioch. The Lance itself became a "holy relic" among Raymond's followers, despite the grave doubts of the papal legate Adhemar and Bohemond's occasional mockery. Raymond refused to relinquish his control of Antioch to Bohemond, reminding Bohemond that he had sworn to return Antioch to Emperor Alexios. A power struggle arose between Raymond's supporters and the supporters of Bohemond, including his nephew Tancred, partly over the genuineness of the Lance, but mostly over the possession of the new Principality of Antioch.

Another important area captured by the "Franks" from the "Saracens" and made into a Crusader state was the County of Edessa, now the Turkish province of Urfa, a landlocked state northeast of Antioch, which straddled the Euphrates River and became the property of Baudouin de Boulogne (1058–1118), a future king of Jerusalem. Edessa was surrounded by Seljuk Turks. In 1097, the Roman Catholic Baudouin de Boulogne left the main Crusading army, which was traveling southeastward towards Antioch and Jerusalem, and went into Cilicia, then east to Edessa, where he convinced its Greek Orthodox Christian lord, Thoros, to adopt him as a son and heir. Thoros was disliked by his Armenian Orthodox subjects; in 1098 he was assassinated. It is not known if Baudouin had any part in this murder. In any event, Baudouin succeeded Thoros, taking the title of Count of Edessa (having also been Count of Verdun as a vassal of his brother in Europe).

From Antioch to Jerusalem

The Seljuk Turks had taken Jerusalem from the Egyptian Fatimids in 1073, but in the summer of 1098, at about the same time as the Crusader capture of Antioch, the Fatimids took Jerusalem back from the Seljuks. Al-Malik Al-Afdal ibn Badr al-Jamali Shahanshah (1066–1121), the Fatmid general, expelled its Seljuk Turkish governor, Najm ad-Din Ilghazi ibn Artuq (died 1122), and placed a Fatimid governor, Iftikhar al-Dawla, in his place. To the Crusaders, however, it made no difference: they were all "Saracens." When the "Franks" arrived in their caliphate in 1099, the bewildered Fatimids attempted to make peace with the *Franj*, on condition that they not continue towards Jerusalem, but this demand was ignored, as Jerusalem was the real goal of the Crusaders.

The Fatimid governor of Jerusalem, Iftikhar al-Dawla, had no idea who the Crusaders were, what they were doing in his country, nor what they wanted. On June 7, 1099, the "Franks," led by Raymond de Saint Gilles de Toulouse and Godefroy de Bouillon, laid siege to "Saracen" Jerusalem. Tancred had left Raymond and was now with Godefroy. The siege of Jerusalem by the "Franks" lasted, almost six weeks, from June 7 to July 15. The Crusaders had some 1,500 knights and 12,000 infantry – a small part of those who had left Europe – while the Fatimid garrison had some 1,000 soldiers. The "Franks" fought with great zeal, being certain that they were doing God's bidding, and liberating the "Holy Sepulcher", in addition to the lucrative territories and titles that awaited them. The besieging Crusaders themselves were traumatized, due to the lack of food and water around Jerusalem. The city was well-prepared for the siege, and the Fatimid governor Iftikhar al-Dawla had expelled most of the Christians from the city.

Soon after the first assault, a number of Christian supply ships sailed into the port at Jaffa, and the Crusaders were able to re-supply themselves for a short time. They also began to gather wood from Samaria in order to build siege engines. They were short of food and water, and by the end of June there was the bad news that a "Saracen" army was marching north from Egypt to Jerusalem. But the "Franks" were encouraged when a traumatized priest named Peter Desiderius claimed to have had a divine vision in which the ghost of Adhemar, the papal legate who had died in 1098, instructed them to fast for three days and then march in a barefoot procession around the city walls, after which the city would fall in nine days, following the Biblical example of Joshua at the siege of Jericho. Although they were already starving, the traumatized pilgrims fasted, and on July 8 they made the procession, with the clergy blowing trumpets and singing psalms, being mocked by the defenders of Jerusalem all the while. The procession stopped on the Mount of Olives and sermons were delivered by monks such as Peter the Hermit, Arnulf of Chocques, and Raymond of Aguilers.

Chapter 8

The Latin Kingdom of Jerusalem as a Psychogeographical Fantasy

On July 15, 1099, the traumatized, frenzied and furious "Franks" finally managed to breach the walls of Jerusalem and take the "Holy City." According to Guillaume de Tyr (died 1185), the archbishop of Tyre and a chronicler of the Crusades, there followed a horrible bloodbath (William of Tyre 1893, 1943, 1986). To the "Franks," as to their pope, the "Saracens" were "a vile race" that had to be eradicated. They split up their world into good and bad, white and black: they were the good "race," the "Saracens" were the devil. Almost every "Saracen" inhabitant of Jerusalem was killed over the course of that afternoon, that evening and the next morning. Muslims, Jews, and even a few of the Christians who looked to the Crusaders like "Saracens" were massacred with indiscriminate violence. Some 40,000 people lost their lives. Raymond d'Aguilers, a chronicler of the Crusade, and the *Gesta Francorum* reported Crusaders wading in rivers of blood. Needless to say, both the survivors and the victors were traumatized.

The impetuous young Tancred d'Hauteville, along with Gaston of Béarn, claimed to have been the first "Frank" to enter Jerusalem. However, the first Crusaders to enter Jerusalem were actually Ludolf of Tournai and his brother Englebert. When the city fell, Tancred gave his banner to a group of citizens who had fled to the roof of what they believed to be the Temple of Solomon. This should have assured their safety, but they were massacred along with the others during the sack of the city. The *Gesta Francorum* records that when Tancred realized this he was "greatly angered." When the Latin Kingdom of Jerusalem was established, Tancred became Prince of Galilee.

Some scholars believe that the local Sunni Muslims had been suffering under the yoke of the Shiite Fatimids, and actually saw the "Franks" as liberators. The Crusader princes, for their part, set up a new kingdom along the European model, which was called *Regnum Hierosolymitanum* in Latin and *Roiaume de Jherusalem* in their medieval French. Modern scholars have used the term "Latin Kingdom of Jerusalem", but that was not what the first Crusaders called it themselves. In fact, this kingdom included not only Jerusalem, but most of the "Holy Land". Why did the Crusaders not call it *Regnum Terrae Sanctae* (Kingdom of the Holy Land)?

DOI: 10.4324/9781003527367-8

The "Latin Kingdom of Jerusalem" was sandwiched between the Seljuk Sultanate of "Rum" (the Arabic name for Byzantium), the Emirate of Damascus, and the Fatmid Caliphate of Cairo. At first the kingdom was little more than a loose collection of "Palestinian" towns and cities captured during the Crusade. It developed like the monarchies of Europe, with which it had close connections, both politically and through the family relationships of its rulers. It was, however, a relatively minor kingdom in comparison and often lacked financial and military support from Europe. The kingdom had closer ties to the neighboring Kingdom of Armenia and to the Byzantine Empire, which had an Orientalizing influence on the western Crusaders.

Some of the Crusading "Franks" at times distinguished between "Saracens" and Arabs or Seljuk Turks. Most of them continued to use the word "Saracens" as a single appellation for all Muslims, Persians, Arabs, Turks, and Mamluks throughout the Crusades (which ended with the expulsion of the Crusaders from Acre by the Mamluks in 1291). Even in the sixteenth century, the great Italian poet Torquato Tasso in his famous poem *La Gerusalemme liberata* used the name *Saraceni* for the Muslims. Tasso imagined a terrible fight to the death between Tancredi, the prince of the Galilee, and his "Saracen" lover Clorinda (hardly an Arab name!), a princess disguised as a "Saracen" warrior. After a bloody duel, Tancredi kills Clorinda, not knowing that she is his lover or even a woman. Before she dies, Tancredi recognizes his lover, who asks him to baptize her a Christian. In 1624 the great composer Claudio Monteverdi wrote a dramatic musical work entitled *Il Combattimento di Tancredi e Clorinda*, using Tasso's poem, in which, at the moment of recognition, the narrator sings Tasso's words, "*Ahi, vista! ahi, cononscenza!*" ("O the view! O the recognition!"). This terrible tragedy may be symbolic or emblematic for the entire Crusades.

The "Frankish" princes divided the spoils among them. Tancred became the hero of many future works of fiction, such as the *Gerusalemme Liberata* of Torquato Tasso, the *Combattimento di Tancredi e Clorinda* of Claudio Monteverdi, and the *Tancred* of Benjamin Disraeli. In reality, he was an ambitious and impetuous young prince who had refused to swear loyalty to the "Roman Emperor of the East," Alexios Komnenos, and with his uncle Bohemond continued to make war on the Byzantines, and even on Baudouin de Boulogne, who had become the Count of Edessa and later King of Jerusalem. His life was recorded in the *Gesta Tancredi*, written in Latin by Raoul de Caen (1080–1120), a Norman chronicler who joined the First Crusade and served under Tancred and Bohemond.

Raymond de Saint-Gilles de Toulouse, the leader of the most important army to capture Jerusalem, was offered the crown of "King of Jerusalem" by his fellow princes. He refused to accept it, saying that he would not rule over the city where Jesus Christ had been tortured and crucified. He shuddered to think of being called "King of Jerusalem" because that should be the title of Jesus Christ himself and not of an earthly king. It is also likely that Raymond wished to continue the siege of Tripoli (now in Lebanon) rather than remain in Jerusalem. Raymond may have hoped that none of his rivals would accept the crown, and that he would still take it eventually.

In the Middle Ages, Bouillon was a lordship within the Duchy of Lower Lorraine and the principal seat of the "Frankish" Ardennes-Bouillon dynasty. In the eleventh century they dominated the area and held the ducal title along with many other titles in the region. Bouillon was the location of the ducal mint and the dominant urban area in the dukes' possession. On July 22, 1099, the rule of Jerusalem was given to the younger prince Godefroy de Bouillon (1060–1100), who was more popular than Raymond, and who was named "Defender of the Holy Sepulcher". Godefroy did not use the title of King of Jerusalem, and he died the following year, almost a year to the day from the taking of Jerusalem. Godefroy de Bouillon had been born around 1060, either in Boulogne-sur-Mer, in France, or in Baisy, in the region of Brabant (now in Belgium).

Godefroy's chief rival, Raymond de Saint Gilles of Toulouse, was reluctant to give up the "Tower of David" in Jerusalem – a mosque which has nothing to do with King David – and which he had taken after the fall of the city, and it was only with difficulty that Godefroy de Bouillon was able to take it from him. After Godefroy de Bouillon became the ruler of Jerusalem, he and Robert de Flandres led their army to Ascalon (now the Israeli city of Ashkelon) to face the Fatimid "Saracens" from Egypt. Raymond of Toulouse and Robert of Normandy stayed behind, either due to a quarrel with Godefroy, or because they preferred to have better information about the Egyptian army from their own scouts. When the Egyptian presence was confirmed, they marched out as well the next day. Near Ramla, they met Tancred and Godefroy's brother Eustace, who had left to capture Nablus earlier in the month. At the head of the army, the monk Arnulf Malecorne of Chocques (died 1118) carried "the relic of the Cross", while Raymond of Aguilers carried the relic of the "Holy Lance" that had been discovered at Antioch the previous year.

The word *mamluk* is an Arabic word meaning "owned." During the European Middle Ages, a Mamluk was a slave soldier who converted to Islam and served the Muslim Fatimid caliphs of Egypt and later the Ayyubid sultans of Syria and Egypt. Some of the Mamluks were Christian children kidnaped by the Egyptian Muslims in Europe, force-converted to Islam, trained as warriors, and made high-ranking soldiers in Egypt. Over time, the Mamluks became a powerful military caste, and, on more than one occasion, they seized power for themselves. During the Crusades, in 1250, they took power from their Ayyubid masters and ruled Egypt until 1517, when the Ottoman Turks conquered it. Their dynasty was established in 1250 by Baybars (1223–1277), a Kipchak Turk Mamluk who took power from his Ayyubid masters.

On August 12, 1099 the "Franks" roundly defeated the army of the Fatimid "Saracens," led by al-Malik al-Afdal ibn Badr al-Jamali Shahanshah, at Ascalon. Shahanshah is a Persian title meaning "King of Kings," and Al-

Afdal was a powerful man, the regent and the chief of the army of the Fatimid caliphs, who had made a puppet of his child-caliph. He had been born in Acre, Palestine (now Acco, Israel), then part of the Fatimid caliphate, the son of Badr al-Jamali, an Armenian Mamluk vizier of the Fatimid caliphate. Badr al-Jamali was the grand vizier for the Fatimid caliphs in Cairo from 1074 until his death in 1094, when his son al-Afdal succeeded him. The Fatimid caliph Ma'ad al-Mustansir Billah (1029–1094) died soon afterwards. Al-Afdal, who was Regent, appointed as caliph al-Musta'li (died 1101), a child, instead of al-Mustali's older brother, Abu Mansur al-Nizar al-Mustafa ad-Din Illah, meaning "the chosen for Allah's religion." This enabled Al-Afdal to control the caliph.

The furious al-Nizar revolted against his younger brother and was defeated by al-Afdal in 1095; his supporters, led by Hassan-i-Sabah, fled to Alamut (the castle of death), a mountain fortress located in central Elburz mountains, south of the Caspian Sea, where Hassan established the Nizari Ismaili community, also known as the Hashshashin or Assassins. Fatimid power in Palestine had been eroded by the arrival of the Seljuk Turks. In 1097 al-Afdal captured Tyre from the Seljuks, and in 1098, as we have seen, he also took Jerusalem, expelling its Seljuk governor, Najm ad-Din Ilghazi ibn Artuq and placing a Fatimid governor in his place. Al-Afdal temporarily restored most of Palestine to Fatimid control. Al-Afdal had taken the "Franks" for Byzantine mercenaries, and this misperception had caused him to conclude that the Crusaders would be his natural allies, as both of them were enemies of the Seljuk Turks. The Fatimid overtures for an alliance with the Crusaders had been rebuffed, however, and the Crusaders had continued southward from Antioch to capture Jerusalem from the Fatimids.

When it became apparent to Al-Afdal that the "Franks" would not rest until they took Jerusalem, Al-Afdal marched from Cairo toward them, but was too late to rescue Jerusalem, which had fallen on July 15, 1099, and, as we have seen, on August 12 the Crusaders under Godefroy of Bouillon surprised al-Afdal at the Battle of Ascalon and routed him. Al-Afdal, however, did not give up. He would re-harass the "Franks" and re-assert Fatimid control of Ascalon, as the Crusaders did not attempt to retain it, and he would utilize it as a staging ground for later attacks on the Crusader states. Al-Afdal marched out every year from Cairo to attack the "Latin Kingdom of Jerusalem", and in 1105 he attempted to ally with Damascus against them, but was defeated at the Battle of Ramla. Al-Afdal and his army enjoyed success only so long as no European fleet interfered, but they gradually lost control of their coastal strongholds. In 1109 Tripoli (now in Lebanon) was lost to the "Franks," despite the fleet and supplies sent by al-Afdal, and the city became the centre of an important Crusader county. In 1110 the governor of Ascalon, Shams al-Khilafa, rebelled against al-Afdal with the intent of handing over the city to the "Latin Kingdom of Jerusalem" (for a large price). However, Al-Khilafa's Berber troops assassinated him and sent his head to al-Afdal. The Crusaders later took Tyre (now in Lebanon) and Acre (now the

Israeli city of Acco) as well, and remained in Jerusalem until the arrival of "Saladin" in 1187.

Al-Afdal Shahanshah was murdered in 1121 during the *eid ul-adha* (the Feast of the Sacrifice). According to the Muslim chronicler Hamza ibn Asad abu Ya'la ibn al-Qalanisi (1070–1160) "it was asserted that the Batinis (the Isma'ili Naziris or Hashshashin) were responsible for his assassination, but this statement is not true. On the contrary it is an empty pretence and an insubstantial calumny." The real cause of the murder was the growing boldness of the young caliph, al-Amir Bi-Ahkamillah (1096–1130), who had succeeded al-Musta'li in 1101, and his resentment of al-Afdal's control of al-Afdal. Ibn al-Qalanisi states that "all eyes wept and all hearts sorrowed for al-Afdal; time did not produce his like after him, and after his loss the government fell into disrepute." He was succeeded as vizier by Al-Ma'mum. The "Franks" called al-Afdal "Lavendalius" or "Elafdalio."

Their victories over the "Saracens," however, did not end the deep and bitter rivalry between the "Frankish" princes, which was no less emotional than the deepest sibling rivalry or father-son struggle in any family. The chief rivalry was between the forty-year-old Godefroy de Bouillon, the ruler of Jerusalem, and the sixty-year-old Count Raymond de Saint Gilles de Toulouse. It ended in 1110 with the death of the former. The "Saracen" chronicler Hamza ibn Asad abu-Ya'la ibn al-Qalanisi was an Arab politician and chronicler in Damascus in the twelfth century. Ibn al-Qalanisi wrote that Godefroy was killed by a Muslim arrow during the siege of Acre, but the German historians Albert of Aachen (flourished 1100), author of *Historia Hierosolymitanae expeditionis*, and Ekkehard of Aura (died 1126), a participant in the Crusade of 1101, reported that Godefroy had contracted an illness in Caesarea. It was later believed that the Muslim emir of Caesarea had poisoned him, but there seems to be no basis for this rumor. Guillaume de Tyr, the archbishop of Tyre and the chronicler of the Crusades, did not mention it. It is also said that Godefroy died after eating a poisoned apple. He died in Jerusalem after a prolonged illness.

Raymond de Saint Gilles de Toulouse survived his younger rival by five years. He continued to fight actively against the "Saracens" until 1105. When Raymond went north, in the winter of 1099–1100, his first act was one of aggression against Bohemond, capturing Laodicea, now Latakia in Syria, from him (Bohemond had himself taken it from Alexios Komnenos of Byzantium). From Laodicea, Raymond went to Constantinople, where he allied with Alexios, Bohemond's most powerful enemy. Bohemond was at the time attempting to expand his Principality of Antioch into Byzantine territory, and blatantly refused to fulfill his oath of allegiance to the Byzantine Empire. Tancred, the Prince of the Galilee, was Bohemond's nephew and natural ally.

By 1100 the Byzantine town of Malatia, which guarded one of the Cilician Gates through the Taurus Mountains, had been captured by an Armenian mercenary. Reports were received that the Turkoman Danishmend Emir, Ghazi Gümüştekin of Sivas, was preparing an expedition to capture Malatia, and the Armenians sought help from Bohemond of Antioch. Afraid to weaken his forces at Antioch, trying to use the chance to extend his domain, Bohemond marched north with only 300 knights and a small force of infantry. Failing to send scouting parties to find out the location of the Seljuk Turks, they were ambushed by the Turks, and completely encircled at the Battle of Melitene. Bohemond managed to send a soldier to seek help from Count Baudouin of Edessa (who would become King of Jerusalem later that year), but was captured by the Turks and imprisoned in Neo-Caesarea (now the Turkish town of Niskar). Bohemond languished in this prison for two years.

Hearing of Bohemond's capture, Emperor Alexios of Byzantium, incensed that Bohemond had broken his sacred oath to him and kept the Principality of Antioch for himself, offered to ransom Bohemond for 260,000 dinars, if Emir Ghazi Gümüştekin handed the prisoner over to him. When Kilij Arslan (1079–1107), the Seljuk Turkish "Sultan of Rum" and overlord of the Emir, heard of the proposed payment, he demanded half of it, or he would attack Byzantium. Bohemond himself then proposed a ransom of 130,000 dinars paid just to the Emir. The bargain was concluded, and Ghazi Gümüştekin and Prince Bohemond exchanged oaths of friendship. Ransomed by Count Baudouin of Edessa, who had become King of Jerusalem, Bohemond returned in triumph to Antioch in 1103, where his nephew Tancred had been ruling in his place for two years.

In 1101 Raymond de Saint Gilles de Toulouse had joined the Crusade of 1101, a minor Crusade of three separate movements, organized in 1100 and 1101 in the successful aftermath of the First Crusade. It is called the "Crusade of the Faint-Hearted" due to the many participants who joined this Crusade after having abandoned the First Crusade. The three groups of "Franks," who were Lombards, Nivernois, and Bavarians, fought the Seljuk Turks in the "Seljuk Sultanate of Rum," in mid-Anatolia. The Lombards were originally the Langobards (long beards), a Germanic tribe that settled in northern Italy, around Mediolanum (Milan) and became Italianized. The Crusaders were roundly defeated. Guillaume de Nevers escaped to Tarsus and joined the rest of the survivors there, as did Raymond of Toulouse.

Under Raymond's command the "Franks" captured "Tortosa" (the Syrian town of Tartous), with help from a Genoese fleet. The Crusade of 1101 was more of a pilgrimage than a war. The survivors arrived at Antioch at the end of 1101, and at Easter 1102 arrived in Jerusalem. Afterwards, many of them simply went home, their vow of pilgrimage having been fulfilled, although some remained behind to help King Baudouin defend the "Latin Kingdom of Jerusalem" against an Egyptian invasion at Ramla. Estienne de Blois was killed during this battle, as was Hugues de Lusignan, the founder of the Lusignan dynasty of Jerusalem and Cyprus. The French nobleman Josselin de

Courtenay (born 1034) also stayed behind and survived to become Count of Edessa in 1118.

The Seljuk defeat of the Crusaders in 1100 allowed the Seljuk sultan Kilij Arslan to establish his capital at Konya, push the Byzantines to Europe, and prove to the Muslim world that the Crusaders were not invincible, as they had appeared to be during the First Crusade. The Crusaders and the Byzantines each blamed the other for the defeat, but neither of them could ensure a safe route to Jerusalem through Anatolia now that Kilij Arslan had strengthened his position. The only open route to the "Holy Land" was the sea route, which benefitted the Italian cities. The lack of a safe land route from Constantinople to Jerusalem also benefitted the Principality of Antioch, where Prince Tancred, ruling for his captive uncle Bohemond, was able to consolidate his power without Byzantine interference.

In 1101 Raymond de Saint Gilles de Toulouse, who had joined the Crusade of 1101, was defeated by the Seljuk Turks at Mersivan in Anatolia. He escaped the Seljuks and returned to Constantinople, where he joined his ally Alexios Komnenos. In 1102 Raymond traveled by sea from Constantinople to Antioch, where he was imprisoned by Tancred, the Regent of Antioch during the captivity of Bohemond, and was only freed after solemnly vowing not to attempt any more conquests in the country between Antioch and Acre. He immediately broke his promise, however, attacking and capturing Tartous, and in 1103 built a castle on the Mons Peregrinus near Tripoli (now in Lebanon). He was aided by the Byzantine Emperor Alexios, who preferred to create a friendly state in Tripoli to balance the hostile state in Antioch.

Raymond de Saint Gilles had an incestuous streak. He was married three times, and was twice excommunicated for marrying within forbidden degrees of consanguinity. His first wife was his cousin, and the mother of his son Bertrand. His second wife was Matilda, the daughter of King Roger of Sicily. Raymond's third wife was Elvira, the illegitimate daughter of King Alfonso of Castile, the Spanish king who also campaigned against the "Moors," just as Raymond fought the "Saracens." Raymond died in 1105 during the siege of Tripoli, before it was captured from the "Saracens." He was succeeded by his nephew Guillaume-Jourdain de Cerdagne (died 1110), who, in 1109, with the aid of King Baudouin of Jerusalem, captured Tripoli. They created the Christian County of Tripoli (1109–1289), the last Crusader state founded in the "Levant." Guillaume, however, was deposed that year by Raymond's son Bertrand, and Tripoli remained in the possession of the counts of Toulouse throughout the twelfth century.

The *Wikipedia* article about Raymond de Saint-Gilles attributes his behavior to conscious motives:

> Raymond of Toulouse seems to have been driven both by religious and material motives. On the one hand he accepted the discovery of the Holy Lance and rejected the kingship of Jerusalem, but on the other hand he could not resist the temptation of a new territory. Raymond of Aguilers,

a clerk in Raymond's army, wrote an account of the Crusade from Raymond's point of view.

In fact, as is often the case, the unconscious motives may have been more powerful. The "account" of Raymond d'Aguilers was a Latin book entitled *Historia Francorum qui ceperunt Iherusalem*. However, Raymond's greed for territory may have masked a deeper unconscious infantile greed such as the greed for mother's milk, her body, and her love.

During the twelfth century, the French literary productions switched from Latin to the Anglo-Norman dialect of Old French. The first period of the "Latin Kingdom of Jerusalem" lasted until 1187. The Oxford manuscript of the *Chanson de Roland*, an epic poem about an eighth-century battle of Charlemagne, was written between 1040 and 1115. This was the first Anglo-Norman literary text. Its earliest extant text is the Oxford manuscript, which holds some 4,000 lines. The *Chanson de Roland*, written by an unknown French troubadour, is a *chanson de geste*, a literary *genre* that flourished in the eleventh and twelfth centuries, and which told the story of some legendary hero of battles and wars.

The battle celebrated in the *Chanson de Roland* is the battle of Roncevaux Pass, which had taken place in 778, between the Franks and the Basques. At the battle of Roncevaux Pass, the Basques had ambushed and defeated the Frankish army under Hruodland (Roland), the chief paladin of Charlemagne and his ruler of the March of Bretagne (the border region of Brittany), on his way home from Spain, in a small Pyrenees mountain pass. Three centuries later, in the eleventh century, this Roland became the central figure not only in the *Chanson de Roland*, but in the entire *matière de France*, a literary cycle of French epic poems. The name "matière" for that poem cycle was bestowed on it by the twelfth-century French poet Jehan Bodel, the author of the *Chanson de Saisnes*, another *chanson de geste* about the war of Charlemagne with the Saxon leader Widukind, whom Bodel called "Guiteclin". In that poem, Bodel famously wrote, "*Ne sont que III matières à nul homme atandant/ de France et de Bretaigne, et de Rome la grant*" ("There are but three matters waiting for no man/ of France, and of Britain, and of Rome the great"). The Matter of France was about Charlemagne and his paladins, that of Britain about King Arthur and his knights, and that of Rome about ancient times.

Most of the *Chanson de Roland* was not about Roland, but about the victories of Charlemagne over the "Saracens." Those "Saracens" are described as mean and cruel. How did the Basques of Roncevaux Pass become "Saracens"? There are two different theories about when the polytheistic Basques were Christianized. One says that Christianity arrived in the Basque Country during the fourth and fifth centuries, the other that the Basques were not fully Christian until the twelfth and thirteenth centuries. Early traces of Christianity can be found in the major urban Basque areas from the fourth century onwards, a bishopric from 589 in Pamplona, and three Basque hermit cave concentrations were in use from the sixth century onwards.

Did the anonymous author of the *Chanson de Roland* use the word "Saracen" to mean anyone who was not Frankish and Christian or anyone who fought the Franks? If the latter, then the fantastic term "Saracen" was not only reserved for Muslims, Arabs, Turks, and Persians, but for all enemies of the Franks. In 1147 the Germans led a "Wendish Crusade" against the "pagan" Slavs east of the River Elbe, in what are now northeastern Germany and Poland. In 1199–1226 the Teutonic Knights, a Germanic chivalric order that was formed in 1190 in Acre, the new capital of the "Latin Kingdom of Jerusalem," conducted the "Baltic Crusade" against the Livs, Letts, Prussians, and other "pagan" peoples in northeastern Germany, Christianizing them by the sword. The Teutonic Knights also called these "pagan" tribes "Saracens." We shall discuss this striking phenomenon again below.

The only historical account of the battle of Roncevaux was written by Einhard (775–840), a Frankish courtier, biographer, and servant of Charlemagne. His biography of his king is entitled *Vita Karoli Magni*. Here is the relevant passage from Einhard's chronicle about the battle of Roncevaux:

> While he was vigorously pursuing the Saxon war, almost without a break, and after he had placed garrisons at selected points along the border, [Charlemagne] marched into Spain [in 778] with as large a force as he could mount. His army passed through the Pyrenees and [Charlemagne] received the surrender of all the towns and fortified places he encountered. He was returning [to Francia] with his army safe and intact, but high in the Pyrenees [at Roncevaux] on that return trip he briefly experienced the Basques. That place is so thoroughly covered with thick forest that it is the perfect spot for an ambush. [Charlemagne's] army was forced by the narrow terrain to proceed in a long line and [it was at that spot], high on the mountain, that the Basques set their ambush [...] The Basques had the advantage in this skirmish because of the lightness of their weapons and the nature of the terrain, whereas the Franks were disadvantaged by the heaviness of their arms and the unevenness of the land. [The seneschal] Eggihard, the overseer of the king's table, Anselm, the count of the palace, and Roland, the lord of the Breton March [border region], along with many others died in that skirmish. But this deed could not be avenged at that time, because the enemy had so dispersed after the attack that there was no indication as to where they could be found.
>
> (Einhard 1998, pp. 21–22)

The fascinating psychological question is, how could the Basques be called "Saracens" in the *Chanson de Roland*, when that was the Frankish name for Arabs and Muslims? The author of the *Wikipedia* article on the *Chanson de Roland* thinks that the centuries of oral tradition about the Basque ambush of the Franks at Roncevaux that had passed from the battle itself to the *chanson* had turned reality into fantasy. "Roland becomes, in the poem, the nephew of Charlemagne, the Christian Basques become Muslim Saracens, and Charlemagne, rather than marching north to subdue the Saxons, returns to Spain and avenges the deaths of his knights. The *Song of Roland* marks a nascent French identity and sense of collective history traced back to the legendary Charlemagne."

Psychologically, that was what had happened to the Crusaders: they too had thought of themselves as "Franks," tracing their identity back to Charlemagne, even thought they were Normans and Frenchmen. Like the late-twelfth-century Anglo-Norman epic poem *Estoire de la guerre sainte* by Ambroise, which described the Crusade of Richard *Coeur-de-Lion* (1157–1199), the king of England and of what later came to be called the "Angevin Empire," the *Chanson de Roland* was written in an Anglo-Norman dialect, which suggests a common origin in northern France, even though some critics believe that the origin of the Oxford manuscript of the epic was farther south, in Provence. (Anonymous 1988). The author of the *Chanson de Roland* seem to have thought of himself as *françois* rather than *franc*, a subtle but important difference.

Human historiography and memory change the reality of events and create legends around them. Those legends depend on who is doing the writing and the remembering. After 778, over centuries, the battle of Roncevaux Pass was romanticized by oral tradition into a major conflict between Christians and Muslims, when in fact it was a minor battle and the Basques were not Muslims. Charlemagne had fought the "Saracens" in Iberia, though not in the Pyrenees. In the oral tradition, however, the Basques were replaced by a force of 400,000 "Saracens." The *Chanson de Roland*, which commemorates this battle, is the earliest surviving of the *chansons de geste* or epic poems of medieval France in the northern French dialect, or *langue d'oïl*. There is a tombstone near the Roncevaux Pass in the Spanish Pyrenees commemorating the area where Roland purportedly died.

The French legend of the battle of Roncevaux Pass as told in the *Chanson de Roland* has a Spanish counterpart in the shape of the Iberian legends about Bernardo del Carpio, a medieval Spanish hero from the Kingdom of León in northwest Spain, whom these legends make the vanquisher of Roland at Roncevaux. Bernardo del Carpio is the son of Sancho, Count of Saldana and brother of King Alfonso II of Asturias (759–842), and of his sister Ximena. Unhappy with the marriage of his sister to Sancho, Alfonso has his brother-in-law Sancho blinded and thrown into a dungeon, and takes Bernardo into his court as his own son. No one must tell the young Bernardo who his real father is. Some of these Spanish legends have Bernardo striving against

Alfonso to release his father from prison. Others have him as the rival and slayer of "Rolando" at Roncevaux. The legends have Alfonso invite Charlemagne into Iberia to defeat the "Moors", promising to name him his heir, but Bernardo's victory at Roncevaux ends that plan. Bernardo joins the "Moors" hoping to force Alfonso into action, but Alfonso secretly has Sancho killed in his prison cell. From a psychoanalytic viewpoint, this legend has a very clear Oedipal theme to it.

Drawing on their own oral traditions, some medieval Muslim historians glorified "their" victory at the battle of Roncevaux Pass. Writing four centuries after the battle, the medieval Iraqi Kurdish Muslim historian Abu al-Hassan Ali ibn Muhammad ibn Muhammad (1160–1233), also known as al-Athir, claimed that the young Frankish king Charlemagne had come to Spain in 778 at the invitation of the Muslim rulers of Zaragoza, Barcelona, and Huesca, who asked him to aid them in their revolt against Abd ar-Rahman, the *emir* of Córdoba. Seeing an opportunity to extend his empire and his religion into Iberia, Charlemagne led his armies across the Pyrenees, subdued the Basques at Pamplona, and proceeded south. Arriving at Zaragoza, however, he found that its ruler Husayn would not surrender the city to him, and that Sulayman al-Arabi of Barcelona had also changed his mind. Charlemagne besieged Zaragoza for some time, then decided not to risk defeat, turned around, took Sulayman al-Arabi prisoner, and headed home to Paderborn. At Roncevaux Pass, al-Arabi's sons collaborated with the Basques to ambush Charlemagne's troops, avenge their defeat, and rescue their father.

However, this story hardly explains the transformation of the Basques into "Saracens" in the *Chanson de Roland*. This was a pure psychohistorical fantasy. The authors of the epic poem needed to identify the "evil race" of people who had attacked Charlemagne as "Saracens" because this was the "evil race" of the eleventh-century Europe. In the same way the first Crusaders needed to see all Muslims, Turks, Persians, and other non-Christian non-Europeans in the "East" as "Saracens." They even killed the Christians in Jerusalem in 1099 because they were dressed like "Saracens" and appeared to them like the "evil race."

The "Latin Kingdom of Jerusalem"

After the capture of Jerusalem by the "Franks" in 1099, and the creation of the "Latin Kingdom of Jerusalem" headed by Godefroy de Bouillon, a "Latin" religious hierarchy was established in the kingdom under a "Latin Patriarch" named Arnulf of Chocques (died 1118), who was replaced after Christmas 1099 with Archbishop Dagobert of Pisa (died 1105). Arnulf became Latin Patriarch again from 1112 to 1118. The Greek word "patriarchos" means "father ruler." Before that time, all the Christians in the Holy Land were under the authority and care of the Greek Orthodox Patriarch of Jerusalem. From 1099 to 1187 the Latin Patriarchate of Jerusalem was divided into four archdioceses – those of Tyre (now in Lebanon), Caesarea and Nazareth, (now in Israel) and Petra (now in Jordan), and a number of suffragan (subordinate) dioceses. The "Latin" Patriarch controlled the "Latin quarter" of the city of Jerusalem (the "Holy Sepulchre" and its immediate surroundings), and had as his direct "suffragans" the bishops of Lydda-Ramla, Bethlehem, Hebron, and Gaza, and the abbots of the Temple, Mount Zion, and the Mount of Olives. After the last vestiges of the "Latin Kingdom of Jerusalem", including its capital of "Saint-Jean d'Acre," were conquered by the Mamluks in 1291, the "Latin" hierarchy was eliminated in the Middle East. However, refusing to face reality, it moved to Cyprus, then to Rome, and for centuries the Roman Catholic Church continued to appoint a "Latin Patriarch of Jerusalem," who, however, was based in Rome from 1374 to 1847.

The first person to formally call himself "king of Jerusalem," Baudouin de Boulogne (1058–1118), Count of Edessa, actually called himself "King of the Latins of Jerusalem." The Crusaders were no more "Latin" than they were "Franks": they were only Latin in the sense of being Roman Catholics and writing in Latin, and not being Greeks. Yet the Patriarch of Jerusalem was called the "Latin" patriarch. Baudouin may have wanted to assert his authority over the "Latins" and reduce that of the patriarch. The Crusader kingdom, which was called the "Latin Kingdom of Jerusalem" (Prawer 1972, 1980), was no more "Latin," or even a kingdom, than the "Holy Roman Empire of the German Nation" was holy, Roman, or German, or even an empire. The "Franks" imported the feudal system to Palestine, but the King of Jerusalem did not have absolute authority over the feudal lords and princes of his kingdom, such as those of Acre, or Ascalon, or the Galilee, who had their own fiefs. The "kingdom" was a loose collection of towns captured by the Crusaders. It was separate from the Crusader states of Edessa (now in Turkey), Tripoli (now in Lebanon) and Antioch (now in Syria).

In 1100, upon the death of Godefroy de Bouillon, his brother Baudouin de Boulogne, the Count of Edessa, claimed the title of "King of the Latins of Jerusalem." Baudouin was opposed by his old enemy Tancred, the Prince of the Galilee and nephew of Prince Bohemond of Antioch, as well as by the "Latin" patriarch, Dagobert of Pisa, who wished to set up a theocratic state in Jerusalem. As soon as he arrived in Jerusalem, however, Baudouin set out on an expedition against the "Saracen" Egyptian Fatimid territory to the south and did not return until the end of December. The showdown with Dagobert was postponed.

On Christmas Day 1100 Baudouin de Boulogne, Count of Edessa, was crowned King of Jerusalem by Latin Patriarch Dagobert, who had given up his opposition to Baudouin, although he refused to crown Baudouin in Jerusalem. The coronation took place in Bethlehem, the place Christians believe to be the birthplace of their Messiah and God, Jesus Christ. The struggle between church and state in Jerusalem continued into the spring of 1101, when Baudouin had Dagobert suspended by a papal legate. Later that the year the two disagreed on the question of the contribution to be made by the patriarch towards the defense of the "Holy Land". The struggle ended in the deposition of Dagobert by

Baudouin. Dagobert died in 1105. Their struggle was similar to that of King Heinrich against Pope Gregorius in the investiture controversy.

Baudouin expanded his kingdom northward into what is now Lebanon. He captured the port cities of Acre (1104), Beirut (1110), and Sidon (1111), while also exerting his suzerainty over the Crusader states to the north – the County of Edessa (which he had founded), the Principality of Antioch, and, after 1109, the County of Tripoli. He successfully defended his kingdom against "Saracen" invasions from the Fatimids in Egypt at the numerous battles at Ramla and elsewhere in the southwest of the kingdom, and from Damascus and Mosul in the northeast in 1113. Baudouin brought with him an Armenian wife, whom he had married to gain political support from the Armenian population in Edessa, but whom he set aside when he found that he did not really need the Armenian support in Jerusalem. He married Adelaide del Vasto, regent of Sicily, in 1113, but divorced her as well in 1117. Adelaide's son from her first marriage, Roger II of Sicily (1095–1154), never forgave Baudouin, and for decades withheld his much-needed naval support from the Crusades.

One of the fascinating aspects of the Crusades is not only that one of the nine major ones (the fourth) never reached the "Holy Land" and ended with the sack of Constantinople, but that they also included numerous minor "Crusades," most of which had nothing to do with "the Holy Land." Among these were the "Italian Crusades," which began with the Mallorca Crusade (1113–1115) and went on for two and a half centuries. They included the Crusade of Jean de Brienne (c. 1170–1237) in Apulia (1229), the Genoese Crusade against Savona and Albenga (1240), the Crusade against Manfred of Sicily (1255–1266), the Crusade against Ezzelino da Romano (1256), the Crusade against King Conradin of Jerusalem and Sicily (1268), the First Crusade against the Aragonese (1309), and the Crusade against Bernabò Visconti (1362–1363). Despite the name "Italian Crusades" some of them involved Spain. Their connection to the "Holy Land Crusades" was tenuous at best.

Other "Crusades" that had little or nothing to do with the "Holy Land Crusades" were the Northern Crusades of the Teutonic Knights and of the Catholic kings of northern Europe against the "pagan" people of the Baltic Sea coast, including the Wends, Sorbs, Obotrites, Livonians, Latgallians, Selonians, Lithuanians, Letts (Latvians), Finns, Estonians, Semigalians, Samogitians, Curonians, Old Prussians, and other "heathen" people. The "northern Crusades" were also known as the "Baltic Crusades." They began in 1171, after Pope Alexander III authorized a Crusade against the "heathen" of the East Baltic coast, or in 1195, after Pope Celestinus III did the same. The Roman Catholic kingdoms of Sweden, Norway, Denmark, Poland, and the "Holy Roman Empire" of Germany had begun subjugating their "pagan" neighbors in 1147 and the "northern Crusades" went on until 1410.

Baudouin, who may have been homosexual or bisexual, died without heirs in 1118, during a campaign against the "Saracens" of Egypt, and the "Latin" kingdom was offered to his brother Eustache de Boulogne, who rejected it. It was then given to Baudouin du Bourg, a former Count of Edessa, who became "King Baudouin II of Jerusalem." Baudouin II was an able ruler who successfully defended his kingdom against the "Saracen" (Fatimid Arab and Seljuk Turk) invasions. The Principality of Antioch was weakened in 1119 by the battle that the "Latins" called the battle of *Ager Sanguinis* (Field of Blood). In that battle, which took place near Sarmada in Syria, the Crusader army of the Principality of Antioch, led by Prince Roger of Salerno, was annihilated by the "Saracen" army of Najm ad-Din Ilghazi ibn Artuq (died 1122), the Seljuk ruler of Aleppo. Roger was killed. Baudouin himself was held captive by the emir of Aleppo from 1122 to 1124, when he was finally ransomed and returned to his throne. In 1125 Baudouin led the Crusader states to victory at Azaz in Syria over a Muslim coalition commanded by the Seljuk atabeg Aqsunqur al-Bursuqi of Mosul, who was murdered in 1126 by the Nizari Ismaili Assassins.

What kind of relations developed between the "Franks" who lived in the "Holy Land" and the "Saracens" whom they were fighting? The Israeli historian Benjamin Kedar believed that there was a "cross-fertilization" between the two communities. He believed that the Crusaders saw themselves as Christian missionaries (Kedar 1984). Before 970, the European Christians were not particularly interested in Muslims, except as "evil Saracens." Later, they sought to convert them to Christianity. Islam, however, forbids the "infidel" from attacking it, considers itself the only true religion, and imposes the death penalty on renegades who abandon it. After the conquest of "the Holy Land" by the Crusaders there were more conversions of Muslims to Christianity, but Kedar thought they came from economic and social motives, not religious conviction.

Jewish converts to Christianity often became "more Catholic than the Pope," embracing their new religion with fanatical zeal. One of them, the Spaniard Petrus Alfonsi (1062–1110), was the most important historical source in Christian Europe about Islam in the eleventh century. Alfonsi was a physician to King Alfonso VI of Castile. His original Hebrew name was Moshe Sephardi (Moses the Spaniard). He was born at Huesca, Aragon, and was forty-four years old when he embraced Christianity. He was baptized at Huesca on St. Peter's Day in 1106, taking the baptismal name of Petrus Alfonsi. Like all the Jewish "apostates" of his time, he sought to show his zeal for his new faith by attacking Judaism and defending the truths of the Christian faith.

Petrus Alfonsi composed twelve dialogues against the Jews, which were praised by Raymund Martin in his *Pugio Fidei*, and by others equally biased against the Jews, but are little known to-day. The works of Petru Alfonsi came to light in the sixteenth century. A fifteenth-century manuscript attributed to him is entitled *De conversione Petrus Alfonsi quondam judaei et libro ejus in Judaeos et Saracenos.* In that manuscript, much material about the "Saracens" can be found. The Israeli historian Benjamin Kedar concluded from it that the Crusader "Latins" were no less missionary in propagating their Christian religion than the Muslim "Saracens" who force-Islamized all those whom they conquered.

We have several documents written in Latin by the "Franks" of the First Crusade: two letters of Count Anselme de Ribemont to Archbishop Manasses II of Reims in France, dated 1098; a letter by Estienne Henry, Count of Blois and of Chartres, to his wife Adele; a letter of the "Latin Patriarch of Jerusalem" to the Latin Church of the West; a letter by the people of Lucca in Italy to all faithful Christians; and a letter by the princes Godefroy, Raymond, and Daimbert to the Pope. Anselme of Ribemont, the count of Ostrevant and Valenciennes, was one of the heroes of the first Crusade; his "glorious" death before Archis (now Arqa in Lebanon) in April 1099, was recorded by all the eye-witnesses of the expedition. He wrote two letters to the archbishop of Reims. In the first letter by Anselme de Ribemont, written in 1098 during the siege of the Antioch by the Crusaders, he repeatedly mentioned the "Turks" rather than the "Saracens."

> We moved our camp from Nicaea on the fourth day before the of July and proceeded on our journey for three days. On the fourth day the Turks, having collected their forces from all sides, again attacked the smaller portion of our army, killed many of our men and drove all the remainder back to their camps. Bohemond, count of the Romans, count Stephen, and the count of Flanders commanded this section. When these were thus terrified by fear, the standards of the larger army suddenly appeared. Hugh the Great and the duke of Lorraine were riding at the head, the count of St. Gilles and the venerable bishop of Puy followed. For they had heard of the battle and were hastening to our aid. The number of the Turks was estimated at 260,000. All of our army attacked them, killed many and routed the rest. On that day I returned from the emperor, to whom the princes had sent me on public business.
> (Robinson & Robinson 1894, vol. 1, no. 4, pp. 2–5)

We do not know whether Count Estienne of Blois placed that mythical chastity belt on his wife before embarking on the First Crusade in 1096. In his letter to her from the siege of Antioch in 1098, we have the following paragraph:

> We found the city of Antioch very extensive, fortified with incredible strength and almost impregnable. In addition, more than 5,000 bold Turkish soldiers had entered the city, not counting the Saracens, Publicans, Arabs, Tulitans, Syrians, Armenians and other different races of whom an infinite multitude had gathered together there. In fighting against these enemies of God and of our own we have, by God's grace, endured many sufferings and innumerable evils up to the present time. Many also have already exhausted all their resources in this very holy passion. Very many of our Franks, indeed, would have met a temporal death from starvation, if the clemency of God and our money had not saved them. Before the above-mentioned city of Antioch indeed, throughout the whole winter we suffered for our Lord Christ from

excessive cold and enormous torrents of rain. What some say about the impossibility of bearing the heat of the sun throughout Syria is untrue, for the winter there is very similar to our winter in the west.

(Robinson & Robinson 1894, vol. 1, no. 4, pp. 5–8)

This letter is fascinating, because, contrary to the general tendency of the European Christians to lump all Muslims, Turks, Arabs, Persians, and other "Easterneres" into one bag called "Saracens," Esteinne of Blois seemed to think that the "Publicans, Arabs, Tulitans, Syrians" were not Saracens. By "Arabs" he may have meant the desert Bedouin. On the other hand, he obviously called the French and Norman Crusaders "Franks," just as the Muslims called them all *al-Franj*. In another paragraph of the same letter, Count Estienne de Blois wrote to his wife Adele about the "Saracen princes," who were really Seljuk Turkish emirs. As the Europeans always did, every Arabic or Turkish named was Latinized:

When truly Caspian [Yaghi Siyán], the emir of Antioch – that is, prince and lord – perceived that he was hard pressed by us, he sent his son Sensodolo [Shams ad-Dawlah] by name, to the prince who holds Jerusalem, and to the prince of Calep, Rodoam [Rodoanus], and to Docap [Duqaq ibn Tutush], prince of Damascus. He also sent into Arabia to Bolianuth [sic] and to Carathania to Hamelnuth [sic]. These five emirs with 12,000 picked Turkish horsemen suddenly came to aid the inhabitants of Antioch. We, indeed, ignorant of all this, had sent many of our soldiers away to the cities and fortresses. For there are one hundred and sixty-five cities and fortresses throughout Syria which are in our power. But a little before they reached the city, we attacked them at three leagues distance with 700 soldiers, on a certain plain near the "Iron Bridge." God, however, fought for us, His faithful, against them. For on that day, fighting in the strength that God gives, we conquered them and killed an innumerable multitude – God continually fighting for us – and we also carried back to the army more than two hundred of their heads, in order that the people might rejoice on that account. The emperor of Babylon also sent Saracen messengers to our army with letters and through these he established peace and concord with us.

(Robinson & Robinson 1894, vol. 1, no. 4, pp. 5–8)

The letter of the "Frankish" princes Daimbert, Godefroy, and Raymond to the Pope was sent from Laodicaea (now the Syrian port city of Latakiya) in September 1099, two months after the bloody capture of Jerusalem, and it mentioned not the "Saracens" and the Turks. It seems, however, that the two names were used as synonyms:

Multiply your supplications and prayers in the sight of God with joy and thanksgiving, since God has manifested His mercy in fulfilling by our hands what He had promised in ancient times. For after the capture of Nicaea, the whole army, made up of more than three hundred thousand soldiers, departed thence. And, although this army was great that it could have in a single day covered all Romania, and drunk up all the rivers and eaten up all the growing things, yet the Lord conducted them amid so great abundance that a ram was sold for a penny and an ox for twelve pennies or less. Moreover, although the princes and kings of the Saracens rose up against us, yet, by God's will, they were easily conquered and overcome. Because, indeed, some were puffed up by these successes, God opposed to us Antioch, impregnable to human strength. And there He detained us for nine months and so humbled us in the siege that there were scarcely a hundred good horses in our whole army. God opened to us the abundance of His blessing and mercy and led us into the city, and delivered the Turks and all of their possessions into our power.

(Robinson & Robinson 1894, vol. 1, no. 4, pp. 8–11)

The letter of the "Frankish" princes seems to imply that they identified the "Saracens" with Arabs, Turks, Persians, and Muslims. They may have distinguished among some groups, such as Bedouin Arabs, Turks, and Muslims in general, but the general tendency was to label them all "Saracens" and treat them as the evil enemies of God.

Chapter 9

The Second Crusade
Persisting Rescue Fantasies

The Turkish title of *Atabeg*, meaning "father prince," was an hereditary title of the Turkish nobility. It was used by the Seljuk Turks and by other Turkish, Turkic, and Turkoman tribes from Central Asia that invaded western Asia in the Middle Ages. The Frankish County of Edessa, founded in 1098 in what is now Urfa in southeastern Turkey when the First Crusaders were on their way to Jerusalem, had been sandwiched between the Seljuk Turkish "sultanate of Rum" that surrounded most of it, the "Dominion of the Atabegs" that ruled parts of what are now Syria and Iraq, the Christian kingdom of Armenia, and the Crusader principality of Antioch.

In 1144 the landlocked County of Edessa, northeast of the Principality of Tripoli, was taken by the Seljuk Turks. The loss of Edessa was a major defeat for the Christians, as Edessa was the first county they had taken and ruled in the first Crusade, and one of the only four states of *Outremer* (the others were the principality of Antioch, the county of Tripoli, and the kingdom Jerusalem). It provoked the Second Crusade. Edessa, which had a centuries-long Christian history, was the first of the Crusader states to have been founded during the First Crusade, and it was the first to fall to the "Saracens." Its fall was traumatic for the Roman Catholic Church.

The Second Crusade was announced in 1145 by the new pope, Eugenius III (Bernardo dei Paganelli di Montemagno, who was Pope until his death in 1153). It lasted four years, until 1149. The pope chose as his legate the French abbot Bernard de Clairvaux (1090–1153) to preach the second Crusade. The new pope granted the same indulgences for the second Crusade which his predecessor Urban II had accorded to the First Crusade. In 1146 a *parlement* was convoked at Vézelay in Burgundy, and Bernard preached before the assembly. The young King Louis VII of France (1120–1180), his wife, Eleanor of Aquitaine, and all the princes and lords present prostrated themselves at the feet of Bernard to receive the pilgrim's cross. Bernard then crossed the Rhine into Germany, and the reported miracles which multiplied almost at his every step undoubtedly contributed to the success of his mission. King Conrad III of Germany and his nephew Friedrich Barbarossa received the cross from the hand of Bernard. Pope Eugenius came in person to France to encourage the enterprise.

Bernard of Clairvaux was the primary builder of the Cistercian order of monks. After the loss of his mother, which was great blow to him, Bernard entered the Cistercian order. *Mater Ecclesia* became his new mother. Three years later, he was sent to found a new house that Bernard named *Claire Vallée* (hence Clairvaux), in 1115. Bernard preached an immediate faith, in which the intercessor was the Virgin Mary (another mother figure). In 1128 Bernard attended the Council of Troyes, at which he outlined the Rule of the Knights Templar, who became the ideal of Christian nobility. On the death of Pope Honorius II in 1130, another schism broke out in the Roman Catholic Church. Cardinal Gregorio Papareschi (died 1143) was hastily elected Pope Innocentius II by most of his fellow cardinals. In protest, the other cardinals elected Cardinal Pietro Pierleoni (died 1138) "Antipope" Anacletus II. In response, King Louis VI of France (*Louis le gros*, 1081–1137) convened a national council of the French bishops at Estampes, and chose Bernard de Clairvaux to adjudicate between the rival popes (father figures) and end the schism.

Portugal, then a region in southwestern Iberia, had been a county and fief of the united Kingdom of León and Castilla. In 868, during the *Reconquista,* the centuries-long process through which the Iberian Christians re-conquered the Iberian peninsula from the Muslims, the First County of Portugal was formed. The Christian rulers of Leon and Castile repeatedly proclaimed that they were re-conquering Christian territory that had been lost to the "Moors," thus insuring that reinforcements would continue to arrive from other Christian realms, especially because the Papacy in Rome continued to support such efforts. Galicia, in northwest Spain, was the "march" or border land of the Kingdom of Leon and Castile.

At the end of the eleventh century, when the First Crusade set out for "the Holy Land" to fight the "Saracens" there, Crusading knights also came from every part of Europe to Iberia to aid the kings of Leon, Castile and Aragon in combating the "Moors." Among these was Henry of Burgundy, who, in 1095, married Theresa de León, a daughter of King Alfonso VI of León. The County of Portugal was included in Theresa's dowry. Count Henry ruled Portugal as a vassal of Alfonso VI, securing his Galician march against Moorish raids. In 1109 Alfonso VI died, bequeathing all his territories to his legitimate daughter, Urraca of Castile. Count Henry of Portugal at once invaded León, hoping to add it to his own dominions at the expense of his suzerain.

In 1112, after three years of war against Urraca and other rival claimants to the throne of León, Count Henry died, leaving his widow Theresa to govern Portugal north of the Mondego River during the minority of her infant son, Afonso Henriques, (1109–1185), the future King Afonso of Portugal. South of the Mondego River, the "Moors" were still supreme. Afonso became Count of Portugal, and in 1139 his victory over the "Saracens" at Ourique, in the Alentejo region of southern Portugal, transformed Portugal into an independent kingdom. Portugal still fought the "Moors" until the thirteenth century, and also had its own internal wars. The Portuguese language developed from one of the dialects of Vulgar Latin, akin to the Gallego language of Galicia in northwestern Spain.

Bernard de Clairvaux devoted himself to the composition of the works which would win for him the title of "Doctor of the Church." In 1139, he attended the Second Lateran Council called by the pope. Bernard denounced the teachings of the "heretical" poet and philosopher Pierre Abelard (died 1142) to Pope Innocent, who called a council at Sens in 1141 to settle the matter. Bernard's disciple, Bernard of Pisa, was elected Pope Eugenius III. Having previously helped end the schism within the Church, Bernard was now called upon to combat heresy. In June 1145, Bernard traveled in Southern France and his preaching there helped strengthen support against heresy. Now he preached the Second Crusade.

For all his religious zeal, Bernard de Clairvaux was neither a bigot nor a persecutor. Yet, as in the First Crusade, his preaching of the Second Crusade led to mob attacks on the Jews; and just as in the First Crusade Pierre l'hermite and Gautier sans avoir had led murderous gangs of Crusades on a rampage through Jewish towns, a fanatical French monk named Rodolphe inspired the massacres of the Jews in the Rhineland cities of Cologne, Mainz, Worms, and Speyer, claiming that the Jews were not contributing financially to the rescue of the "Holy Land". Bernard of Clairvaux, the Archbishop of Cologne and the Archbishop of Mainz were vehemently opposed to these attacks, and Bernard traveled from Flanders to Germany to deal with the problem and calm the mobs. Bernard found Rodolphe in Mainz and was able to silence him, returning him to his monastery.

The Second Crusade was the first of the Crusades to be led by European Christian kings – Louis VII of France (1120–1180) and Conrad III of Germany (1093–1152) – with help from some other important European nobles. While Louis was the undisputed king of France, Conrad was never crowned emperor of the "Holy Roman Empire" by the pope. He continued to style himself *Rex Romanorum* until his death. The armies of these two unfortunate kings marched separately across Europe toward Constantinople, and were alternately and ambivalently helped and hindered by the Byzantine emperor Manuel Komnenos, who was afraid they would take his territories.

One of the leaders of the Second Crusade was Count Josselin de Courtenay (died 1159), the son of the first Josselin de Courtenay. The young Josselin had been taken prisoner by the Seljuk Turkish "Saracens" at the Battle of Azaz in 1125, but was ransomed by Baudouin, the "Latin King of Jerusalem." In 1131, Josselin's father, Josselin de Courtenay, was gravely injured in battle with the Turkoman Danishmend emir Ghazi Gümüshtigin. The Danishmends were a Turkoman dynasty that ruled north-central and eastern Anatolia in the eleventh and twelfth centuries, and Edessa passed to his son. The feared to march the small Edessan army out to meet the powerful Danishmends. His father, in his last act, did so, and forced Gümüshtigin to retreat, dying soon thereafter. The landlocked Edessa was the weakest and most isolated of the Crusader states.

In 1138 Josselin II of Edessa allied himself with the Prince of Antioch and with the Byzantine emperor Johannes II Komnenos to attack the *atabeg* of Mosul and Aleppo, Imad ad-Din Zengi al-Malik al-Mansur (1085–1146), who ruled under the Abbasid caliphs. The *atabeg* was the governor of a nation or province who was subordinate to the *sultan* and charged with raising the crown prince. The title first appeared among the early Seljuk Turks, and was later used by the Armenians. Zengi defeated the "Franks" and drove them back. In the "Frankish" principality of Antioch, popular sentiment against the Byzantine Empire, which Johannes Komnenos was trying to extend into the northern Crusader states of Edessa, Tripoli and Antioch, led to a riot, engineered by Josselin. The Byzantine emperor was forced to return home.

In 1143 Emperor Johannes Komnenos of Byzantium and King Foulques of Jerusalem, who had expanded the Latin Kingdom of Jerusalem to its largest territorial extent, both died, leaving Count Josselin with no powerful allies to help him defend Edessa against the "Saracens." In 1144 Atabeg Zengi of Aleppo and Mosul invaded and captured Edessa. Josselin fled to Turbessel (now the southeastern Turkish town of Gündoğan), where he held the remnants of the county.

In 1146 Atabeg Zengi of Aleppo and Mosul was assassinated by his Frankish slave, Yaranqash. The murder was described by the Muslim historian Ibn al-Qalanisi of Damascus as follows:

> [...] one of [Zengi's] attendants, for whom he had a special affection, and in whose company he delighted [...] and who nursed a secret grudge against him on account of some injury previously done to him by the atabeg, had, on finding an opportunity when he was off his guard in his drunkenness, and with the connivance and assistance of certain of his comrades amongst the attendants, assassinated him in his sleep on the eve of Sunday, the 6th of Rabi al-Thani [September 15, 1146].
>
> (Ibn al-Qalanisi 1932)

According to Ibn al-Qalanisi, Yaranqash stabbed the *atabeg* numerous times, killed him, fled to the fortress of Dawsar (now the Syrian fortress of Qala'at Ja'abar), and then went to Damascus, "in the confident belief that he would be secure there, openly putting forward his action as a claim to consideration, and imagining that he would be made welcome." Instead, the Turkoman governor of Damascus, Mu'in ad-Din Unur al-Atabeki (died 1149), a former slave of the Burid emirs, had Yaranqash arrested and sent him in chains to Zengi's son, Nur ad-Din Mahmud Zengi (1118–1174), in Aleppo. Nur ad-Din sent Yaranqash on to his elder brother, Sayf ad-Din Ghazi (died 1149), in Mosul, who had Yaranqash beheaded.

In 1150 Count Josselin de Courtenay of Edessa, the former Lord of Turbessel and Prince of Galilee, tried in vain to take Edessa back from the Seljuk Turks. Zengi's son and successor, al-Malik al-Adil Nur ad-Din Abu al-Qasim

Mahmud Ibn Imad ad-Din Zengi, defeated and captured Josselin, who languished in the Citadel of Aleppo and died in 1159. His daughter, Agnes de Courtenay (c. 1138–1184), was engaged to the Crusader nobleman Hugues d'Ibelin. Instead, she married Amalric (1136–1174), Count of Jaffa and of Ascalon.

In 1162 King Baudouin III of Jerusalem (1130–1162) died, and the "Latin" kingdom passed to Amalric. Although there was some opposition among the nobility to Agnes; they were willing to accept the marriage in 1157, when Baudouin III was still capable of siring an heir, but now the *Haute Cour* refused to endorse Amalric as king unless his marriage to Agnes was annulled. The nobles' hostility to Agnes may have been exaggerated by Guillaume de Tyr, whom she prevented from becoming the "Latin Patriarch of Jerusalem" decades later, as well as by Guillaume's "continuators," like Ernoul, the author of a chronicle of the late twelfth century dealing with the fall of the Crusader Kingdom of Jerusalem, who hints at a slight on her moral character: *"car telle n'est que roine doie iestre di si haute cite comme de Jherusalem"* ("for there should not be such a queen for so high a city as Jerusalem") (Ernoul 1982).

Consanguinity, which to them meant incest, had led to the nobles' opposition to Amalric's marriage with Agnes. Amalric then agreed to annul his marriage to Agnes and ascended the throne single. Agnes continued to hold the title Countess of Jaffa and Ascalon and received a pension from that fief's income. She married Hugues d'Ibelin, to whom she had been engaged before her marriage to Amalric. The church ruled that Amalric's and Agnes' children Sibylla, Baudouin and Alix were legitimate and preserved their place in the order of succession. Through her children Agnes exerted influence in Jerusalem for almost two decades. After her divorce from Amalric, she held the lands and incomes of the County of Jaffa, while Josselin's son Josselin III held the nominal title Count of Edessa, being in reality the lord of a small seigneurie near Acre.

Josselin II's grandchildren, Sibylla (c. 1160–1190) and her brother Baudouin IV (1161–1181), the Leper King, both children of Amalric and Agnes, were monarchs of Jerusalem, as was Josselin's great-grandson, Baudouin V, who led a Crusade in the East. In early 1147 the French Crusades met at Estampes to discuss their route. The Germans had already decided to travel overland through Hungary, as King Roger II of Sicily was an enemy of Conrad, and the sea route was politically impractical. Many of the French nobles distrusted the land route, which would take them through the Byzantine Empireand through the "Saracen Sultanate of Rum," the reputation of which still suffered from the accounts of the First Crusades. Nevertheless, it was decided to follow Conrad, and to set out on 15 June 1147.

Roger II of Sicily was offended and refused to participate any longer. In France, Abbot Suger and Count Guillaume II of Nevers were elected as regents while the king was on Crusade. In Germany, further preaching was done by Adam of Ebrach, and Otto of Freising also took the cross. In March

1147, at Frankfurt, Conrad's son Heinrich Berengar was elected king, under the regency of Henry, Archbishop of Mainz. The Germans planned to set out at Easter but did not leave until May.

Baltic "Saracens"

One of the fascinating things about the Crusades was their fantastic use of the word "Saracens" for any enemy of the Franks, as well as their turning away from their initial goal of rescuing the "Holy Sepulcher," the "Holy City," and "the Holy Land" from the "evil Saracens" and waging a "holy war" against "pagan idolaters" in Europe itself. By the twelfth century, the peoples inhabiting the Baltic lands (now Estonia, Latvia, and Lithuania) formed a pagan wedge between increasingly powerful Christian states, Greek Orthodox to their east and Roman Catholic to their west. The conflict and difference in creeds between the Roman Catholic and Greek Orthodox churches was one of the reasons they had not been Christianized. During a period of more than 150 years leading up to the arrival of the German Crusades in the region, Estonia was attacked 13 times by Russian Orthodox principalities, and by Denmark and Sweden as well. The Estonians for their part raided Denmark and Sweden. There were some peaceful attempts by the western Christians to convert the Estonians, starting with missions dispatched by Adalbert, Archbishop of Bremen from 1045 to 1072. However, these peaceful efforts had very limited success.

In 1147, with new religious fervor, Pope Eugenius III, who, along with Bernard of Clairvaux, had preached the Second Crusade, authorized the "Wendish Crusade", a campaign of German Crusaders against the Polabian Slavs or "Wends" in northeastern Germany (as well as an Iberian Crusade against the "Moors" of Spain). In the case of the Wendish Crusade, the "Saracen" enemy was no longer Muslim, but rather "pagan." The Christians saw it as a "holy war" for Jesus Christ. The "Wendish Crusade" may have begun in the mid-twelfth century, but it went on for centuries, not ending until the sixteenth century and the Reformation. As always, internal conflicts within the Christian world led to "holy wars" on non-Christians, who were force-converted by the sword.

In 1180, moving in the wake of German merchants who followed the old trading routes of the Vikings, a German monk named Meinhard had landed at the mouth of the Daugava River (now in Latvia) and was made Bishop in 1186. In 1193 Pope Celestinus III proclaimed a Crusade against the Baltic "heathen." A Crusading expedition led by Meinhard's successor, Bishop Berthold, landed in Livonia (now in Estonia and Latvia, surrounding the Gulf of Riga) in 1198. Although the Crusaders won their first battle, Bishop Berthold was mortally wounded, and the Crusaders were repulsed by the "Saracens." The first "Baltic Crusade" (1199–1266), which had been called by Pope Celestinus III (died 1198) six years earlier, was directed against the Balts, Livs, Letts, Prussians, and other "pagans" – who were incredibly called "Saracens" by the German knights who converted them by the sword. The Arabs and Muslims were forgotten. The "Saracens" were now the Baltic peoples.

One of the Baltic Crusades, the so-called "Livonian Crusade" (1198–1290), was the German and Danish conquest and colonization of Livonia. The lands on the eastern shores of the Baltic Sea were the last corners of Europe to be Christianized. During the "Livonian Crusade" (1198–1290) Livonia was colonized by the *Fratres militiae Christi Livoniae* (literally the Brothers of the Livonian army of Christ), called in German the *Schwertbrüderorden* (the Order of the Brothers of the Sword), and later called the Livonian Knights. The name Livonia came to designate a larger territory: the Livonian Confederation on the eastern coasts of the Baltic Sea. Its frontiers were the Gulf of Riga and the Gulf of Finland in the northwest, Lake Peipus and Russia to the east, and Lithuania to the south.

Before they were united in 1237, the Livonian Knights and the Teutonic Knights, both Germanic orders, vied for the Christianization of the Baltic tribes. The "Baltic Crusades" lasted several centuries, along with the "Holy Land Crusades," and long after the latter ended. The Teutonic Knights, who had been formed in Acre in 1190, and the Livonian Knights sought to Christianize many "heathen" tribes: the Polabian Slavs and Sorbs (Christianized by the by the Saxons, Danes, and Poles, beginning with the "Wendish Crusade"), the Finns (in 1154, in 1249, and in 1293, Christianized by the Swedes), the Estonians, Latgalians, and "Livonians" (Christianized by the Germans and Danes from 1193 to 1227), the Lithuanians (Christianized by the Germans, unsuccessfully, in 1316), the Curonians and Semigallians, the Old Prussians, the Polabian Wends, and Obotrites (between the Elbe and Oder rivers).

Meanwhile, the only apparent success of the Second Crusade was not in the "Holy Land" but in Europe, in 1147, when Flemish, Frisian, Norman, English, Scottish, and some German Crusaders, on the way by ship to the "Holy Land", fortuitously stopped and helped the Portuguese in the capture of Lisbon from the "Saracens." Some, who had departed earlier, helped capture Santarém earlier in the same year. Later they also helped to conquer Sintra, Almada, Palmela, and Setúbal, and were allowed to stay in the conquered lands, where they had offspring. After crossing Byzantine territory from Constantinople into Anatolia, the French and German armies were defeated in 1148 by the Seljuk Turks. Louis and Conrad and the surviving remnants of their armies did reach Jerusalem and, in 1148, participated in another ill-advised attack on Damascus, which also failed. The Second Crusade was a traumatic defeat for the Crusaders and a great victory for the Muslims. It would ultimately lead to the fall of Jerusalem in 1187 and to the Third Crusade that followed, at the end of the twelfth century.

Meanwhile, in northeastern Europe, the first Baltic Crusade (1199–1266) began, with the intent of converting the "pagan" Baltic tribes to Christianity. The official beginning of the Northern Crusades was Pope Celestinus III's call in 1193 to Christianize the "heathen" peoples of the Baltic, but the already

Christian kingdoms of Scandinavia and the "Holy Roman Empire" of Germany had started to move to subjugate their "pagan" neighbors earlier. These Crusades would last four centuries, but they had nothing to do with the Crusades in the Holy Land. These "Northern Crusades" were undertaken by the Catholic kings of Denmark and Sweden, the German Livonian and Teutonic military orders, and their allies, against the "pagan" peoples of Northern Europe around the southern and eastern shores of the Baltic Sea (including the Prussi, Letts, Finns, Livs, and Eesti). Some of these wars were called Crusades during the Middle Ages; others, including the Swedish ones, were first dubbed Crusades by nineteenth-century romantic historians. The eastern Baltic was transformed by military conquest: first the Livs, Letts, and Estonians, then the Prussians and the Finns underwent defeat, baptism, military occupation, and sometimes extermination by groups of Germans, Danes, and Swedes.

The Latin documents of the "Baltic Crusade" of 1199–1266 give us a flavor of the fantastic quality of the Crusader ideas about the "Saracens" whom they were fighting to Christianize and of what went through their minds as they set out on their Crusade. For example, in 1211 Pope Innocentius III signed an agreement with the Brothers of the Sword in which nothing was said about the people to be force-converted, but very much was said about lands, property, wealth, and titles:

> As for lands which the Brothers acquire with the help of God outside Livonia or Lettia, they will not answer to the Bishop of Riga for these, nor will he trouble them in any way over them. But they will obey what the Apostolic See tells them. The Brothers will obey the rule of the Knighthood of the Temple, but will have a different symbol on their habit, to show that they are not subject to them.
> (Migne 1844–1864, 1965, online translation by Helen Nicholson)

In 1266, at the end of the first Baltic Crusade, the thirteenth-century English Franciscan monk Roger Bacon, also known as *Doctor Mirabilis*, one of the most famous Franciscan friars of his time, wrote his Latin-language *Opus Maius*, in which he described the "Baltic Crusade" and referred to the "heathen" as "Saracens." Bacon discussed the importance of learning foreign languages, arguing that the third reason for needing to learn languages is to be able to convert the infidel by speaking to them in their own tongue:

> And so an infinite number of Jews perish among us, because no one knows how to preach to them, nor to interpret the scripture in their language, nor to confer with them nor dispute.
> (*Medieval Sourcebook: Documents relating to the Baltic Crusade 1199–1266*, Fordham University, online translation by Helen Nicholson)

A very learned man, Roger Bacon argued that the Christian religion came from the Jewish one, that the Jews were from the seed of the patriarchs and prophets, that Jesus Christ Our Lord was a Jew, as were the Virgin Mary and the apostles and innumerable saints. Also, he wrote:

> the Greeks and the Russians and many other "schismatics" (the Greek Orthodox Christians who call themselves Christian but do not acknowledge papal authority) remain in error because there is no one to preach the truth to them in their own language. Similarly, with the "Saracens" and pagans and Tatars and other infidels throughout the whole world.
> (*Medieval Sourcebook: Documents relating to the Baltic Crusade 1199–1266*, Fordham University, online translation by Helen Nicholson)

Bacon believed that war would not solve the problem of Christianization:

> Nor is war against them any use, since sometimes the Church loses out in Christians' wars, as often happens Overseas [in the Holy Land] and especially in the last expedition, i.e. the lord King of France's, as the whole world knows [the Seventh Crusade, or "Louis IX's first Crusade"]; and even if the Christians conquer, there is no one who defends the occupied lands. Nor are the infidels converted thus but killed and sent to hell. But as for the rest [of the infidels] who survive after the battle, their sons are stirred up more and more against the Christian faith because of those wars, and move an infinite distance away from the faith of Christ, and are inflamed to do every evil which they can against the Christians.
> (*Medieval Sourcebook: Documents relating to the Baltic Crusade 1199–1266*, Fordham University, online translation by Helen Nicholson)

Bacon denounced the violence of the Teutonic Knights while using the term "Saracens" to refer to all "infidels," including the Baltic ones:

> So the Saracens, because of this, become impossible to convert in many parts of the world, and especially Overseas and in Prussia and the lands bordering Germany, because the Templars and Hospitallers and the brothers of the Teutonic order much disturb the conversion of infidels because of the wars which they are always starting, and because of the fact that they wish to dominate them absolutely. For there is no doubt that all the infidel nations beyond Germany would have been converted long ago, if it was not for the violence of the brothers of the Teutonic order. The pagan race has many times been ready to receive the faith in peace after preaching, but those of the Teutonic order do not wish to allow this, because they wish to subjugate them and reduce them to

slavery. By subtle persuasions they have already deceived the Roman Church for many years ... Besides, faith does not come into this world through weapons but by simple preaching, as I have shown. And we have many times heard and we are certain that many, however imperfectly they know languages and have poor interpreters have nevertheless done much useful work by preaching, and converted many to the Christian faith.
(*Medieval Sourcebook: Documents relating to the Baltic Crusade 1199–1266*, Fordham University, online translation by Helen Nicholson)

Chapter 10

Templars and Hospitallers
Monastic Knights?

King Baudouin's reign in Jerusalem, which lasted from 1118 to 1131, saw the establishment of the Crusader military orders, the Knights Hospitaller and the Knights Templar. These extraordinary orders combined knighthood with monasticism in a way which had not been known in Europe, where you were either a monk or a knight, but not both. The *Ordre des Hospitaliers* was first known as "the Order of the Knights of the Hospital of St. John of Jerusalem," later as "the Sovereign Military Hospitaller Order of St. John of Jerusalem," and later still, as its members fled the "Saracens" and the "Holy Land," the Order of St. John, the Knights of Rhodes, and the Knights of Malta.

This unique Christian organization began as an "Amalfitan" hospital, founded by southern Italian merchants from Amalfi in Jerusalem in 1080, under "Saracen" rule, to care for poor, sick, or injured Christian pilgrims to the "Holy Land". They dedicated the hospital to St. John the Baptist, whom the Knights Hospitaller later called Saint John of Jerusalem. After the Christian conquest of Jerusalem in 1099, it became a religious-military order under its own charter, and was charged with the care and defense of the "Holy Land." How could those monkish knights whose job was to take care of sick people defend the Holy Land against the "Saracens"?

The headquarters of the Knights Hospitaller in "the Holy Land" during the Crusades was a mighty fortress called Kerak in what is now Jordan. The name *Kerak* came from the old Syriac *karak* meaning fortress. The French called it *Le Crac des Chevaliers* and the Arabs called it *Qala'at al-Hisn*. The nearby *Qala'at Salah ed-Din* (The fortress of "Saladin") was in the Principality of Antioch but was taken from the "Franks" by the "Saracens" in 1188. Kerak was expanded between 1150 and 1250 and housed a garrison of 2,000 knights Hospitaller. The inner curtain wall was up to 100 feet thick at the base on the south side, with seven guard towers 30 feet in diameter. King Edward I of England (1239–1307), while on the Ninth Crusade in 1271, saw the fortress and used it as an example for his own castles in England and Wales.

DOI: 10.4324/9781003527367-10

The *Ordre des Templiers* was founded in 1119 by the French knight Hugues de Payens and his relative Godefroy de Saint-Omer. They proposed the creation of a monastic order for the protection of the pilgrims. King Baudouin accepted their proposal. The order was formally called *Pauperes commilitones Christi Templique Solomonici* (The Poor Fellow-Soldiers of Christ and of the Temple of Solomon). Its original purpose was to ensure the safety of the many European Christians who made the pilgrimage to Jerusalem after its conquest. The Crusaders called the site of the Dome of the Rock *Templum Solomonis*. Around 1129 the Templars were officially endorsed by the Roman Catholic Church. Their Order became a favored charity across Europe and grew rapidly in membership and power. Knights Templar, in their distinctive white mantles with a large red cross on it, were among the most skilled fighting units of the Crusaders, and the most warlike. Non-combatant members of the Order managed what became the largest economic infrastructure throughout Christendom, innovating financial techniques that were an early form of banking, and building many fortifications across Europe and the "Holy Land".

The Hospitaller order was founded by a monk named Gerard (1040–1120), who went to Jerusalem in 1097, either as a soldier or as a merchant, where the hospice of St. John had existed since 1080 for the convenience of those who wished to visit the Christian holy places. Gerard joined the monastery of St. Mary of the Latins, became the guardian or provost of this institution around 1100, and organized the religious order of St. John which received papal recognition from Pope Paschal II in 1113, by the papal bull entitled *Geraudo institutori ac praeposito Hirosolimitani Xenodochii*. It was renewed and confirmed by Pope Calixtus II shortly before the death of Gerard in 1120.

The first Grand Master of the *Templiers* was Hugues de Payens, the French knight from the Champagne region, and the co-founder with his relative Godefroy de Saint-Omer of the Order of the Knights Templar. With Saint Bernard of Clairvaux, he created the Latin Rule, the code of behavior for the Order. The fortunes of the Templars, being the foremost Crusader fighters, were tied closely to those of the Crusades. At first victorious, the Second Crusade in 1144 brought them defeat and trauma. In 1187 they lost a major battle at Hattin to the "Saracens" under "Saladin," who went on to take Jerusalem from "*al-Franj*." This was the worst collective trauma of the Crusades. In 1291 the last Crusaders were forced out of "the Holy Land" after the capture and destruction of their capital, "Saint-Jean d'Acre," by the Mamluks, and the Latin "Kingdom of Jerusalem" was no more. After that, support for the Order waned. False rumors about "un-Christian" acts at the Templars' secret initiation ceremony created mistrust, and King Philippe le Bel of France, who was deeply in debt to the Order, pressured Pope Clement V to take action.

In 1307, using the false pretext of the initiation ceremonies, King Philippe le Bel had many of the Order's members in France arrested, tortured into giving false confessions, and burned at the stake, including their last Grand Master, Jacques de Molay. In 1312, Pope Clement, under continuing pressure from King Philip, disbanded the Order.

The abrupt disappearance of a major part of the European infrastructure of the *Templiers* gave rise to much speculation and legends about the Templars' subsequent fortunes, which have kept the "Templar" name alive into the modern day. The freemasons believed they too were Templars. The York Rite of Freemasonry has incorporated some Templar symbols and rituals, and it has a modern degree called "the Order of the Temple." The Sovereign Military Order of the Temple of Jerusalem, founded in 1804, has achieved United Nations NGO status as a charitable organization. There is no clear historical link between the Knights Templar, which were dismantled in the 1300s, and any of these newer organizations, of which the earliest emerged in the 1700s.

In 1854 Christoph Hoffmann, a Lutheran clergyman, started the paper *Süddeutsche Warte*, an "organ for the gathering of the children of God in Jerusalem." In 1861 the *Tempelkirche* or Temple Church, also called *Deutscher Tempel* or *Jerusalemsfreunde*, was organized by Christoph Hoffmann at a meeting of the Friends of Jerusalem at Ludwigsburg, near Stuttgart, in Germany. The movement was rooted in Württemberg Pietism. Gottlieb W. Hoffmann, the father of Christoph Hoffmann, had founded the separatist settlement of Korntal, near Stuttgart. Philipp M. Hahn influenced Christoph Hoffmann regarding the establishment of the kingdom of God on earth and called all true believers "out of Babel," later adding the notion of gathering them in Palestine in order to "build the temple of God." Around 1870, a group of German Mennonites called themselves *Templer* and set out to the Holy Land. They established colonies in Jerusalem, Haifa, Jaffa, "Wilhelma" and other places. During both World Wars the *Templer* were interned as German citizens. During World War II their German Nazi descendants were deported to Australia by the British mandatory government of Palestine.

The earliest surviving laws of the "Latin Kingdom of Jerusalem" were compiled at the Council of Neapolis convened by Latin Patriarch Warmund and King Baudouin II in 1120, and its first commercial treaty with Venice, the *Pactum Warmundi*, was written in 1124; the increase of naval and military support from Venice led to the capture of Tyre from the "Saracens" that year. The influence of the "Latin Kingdom of Jerusalem" was also further extended over the county of Edessa and the principality of Antioch, where Baudouin II acted as regent when their leaders were killed in battle, although there were regency governments in Jerusalem as well during Baudouin's captivity. Baudouin was married to the Armenian princess Morphia of Melitene, and had four daughters by her: Hodierna and Alice, who married into the noble families of the Count of Tripoli and Prince of Antioch; Ioveta, who became an influential nun and abbess; and the eldest, Melisende, who was his heir, and succeeded him upon his death in 1131, with her husband, Foulques V of Jerusalem, the former Count Foulques of Anjou, as her king-consort. Foulques died in 1143. Their son, the future Baudouin III, was also named co-heir by his grandfather.

Chapter 11

The "Saracens" Look at the "Franks"

After two centuries of studying the European sources for the Crusades a few scholars, both "Western" and Muslim, collected and translated the Arabic sources about the Crusades into English and other European languages. This has given us an understanding of how the Muslim "Saracens" saw themselves and their "Frankish" enemies. An Italian scholar, Francesco Gabrieli, translated the Muslim historians of the Crusades from Arabic into Italian and his book was translated into English (Gabrieli 1969). Amin Maalouf (born 1949), a Lebanese Arab journalist and writer, and a former editor of *An-Nahar*, the leading Arabic-language daily in Lebanon, brought together various Arabic sources on the Crusades (Maalouf 1984). Some scholars, however, see this book as an inaccurate historical novel.

Carole Hillenbrand, an Arabic-speaking Islamic Studies scholar at the University of Edinburgh has published translations of Muslim *jihad* (holy war) poetry from the time of the Crusades and of Muslim writings on the Crusades, augmented by Muslim paintings of the Crusaders (Hillenbrand 1991, 1999). Her studies highlight and explain the Muslim tenacity in the Crusader wars. Hillenbrand pointed out that medieval Muslims considered their civilization, with its medicine, mathematics, art, and religion, far above that of the "Franks," and felt that they had little to learn from the Europeans:

> Western Europe held few attractions to the medieval Muslims; from their perspective their own culture was so obviously more sophisticated and advanced. The medieval Muslim felt superiority and condescension toward Christians. For him it was indisputable that Christianity, an incomplete and imperfect revelation, had been superseded and perfected by Islam, the final Revelation, and that the Prophet Muhammad was the seal of the prophets.
>
> (Hillenbrand 1999, p. 267)

Before Hillenbrand's ground-breaking work, the history of the Crusades had been written by Western historians and had been based mainly on Western sources. Arabic documents had been used sparingly because they were hard for most westerners to read and because many of them were inaccessible. "Carole Hillenbrand set out to re-evaluate the sources for the Crusading period, not only looking with fresh eyes at known accounts, but also locating and utilizing new sources that had previously been overlooked" (Houghton & Peters 2017). She evaluated the new sources carefully, assessing their arguments, their evidence, and their value in order to place them correctly in the context of Crusade studies as a whole.

> The result is not only a history that is more balanced, better argued and more adequate than most that have gone before it, but also a work with relevance for today. At a time when Crusading imagery and mentions of the current War on Terror as a "Crusade" help to fuel political narrative, Hillenbrand's evaluative work acts as an important corrective to oversimplification and misrepresentation.
>
> (Houghton & Peters 2017)

Unlike Westerners, whose solar calendar begins with the birth of Jesus Christ, and Jews, who use a lunar calendar with occasional 13-month leap years to keep up with the solar calendar, the Arabs and Muslims still use a strictly lunar calendar beginning at the time of the *Hijra*, the year of the emigration of the Prophet Muhammad and his followers to the city of Medina (622 CE), marking it as the first year of the Islamic calendar. One of the first Muslim historians to write about the Crusades was the Damascus scholar Hamza ibn Asad abu-Ya'la ibn al-Qalanisi (1070–1160), who saw the "Frankish" armies entering his country when he was in his twenties. His chronicle, *Dhail Ta'rikh Dimashq* (Continuation of the Chronicle of Damascus), was an extension of the chronicle of his predecessor Hilal al-Sabi (died 1055), covering the years 363 to 555 of the Muslim *Hijrah*, to Ibn al-Qalanisi's death in 1160 (Ibn al-Qalanisi 1932). His chronicle is one of the few contemporary accounts of the First Crusade and its immediate aftermath from the Muslim perspective. It is a valuable source for modern historians, and was also an important source for later Muslim chroniclers, including the Kurdish Muslim chronicler Abu al-Hassan Ali ibn Muhammad ibn Muhammad, also known as Ali 'izz al-Din ibn al-Athir al-Jazari (1160–1233) or, for short, Ibn al-Athir. In addition to the Crusades, Ibn al-Qalanisi wrote about the rivalries and wars among the petty Arab princes, the terrible, murderous and burning hatred between Radwan and Duqaq in Syria, and the helplessness of the Abbasid caliphate in Baghdad, which also ruled Damascus, in the face of the "Franks."

We learn from Ibn al-Qalanisi that in the summer of the year 492 of the *Hijra* (August 1099 CE), after the fall of Jerusalem to the "Franks," al-Harawi, the chief *qadi* of Damascus in Syria, preached a sermon in the Great Mosque in Baghdad, crying, "Your brethren in Syria have no home other than the saddles of their camels or the entrails of vultures." Al-Harawi was surrounded by a throng of Syrian and Palestinian refugees who wept as he spoke, and their weeping made others in turn weep. Al-Harawi was preaching about the need to fight the armies of the First Crusade, which had arrived in Syria in 1097 and had later occupied Antioch, Edessa, and finally, in 1099, Jerusalem. Muslims from places that had fallen to the "Franks" had fled to the larger Muslim cities of the hinterland, in particular to Damascus and Aleppo in Syria. At the end of the eleventh century, Syria and Palestine were, theoretically at least, part of the Seljuk Turkish sultanate, and as such subject to the authority of the Abbasid caliph in Baghdad and of the Seljuk sultan in Isfahan.

Al-Harawi's mission in Baghdad was to pressure the Abbasid Caliph, al-Mustazhir Billah (1078–1136), to send an army to help the Muslims against the Crusaders. However, Baghdad was a long way from Jerusalem and, moreover, al-Mustazhir had no troops to speak of. In fact, as we have seen, the Fatimids of Egypt had taken Jerusalem from the Seljuks before being defeated by the "Franks." Muslim preachers traveled throughout the Abbasid caliphate proclaiming the tragedy and rousing men to recover the Al-Aqsa Mosque, the scene of the Prophet's heavenly flight, from infidel hands. But whatever the success elsewhere, the mission failed in the eastern provinces, which were preoccupied with their own troubles, and moreover cared little for the Holy Land, dominated as it was by the Fatimid Shiite faith. Crowds of exiles, seeking refuge in Baghdad, joined there with the populace in crying out for war against the "Franks." For two Fridays in 1111 the insurgents, incited by Ibn al-Khashshab, the *qadi* of Aleppo, stormed the Great Mosque, broke the pulpit and throne of the Caliph in pieces, and shouted down the service, but neither the Sultan nor the Caliph were interested in sending an army to the "west."

One of the most important Arab historians of the Crusades was Usamah ibn Munqidh (1095–1188), a Muslim *emir* and counselor of the statesman and general Imad ad-Din Zengi al-Malik al-Mansur (1085–1146), the *atabeg* of Mosul and Aleppo. (Irwin 1998; Cobb 2005). Zengi himself ruled under the Seljuk Turkish sultan before being murdered by his Frankish slave, Yarankash. Ibn Munqidh wrote a memoir entitled *Kitab al-i'tibar* (the book of learning by example) which was published in English by Philip Khuri Hitti (1886–1978), a Lebanese-born Arab-American scholar (Ibn Munqidh 1929). This book tells us a great deal about the Muslim attitude toward the "Franks" in the twelfth century. The Muslims compared the "Frankish" culture to their own and found it inferior.

Hitti thought that the "Franks'" apparent lack of jealousy in sexual matters shocked the Muslims, for whom female sexual honor or *'ird* was paramount. Indeed, in Muslim and Arab society *'ird* was (and still is) more important than *sharaf* (honor). *'Ird* translates roughly into English as "chastity" or "purity." *'Ird* was the honor of women, depending on their chastity and faithfulness. Its value could only decrease. Exemplary sexual and moral behavior could not increase a woman's *'ird*, but sexual misconduct reduced or killed it. The honor of the Arab family, clan or tribe, the respect accorded to it by others, can be gravely damaged when one of its women's *'ird* is violated or when her reputation is tainted. If an Arab woman became pregnant out of wedlock, she would be killed in an "honor killing" by her own father or brother, to save the family's honor (Patai 1974, pp. 120–125; Feldner 2000).

The "Franks" had no such notion, and the Muslims did not understand them at all. Like other Muslims, Ibn Munqidh was amazed by "Frankish" customs. When his "Frankish" friend, a knight in the army of King Foulques of Jerusalem offered to take away his son to the "Frankish" lands, Ibn Munqidh thought him foolish:

> In the army of King Foulques, son of Foulques, was a Frankish reverend knight who had just arrived from their land in order to make the holy pilgrimage and then return home. He was of my intimate fellowship and kept such constant company with me that he began to call me "my brother." Between us were mutual bonds of amity and friendship. When he resolved to return by sea to his homeland, he said to me: "My brother, I am leaving for my country and I want you to send with me thy son (my son, who was then fourteen years old, was at that time in my company) to our country, where he can see the knights and learn wisdom and chivalry. When he returns, he will be like a wise man." Thus there fell upon my ears words which would never come out of the head of a sensible man; for even if my son were to be taken captive, his captivity could not bring him a worse misfortune than carrying him into the lands of the Franks.
>
> (Ibn Munqidh 1929)

Ibn Munqidh also relates that the Muslims mocked the "Frankish" justice system. When a dispute arose among two "Franks", they fought a duel to settle it. To test the veracity of a man's statements in a trial, they tried to drown him in a cask of water. Here is a typical passage from *Kitab al-'itibar*:

> I once went in the company of *al-Amir* Mu'in-al-Din (may Allah's mercy rest upon his soul!) to Jerusalem. We stopped at Nablus. There a blind man, a Muslim, who was still young and was well dressed, presented himself before the *amir* carrying fruits for him and asked permission to be admitted into his service in Damascus. The *amir* consented. I inquired about this man and was informed that his mother had been married to a Frank whom she had killed. Her son used to practice ruses against the Frankish pilgrims and cooperate with his mother in assassinating them. They [the Franks] finally brought charges against him and tried his case according to the Frankish way of [legal] procedure. They installed a huge

cask and filled it with water. Across it they set a board of wood. They then bound the arms of the man charged with the act, tied a rope around his shoulders and dropped him into the cask, their idea being that in case he was innocent, he would sink in the water and they would then lift him up with the rope so that he might not die in the water; and in case he was guilty, he would not sink in the water. This man did his best to sink when they dropped him into the water, but he could not do it. So he had to submit to their sentence against him – may Allah's curse be upon them! They pierced his eyeballs with red-hot awls.

(Ibn Munqidh 1929)

Obviously, to the Muslims of the twelfth century, their own system of justice, based on *Shari'a* law, was much more fair and advanced. Ibn Munqidh saw the "Frankish" culture as far inferior to his own. Their medicine was hopelessly primitive, ignorant, and cruel. There were patients whom Ibn Munqidh personally and successfully treated with simple, natural means, and whom the "Frankish" physicians killed with their ignorant, superstitious, and brutal treatments. On the other hand, Ibn Munqidh also cited a case in which the "Frankish" physicians knew how to cure their patients:

The king of the Franks had for treasurer a knight named Bernard, who (may Allah's curse be upon him!) was one of the most accursed and wicked among the Franks. A horse kicked him in the leg, which was subsequently infected and which opened in fourteen different places. Every time one of these cuts would close in one place, another would open in another place. All this happened while I was praying for his perdition. Then came to him a Frankish physician and removed from the leg all the ointments which were on it and began to wash it with very strong vinegar. By this treatment all the cuts were healed and the man became well again. He was up again like a devil.

(Ibn Munqidh 1929)

There was yet another case of a patient in which Ibn Munqidh admitted that he had learned medicine from his "Frankish" colleagues:

Another case illustrating their curious medicine is the following: In Shayzar we had an artisan named Abu-al-Fath, who had a boy whose neck was afflicted with scrofula [swellings of the lymph nodes]. Every time a part of it would close, another part would open. This man happened to go to Antioch on business of his, accompanied by his son. A Frank noticed the boy and asked his father about him. Abu-al-Fath replied, "This is my son." The Frank said to him, "Wilt thou swear by thy religion that if I prescribe to you a medicine which will cure thy boy, thou wilt charge nobody fees for prescribing it thyself? In that case, I shall prescribe to you a medicine which will cure the boy." The man took the oath and the Frank said: "Take uncrushed leaves of glasswort, burn them, then soak the ashes in olive oil and sharp vinegar. Treat the scrofula with them until the spot on which it is growing is eaten up. Then take burnt lead, soak it in ghee butter and treat him with it. That will cure him." The father treated the boy accordingly, and the boy was cured. The sores closed and the boy returned to his normal condition of health. I have myself treated with this medicine many who were afflicted with such disease, and the treatment was successful in removing the cause of the complaint.

(Ibn Munqidh 1929)

Nonetheless, the unconscious process of *dehumanization* operated in full force. Ibn Munqidh saw the *Franj* as animals. They had the qualities of courage and fighting, but no other. Just as the early Crusaders thought of the Muslims as "that evil race," the Muslims looked down on the *franj* and thought them foolish. The Muslims were willing to cooperate with the *Franj* when it served their interests. Some Muslim rulers allied themselves with Crusader states against their rival Muslims. They also treated newly-arrived "Franks," who were still of fanatical hatred for the "Saracens," quite differently from those who had been in their country for years, and who had got used to Muslim ways. Here is a significant passage:

Among the Franks are those who have become acclimatized and have associated long with the Muslims. These are much better than the recent comers from the Frankish lands. But they constitute the exception and cannot be treated as a rule. Here is an illustration. I dispatched one of my men to Antioch on business. There was in Antioch at that time *al-Ra'is* [the ruler] Theodoros Sophianos, to whom I was bound by mutual ties of amity. His influence in Antioch was supreme. One day he said to my man, "I am invited by a friend of mine who is a Frank. Thou shouldst come with me so that thou mayest see their fashions." My man related the story in the following words: "I went along with him and we came to the home of a knight who belonged to the old category of knights who came with the early expeditions of the Franks. He had been by that time stricken off the register and exempted from service, and possessed in Antioch an estate on the income of which he lived. The knight presented an excellent table, with food extraordinarily clean and delicious. Seeing me abstaining from food, he said, 'Eat, be of good cheer!' I never eat Frankish dishes, but I have Egyptian women cooks and never eat except their cooking. Besides, pork never enters my home. I ate, but guardedly, and after that we departed. As I was passing in the market place, a Frankish woman all of a sudden hung to my clothes and began to mutter words in their language, and I could not understand what she was saying.

This made me immediately the center of a big crowd of Franks. I was convinced that death was at hand. But all of a sudden that same knight approached. On seeing me, he came and said to that woman, "What is the matter between you and this Muslim?" She replied, "This is he who has killed my brother Hurso." This Hurso was a knight in Afiimiyah who was killed by someone of the army of Hamah. The Christian knight shouted at her, saying, "This is a bourgeois (i.e., a merchant) who neither fights nor attends a fight." He also yelled at the people who had assembled, and they all dispersed. Then he took me by the hand and went away. Thus the effect of that meal was my deliverance from certain death.

(Ibn Munqidh 1929)

Ibn Munqidh's *kitab al i'tibar* is an important source for our understanding of how the Muslims perceived the "Franks" who had invaded their lands (which they had taken from the Byzantines in the seventh century).

Other important Muslim and Arab chroniclers of the Crusades were Imad ad-Din Muhammad ibn Muhammad al-Katib al-Isfahani (1125–1201), who related the exploits of Sultan Salah ed-Din ("Saladin"), Baha ad-Din ibn Shaddad (1145–1234), whose honorific *Baha ad-Din* means "splendor of the faith," a Muslim jurist and scholar who wrote a biography of "Saladin," whom he knew well (Ibn Shaddad 2001), and Muhyi ad-Din ibn Abd az-Zahir (1223–1292), one of the historians of Mamluk Egypt, who served under two early Mamluk sultans. The Lebanese writer Amin Maalouf claimed that medieval Arab historians enjoyed a high social and political standing in their society.

The Muslim historian Imad ad-Din Muhammad ibn Muhammad al-Katib al-Isfahani (1125–1201), who chronicled the exploits of Sultan Salah ed-Din ("Saladin"), described in gory detail how in 1187 "Saladin" personally beheaded the "Frankish" leader Reynauld de Chastillon (1125–1187), who had been raiding "Saracen" caravans in the "Holy Land." Reynauld de Chastillon was a very violent Knight Templar who had served in the Second Crusade from 1145 and remained in "the Holy Land" after its defeat. He had ruled as Prince of Antioch from 1153 to 1160 and through his second marriage became Lord of Oultre-Jordain. He was a controversial character in his own lifetime and beyond, being violent and unruly and inciting to war.

Reynauld de Chastillon had served as King Baudouin IV of Jerusalem's envoy to Emperor Manuel Komnenos of Byzantium. As his wife Constance had died in 1163, he was rewarded with marriage to another wealthy widow, Stephanie, the widow of both Humphrey III of Toron (now Latrun) and Miles of Plancy, and the heiress of Oultre-Jordain (Trans-Jordan), including the castles of Kerak and Montréal in the hills of Moab southeast of the Dead Sea. These fortresses controlled the trade routes between Egypt and

Damascus and gave Reynauld access to the Red Sea. He became notorious for his violence and cruelty at Kerak, often having his enemies and hostages flung from its castle walls to be dashed to pieces on the rocks below.

One of the characters of the "Latin Kingdom of Jerusalem" was Balian of Ibelin (died 1193), around whose figure the historical film *Kingdom of Heaven* was made. The Arabic sources call him Balian ibn Barzan. The site of Ibelin had been occupied since ancient times; the Romans called it Iamnia, the Jews Yavneh or Jabneh. The Crusader castle was built in 1141 between Jaffa and Ascalon (Ashkelon), near Montgisard (now Gezer) and Ramla (now the Israeli town of Yavneh). At that time Ascalon was still controlled by Fatimid Egypt, and the Egyptian armies marched out every year from Ascalon to attack the Crusader kingdom. The Castle of Ibelin was constructed in order to contain these attacks. The original castle, built by King Foulques of Jerusalem, had four towers.

In 1186 Reynauld de Chastillon allied himself with Queen Sibylla, the surviving sister of the leprous King Baudouin IV of Jerusalem (1161–1185), and with her husband, Guy de Lusignan, in their struggle for the throne of Jerusalem. Reynauld's influence and power contributed to the recognition of Guy as King of Jerusalem, although Raymond III of Tripoli and the Ibelins had been attempting to advance the claim to the throne of Princess Isabella, the wife of Onfroi IV de Toron, who remained loyal to Guy. Reynauld attacked a "Saracen" caravan traveling between Cairo and Damascus, breaking the truce between Sultan "Saladin" and King Baudouin. In March 1187 "Saladin" sent troops to protect another caravan, in which his own sister was returning from a pilgrimage to Mecca. The caravans became a major issue which led to the great battle of Hattin of 1187 and to Reynauld de Chastillon's execution by "Saladin" himself.

The "Latin Kingdom of Jerusalem" included several *seigneuries* (lordships), one of which was the *Seigneurie d'Ibelin*, in the castle of Ibelin. Ernoul, the squire of Balian d'Ibelin, was also an historian. He continued the Latin chronicle of Guillaume de Tyr, *Historia rerum in partibus transmarinis gestarum* (William of Tyre 1943), in Old French. The *Chronique d'Ernoul* covered the fall of the "Latin Kingdom of Jerusalem" in 1187, the Third Crusade of 1189–1192, the reign of King Corrado del Monferrato in the "Latin Kingdom of Jerusalem" in 1190–1192, the creation of the Kingdom of Cyprus in 1192, and the Byzantine Empire until the Fourth Crusade in 1202–1204.

Another French author (or authors) wrote the *Estoire d'Eracles* (History of Heraclius), a thirteenth-century translation into Old French of Guillaume's Latin chronicle, as well as a chronicle of Jerusalem from 630 to 1184 and a continuation of the history of the Crusades from 1187 to 1277. The *Estoire d'Eracles* described the march of the "Franks" to "the Holy Land" and their campaigning in it, focusing on the suffering and heroism of the First

Crusaders as they sought to gain glory for God and Jesus Christ and establish a Christian state in a distant and misunderstood environment.

The *Chronique d'Ernoul* consists of several separate but similar manuscripts, supposedly stemming from an original source that has not survived, but was assumed to have been written by Ernoul. The basis for assuming the existence of these manuscripts is the *Estoire d'Eracles*. This translation and continuation of Guillaume's work, of which there are forty-nine surviving manuscripts, was called the *Estoire d'Eracles* because it began with the reign of Byzantine emperor Heraclius (c. 575–641), who took Jerusalem from the Persians in 627–628 and in 629 restored what the Byzantine Christians believed to have been "the True Cross" on which Jesus Christ was crucified to the "Church of the Holy Sepulcher".

One of the important manuscripts of the *Estoire d'Eracles* is the *Eracles de Lyon* and is the basis of the modern editions of Ernoul (Ernoul 1973, 1982). This manuscript continues until 1248, and the section containing the years 1184–1197, which covers the great battle of 1187, is not found in any other manuscript. The nineteenth-century *Recueil des historiens des croisades*, a collection of Crusader texts, used a different version of the *Eracles* (Académie des inscriptions et belles-lettres 1841). There is also a shorter manuscript of the *Estoire d'Eracles* known as the *abrégé*, and a Florentine *Eracles*, which has a unique section from 1191 to 1197 and continues until 1277.

The thirteenth-century Old French and Latin chroniclers who "continued" the *Historia rerum in partibus transmarinis gestarum* by Guillaume de Tyr, the Crusader archbishop of Tyre, conflated the two caravan incidents mentioned earlier, claiming erroneously that "Saladin's" sister, aunt, or mother, had been taken prisoner by Reynauld de Chastillon. This is contradicted by Arabic sources, such as Abu Shama and Ibn al-Athir, who say that she made it home safely to Damascus.

King Guy de Lusignan of Jerusalem publicly chastised Reynauld de Chastillon for his attacks on the caravans, in an attempt to appease "Saladin," but a haughty Reynauld replied that he was the lord of his own lands and that he had made no peace with "Saladin." A furious "Saladin" swore that Reynauld de Chastillon would be executed if he was ever taken prisoner. In 1187 "Saladin" invaded the "Latin Kingdom of Jerusalem" from Damascus, defeating the Crusaders at the Battle of Hattin, which took place near Tiberias, on the Sea of Galilee, in what is now Israel. The battlefield, near the town of Hittin, had as its chief geographic feature a double hill named *Karney Hittin* (Hebrew for the Horns of Hattin) beside a narrow pass through the northern hills between Tiberias and the road from Acre to the west. That road, built by the Romans, served as the main east-west passage between the Jordan fords, the Sea of Galilee, and the Mediterranean coast.

One of the worst things for the traumatized "Franks" about the battle of Hattin in 1187 was their loss of what they believed to be "the relic of the True Cross" upon which Jesus Christ had been executed. The Australian medievalist Megan Cassidy-Welch thought that this loss traumatized the Crusaders more than their loss of the battle itself (Cassidy-Welch 2017). The battle of Hattin left "Saladin" with many "Frankish" prisoners. Most prominent among these were Reynauld de Chastillon and King Guy de Lusignan, both of whom "Saladin" ordered brought to his tent. Guy was the king of the "Latin Kingdom of Jerusalem". Reynauld was the former Prince of Antioch from 1153 to 1160 or 1161, when his principality was taken by the "Saracens," and the Lord of *Oultrejordain* (Trans-Jordan), with his castle at Kerak, from 1175 until his death. The Persian-born Muslim Arab chronicler Imad ad-Din al-Isfahani (1125–1201), who was present at the scene, related it as follows:

> Saladin invited the king [Guy de Lusignan] to sit beside him, and when Arnat [Reynauld de Chastillon] entered in his turn, he seated him next to his king and reminded him of his misdeeds. "How many times have you sworn an oath and violated it? How many times have you signed agreements you have never respected?" Raynald [who was not a king] answered through a translator: "Kings have always acted thus. I did nothing more."
>
> (Al-Isfahani 1972)

Al-Isfahani continued his description of the terrible scene between the "Saracen" victor and the defeated "Frankish" rulers:

> During this time King Guy [de Lusignan] was gasping with thirst, his head dangling as though drunk, his face betraying great fright. Saladin spoke reassuring words to him, had cold water brought, and offered it to him. The king drank, then handed what remained to Raynald, who slaked his thirst in turn. The sultan then said to Guy: "You did not ask [me for] permission before giving him water. I am therefore not obliged to grant him mercy." After pronouncing these words, the sultan smiled, mounted his horse, and rode off, leaving the captives in terror. He supervised the return of the troops, and then came back to his tent. He ordered Raynald brought there, then advanced before him, sword in hand, and struck him between the neck and the shoulder-blade. When Raynald fell, he cut off his head and dragged the body by its feet to the king [Guy de Lusignan], who began to tremble [with fear]. Seeing him thus upset, Saladin said to him in a reassuring tone: "This man was killed only because of his maleficence and perfidy."
>
> (Al-Isfahani 1972)

Outremer (beyond the sea) was the fantastic name given by the "Franks" to the four Crusader states they had established in the First Crusade: the County of Edessa, the Principality of Antioch, the County of Tripoli, and the "Latin Kingdom of Jerusalem". The name was also used as an equivalent for the Levant, Syria or Palestine, and incorporated areas that are today part of Israel, Jordan, Syria, Turkey, and Lebanon. But the term *outre-mer* was also used for any other French land that was "overseas." Louis IV of France was called "Louis d'outre-mer," as he had been raised in England.

King Guy de Lusignan of Jerusalem was spared by Saladin. He was taken to Damascus for a time, then allowed to go free. To some Christians of his time, Reynauld de Chastillon was a martyr killed at the hands of the "evil Saracens." However, documentary evidence tends to give an impression of Reynauld as a freebooter and pirate who had little concern for the welfare of the "Latin Kingdom of Jerusalem". Some scholars think that the successes of the "Latin Kingdom of Jerusalem" were undone in large measure by Reynauld's recklessness, which needlessly provoked the Muslim states surrounding *Outremer*. "Saladin," however, had acted in accordance with his own interests. He killed Reynauld, his bitter enemy, and spared the life of Guy, knowing that to kill him was to end the factional struggle in the remnants of the "Latin Kingdom of Jerusalem". He kept him in Damascus until he was sure that he would not be able to destroy all of the Kingdom outright. The factional struggle later greatly diminished the potency of the Third Crusade, which followed the loss of Jerusalem to the "Saracens" in 1187.

Chapter 12

The Third Crusade
A Lionheart in Search of a Holy Land?

After their defeat at Hattin in 1187, the Crusaders temporarily lost their seaport of Acre as well, though "Saladin" allowed its Christian inhabitants to move north to Tyre. The Crusades did not give up on Acre, however, as it was their major seaport access to the "Holy Land." In 1189 they began their efforts to take it back. In 1191, during the Third Crusade, Richard Coeur-de-Lion, the French king of England and of the "Angevin Empire," besieged Acre and took it back from the "Saracens." Jerusalem, however, remained in the hands of the "Saracens," and Richard was unable to take it back from "Saladin." He had to settle for Acre. This created a bizarre situation where the "Latin Kingdom of Jerusalem" was mainly the Crusader city of Acre, with Jerusalem not even part of it, let alone its capital.

When the Crusades began, the island of Cyprus was part of the Byzantine empire. In 1185, the last Byzantine governor of Cyprus, Isaac Comnenos of Cyprus, from a minor line of the Imperial house of Constantinople, rose in rebellion against his emperor and attempted to seize the throne. His attempted coup was unsuccessful, but Comnenos was able to retain control of the island. Byzantine actions against Comnenos failed because he enjoyed the support of King Guillaume le Bon of Sicily. The Emperor of Byzantium had agreed with the sultan of Egypt to close the Cypriot harbors to the Crusaders. That, however, did not deter Richard Coeur-de-Lion.

During the Third Crusade, the Crusaders founded the Kingdom of Cyprus. Richard of England conquered Cyprus from the Byzantines on his way to the Holy Land. The island was made into a kingdom and, after the Crusader defeat at Hattin in 1187, it was given to the displaced King of Jerusalem, Guy of Lusignan, in 1192. He proclaimed Acre the new capital of the "Latin Kingdom of Jerusalem" and Richard left the Holy Land to pursue his wars in Europe. Henceforth the "Latin Kings of Jerusalem," who ruled in Acre, were also the kings of Cyprus. The island was later awarded to the Knights Hospitallers. Acre was a major city in the thirteenth-century Christian world. In 1229 it was placed under the control of the Knights of Saint John (whence came its French name, *Saint-Jean d'Acre*). It finally fell to the Egyptian Mamluks in 1291.

DOI: 10.4324/9781003527367-12

The Third Crusade began two years after the fall of Jerusalem to "Saladin" in 1187. In October of that year the new old pope, Gregorius VIII (Alberto di Morra), who only ruled for less than two months before his death later that year, proclaimed that the capture of Jerusalem by the "Saracens" was God's punishment for the sins of the Christians across Europe. The cry went up for a new Crusade to the Holy Land. King Henry II of England (1133–1189) and King Philippe II of France (1165–1223) ended their war with each other, and both imposed a "Saladin tithe" on their citizens to finance the great venture. In Britain, Baldwin of Exeter, the archbishop of Canterbury, made a tour through Wales, convincing 3,000 men-at-arms to take up the cross, as recorded in the *Itinerarium Cambriae* of Gerald of Wales (1146–1223).

The first European Christian king to respond to Pope Gregory's call for a Third Crusade was neither Richard of England nor Philippe of France but the German king and "Holy Roman Emperor" Friedrich Barbarossa (Red Beard, 1122–1190), who led a massive army across Anatolia into the "Saracen" lands but drowned in a river before reaching the "Holy Land". Many of his discouraged troops went home. The same Barbarossa had undertaken several expeditions to Lombardy in Italy, where he had been repeatedly defeated. Nonetheless, the Germans created a national legend around Barbarossa, that of the sleeping hero, much like the older British Celtic legends of King Arthur. The German legend says that Barbarossa is not dead, but asleep with his knights in a cave in the Kyffhäuser mountain in Thuringia or in Mount Untersberg in Bavaria, and that when the ravens cease to fly around the mountain, he will awake and restore Germany to its ancient greatness. According to the story, his red beard has grown through the table at which he sits. His eyes are half closed in sleep, but now and then he raises his hand and sends a boy out to see if the ravens have stopped flying. Adolf Hitler named his ill-fated invasion of the Soviet Union in 1941, which ultimately led to his defeat and suicide, Operation Barbarossa.

Richard Coeur-de-Lion came from the royal House of Plantagenet, also known as the House of Anjou, later called the "Angevins" after their French capital of Angers. The Plantagenets were a noble family of counts from western France that ruled Anjou, a county around the city of Angers in the lower Loire Valley of western France. Later, the Angevins or Plantagenets ruled the Duchy of Normandy (1144–1204 and 1415–1450), the Kingdom of England (1154–1485), the "Latin Kingdom of Jerusalem" (1131–1205), the Duchy of Aquitaine (1153–1453), and the Lordship of Ireland (1171–1485). Much later, the European lands of the Angevins were called the "Angevin Empire," but they were not an empire in any modern sense, nor were they called that at the time.

After the failure of the Second Crusade, Zengi's dynasty controlled a unified Syria and constantly fought the Fatimid rulers of Egypt, which ultimately resulted in the unification of Egyptian and Syrian forces under the command of the Sultan "Saladin," who employed them to reduce the Christian states and to recapture Jerusalem in 1187. The Third Crusade began in 1189 and ended three years later, in 1192. Even though the Second Crusade had been led by the kings of France and of Germany, the Third Crusade was known as the Kings' Crusade. It was an attempt by European Christian leaders to reconquer the "Holy Land" from "Saladin" and his "Saracens." Spurred by Christian religious zeal, King Henry II of England (1133–1189) and King Philippe II of France (1165–1223) ended their conflict to lead a new Crusade.

Henry II of England died in 1189, and his English contingent of the Third Crusade came under the command of his son and heir, Richard Coeur-de-Lion (1157–1199), who had been a great military leader from a very young age. At the age of 16, Richard had his own command, putting down rebellions in Poitou against his father. Richard was not only the king of England, which he rarely saw, but also the "emperor" of what was later called the "Angevin Empire," a collection of French states ruled by the Plantagenet dynasty of Anjou. That "empire" stretched from the Pyrenees to Ireland during the 12th and early 13th centuries. It was roughly half of medieval France, as well as all of England and Ireland.

With the failure of Barbarossa's Crusade, the Third Crusade had begun inauspiciously. The Crusaders began to besiege Acre, which was occupied by the "Saracens." Barbarossa's successor as German king and "Holy Roman Emperor" was his son Heinrich VI of Germany (1165–1197), who did not wish to leave on a Crusade and suffer his father's fate. Instead, with Swabia and Austria being part of his empire, Heinrich sent as his representatives to the Third Crusade Duke Friedrich VI of Swabia (1167–1191) and Duke Leopold V of Austria (1157–1194). Friedrich was killed at the siege of Acre in 1191. Leopold also arrived to take part in the siege of Acre by the Crusaders in 1191, having sailed from Zadar on the Adriatic coast (now in Croatia).

Duke Leopold of Austria took over command of what remained of the Holy Roman Imperial forces after the death of Duke Friedrich of Swabia. In July 1191, after an initial military success, the Christian leaders fell to disputing the spoils of war. After Acre surrendered to the "Franks," the banners of the "Latin Kingdom of Jerusalem", England, France, and Austria were raised in the city by Leopold's cousin, Corrado del Montferrato (King Conrad of Jerusalem, died 1192), a Piedmontese nobleman. However, an angry Richard, who believed that as King he took precedence over Duke Leopold, and that he deserved more credit for the capture of Acre, removed Leopold's flag. Richard may also have instigated the murder of Conrad of Monferrat shortly after his election as "King of Jerusalem" in April 1192.

Frustrated with Richard Coeur-de-Lion, Duke Leopold V of Austria and King Philippe II of France left the "Holy Land" and sailed back to Europe. Richard kept fighting Sultan "Saladin" of Syria over "the Holy Land" for a few more months but failed to take Jerusalem from the "Saracens." Finally, in early September 1192, Richard and "Saladin" signed a peace treaty in Jaffa by which Jerusalem would remain under Muslim control, but unarmed Christian pilgrims would be allowed to visit the city. Richard sailed home from Acre on October 9, 1192. This was the sad end of the Third Crusade.

Duke Leopold of Austria had been humiliated by Richard and he sought vengeance. On his journey back to Europe in 1193, the thirty-five-year-old King Richard of England, traveling in disguise, stopped in Vienna, was recognized by his signet ring, and was arrested by Duke Leopold's men in Vienna's Erdberg district. For some time Richard of England was imprisoned in Dürnstein castle, after which he was brought for trial before the German king and "Holy Roman Emperor" Heinrich VI, and accused of King Conrad's murder in the Holy Land. The emperor found Richard guilty of the murder and imposed an enormous ransom on him – reportedly 150,000 silver marks, three times the annual income of the English crown. This immense ransom, which was paid in 1194, became the foundation for the Viennese mint and was used to build new city walls for Vienna as well as to build the *Wiener Neustadt* (new city of Vienna). However, Duke Leopold V of Austria was excommunicated by Pope Celestinus III (died 1198) for having taken a fellow Crusader prince prisoner. Leopold died from gangrene after a foot amputation on the last day of 1194.

The Third Crusade, while a large act of war in reality, was the collective unconscious acting out of yet another psychogeographical fantasy. Seeking to "liberate" the "Holy Land," the "Holy City," and the "Holy Sepulcher" from the "evil Saracens," it had failed in all its goals. The "Latin Kingdom of Jerusalem" had become the *de facto* Kingdom of Acre. Like the previous Crusades, the Third Crusade produced many other fantasies in the form of legends and literary works on the greatness of "Saladin," Richard *Coeur-de-Lion* and other heroes. In reality, like most other "holy wars," it led to great trauma and to the tragic loss of many human lives. The failure of the Third Crusade would lead to the papal call for a Fourth Crusade six years later, in 1198, and that Crusade would begin in 1202.

How did the Third Crusaders view the Muslims? Around 1195 the Norman poet Ambroise, who had accompanied Richard Coeur-de-Lion on his Crusade, wrote his famous *Estoire de la Guerre Sainte* (Ambroise 1897, 1941, 2003). This was an epic poem in Anglo-Norman, a dialect of twelfth-century French, and holding some 12,000 lines. Being Richard's court poet, Ambroise denounced the "evil Saracens," but also the Frenchmen and Richard's enemies. Ambroise described the horrors and trauma of the war, including famine, and its great pain and suffering. From his poem, we can learn how the Crusaders viewed the Arabs, Muslims, and other "Saracens" they were fighting. For the most part, they spoke ill of the "Saracens," depicting them as cruel, evil, and ruthless. The occasions on which the "Franks" spoke well of "Saracens" were few and far between. The "Saracens" were the psychological repository on which the "Franks" could unconsciously project, externalize, and displace all their own unacceptable qualities and actions, including their massacres of innocent civilians, women, and children.

Chapter 13

The Fourth Crusade
"Latin" Christians Kill "Greek" Christians

Among the best known secondary sources for the history of the Fourth Crusade are Donald Queller and Thomas Madden's book (Queller & Madden 1997) and Warren Treadgold's history of the Byzantine empire (Treadgold 1997). Queller & Madden thought that the fall of Constantinople was "a historical accident." If we accept this view, then all history is "an accident." In fact, however, there are no accidents: if we examine the preceding events closely, we shall find how they led up to an inevitable historical outcome. The Fourth Crusade, which lasted from 1202 to 1204, was a fantastic, incredible, and tragic series of events. It was originally designed to conquer "Saracen" Jerusalem by means of an invasion of European Christian forces through Egypt. Instead, in 1204, the "Latin Crusaders" of Western Europe and their Venetian allies invaded, conquered, and sacked the Byzantine capital and Eastern "Roman" Christian city of Constantinople, the capital of the Byzantine Empire, the eastern rival of the Roman Catholic Church and of the "Holy Roman Empire."

Some historians think that the sack of Constantinople in 1204 was one of the final acts in the Great Schism between the Roman Catholic and Greek Orthodox churches, which had begun in 1054 and which had led to the creation of the Greek-speaking Eastern Orthodox church in Constantinople. The historian Jonathan Phillips called it one of the most profitable and disgraceful sacks of a city in all of human history (Phillips 2004, p. xiii). In fact, the psychological schism between "Latins" and "Greeks" had begun in the fifth century, if not earlier.

Germany, whose king was elected by its powerful *Curfürsten*, was often divided by the death of its king, which at times led to civil war. After the death of the German king and "Holy Roman Emperor" Heinrich VI in 1197, two rival groups of German *Curfürsten* elected two rival kings: Philip von Schwaben of the Hohenstaufen family, and Otto von Braunschweig of the Welf or Guelph family. Like Duke Leopold V of Austria, Philip of Swabia had been excommunicated by Pope Celestinus III, and had not been crowned in Aachen as the German kings were. In 1198 Lotario Cardinal de' Conti di Segni (1161–1216) was elected Pope Innocentius III. In 1201 the new pope openly supported Otto of Brunswick; he threatened all those who refused to acknowledge Otto with excommunication.

In 1202 Innocentius III issued his papal bull entitled *Per Venerabilem*, which made clear to the German princes his view of the relationship between the empire and the papacy – namely that as God's vicar, the pope was above the emperor (this decree was afterwards embodied in the *Corpus Juris Canonici*). The decree asserted the papal rights to decide whether a German king is worthy of the Roman imperial crown, and to arbitrate or to pronounce in favor of one of the claimants in case of a double election, which was the current situation. He argued in his bull that the *translatio imperii* – the transition of the ancient Roman Empire to the Holy Roman Emperor – had taken place only under papal blessing, and therefore all blessing, coronation, and investiture of the emperor depended upon the pope.

The Fourth Crusade was the great ambition of Pope Innocentius III. The new Crusade became the main goal of his pontificate. He issued his call for the Fourth Crusade soon after his accession to the Throne of Saint Peter. The pope directed his call to the knights and nobles of Christian Europe rather than to its kings, as he wished that neither Richard I of England nor Philippe II of France, who were still engaged in war, nor especially his German enemies, should participate in the Crusade. Indeed, his call was largely ignored by the European monarchs. There were two German kings, struggling for the office of "Holy Roman Emperor", while England and France were warring on each other. However, due to the fiery preaching of Foulques de Neuilly (died 1201), the priest of Neuilly-sur-Marne, in 1199 a Crusading army had been organized by the nobles and knights at a tournament held at Escry-sur-Aisne by Count Thibault III de Champagne (1179–1201).

Thibault was elected the leader of the Crusade, and was going to go on the Crusade with his brother-in-law, Count Baudouin de Flandre, and with his cousin, Count Louis de Blois, a son of Queen Alix of France. Thibault, however, died in 1201, and was replaced by an Italian count, Bonifacio del Monferrato (died 1207). Bonifacio was an experienced soldier, and it was an opportunity for him to restore his dynasty's reputation after several military defeats at home in Italy. Bonifacio's family was well-known in the "East": his brother Corrado (died 1192) and their nephew Baudouin (1177–1186) had both been Kings of Jerusalem, and his niece, Maria del Monferrato (1192–1212), who married Jean de Brienne (c. 1170–1237) in 1210, was the heiress of the "Latin Kingdom of Jerusalem". But Thibault had died at age twenty-two, Baudouin had died aged nine, and Corrado had been murdered. Bonifacio was either very courageous or foolhardy.

Bonifacio del Monferrato and the other leaders of the Fourth Crusade sent envoys to Venice, Genoa, and to other port cities to negotiate the sea transport of the Crusaders to Egypt, the object of their Crusade, where they planned to attack and defeat the "Saracens" and then take the "Holy Land".

One of the chief envoys was Geoffroy de Villehardouin (died 1213), a soldier-historian, the future *seneschal de Champagne,* who had joined the Crusade in 1199 during the tournament held by Count Thibault of Champagne. (Morris 1968). Thibauld had named Geoffroy one of his ambassadors to Venice to procure ships for the voyage, and Geoffroy helped to elect Bonifacio del Montferrato as the new leader of the Crusade when Thibault died. Geoffroy was one of the architects of the diversion of the Crusade first to Dalmatia and then to Constantinople. While at Constantinople, he also served as an ambassador to the Byzantine emperor Isaakios II Angelos, and he was in the embassy that demanded that Isaakios appoint Alexios IV Angelos his co-emperor in 1203.

The Republic of Genoa was not interested in joining the Crusade, but in 1201 Bonifacio del Montferrato and his fellow leaders negotiated fruitfully with Enrico Dandolo (died 1205), the old and blind *doge* of the Republic of Venice, a great maritime and naval power, who agreed to build ships to transport 33,500 Crusaders to Egypt, a very ambitious number for that time. Venice was to be paid an enormous amount of money for its services: 85,000 silver marks. This agreement required a full year of preparation on the part of the Venetians to build numerous ships and train the sailors who would man them, all the while curtailing the city's commercial activities.

The Crusading army was expected to comprise 4,500 knights (with their horses), 9,000 squires (two for each knight), and 20,000 foot-soldiers. It was ready by the fall of 1202, but it did not sail for Egypt. The majority of the Crusading army that set out from Venice in October 1202 originated from France. There were men from Blois, Champagne, Amiens, Saint-Pol, the Isle-de-France, and Burgundy. Several other European regions such as Flanders and Montferrat sent substantial military contingents as well. Other Crusader groups came from the "Holy Roman Empire" of Germany, including groups led by Abbott Martin Litz of the Alsatian Cistercian monastery of the source of the *Historia Constantinopolitana* by Gunther of Pairis (died 1220), and by Conrad von Krosigk (died 1225), the bishop of Halberstadt (Andrea 1987), and a group of Venetian soldiers and sailors led by Enrico Dandolo, the old *doge* of the Republic of Venice.

The Fourth Crusade was to sail directly to Alexandria and then march on "Saracen" Fatimid Cairo, which the Europeans took to be the center of the "Saracen" world. Its leaders were ready to sail on June 24, 1202. Their agreement with Venice was ratified by Pope Innocentius III, but with a solemn ban on attacks on Christian states, which had often happened in the previous Crusades. (Hughes 1934, New edition 1948, p. 370). This ban, however, was broken by the Crusader leaders, who not only attacked the Christian Dalmatian city of Zara (now Zadar in Croatia), but also sacked Constantinople herself. The pope sent a personal legate to the Fourth Crusade, Pietro Cardinal di Capuano (died 1214), who, however, was more indulgent about attacking Christian states than his boss in Rome.

One of the first blunders of the Fourth Crusade leaders was not requiring all their men to sail from Venice. Being far away from Venice, many Crusaders chose to sail for Egypt from other European ports, such as Antwerp, Marseille, or Genoa. By 1201 the Crusader army had gathered at Venice, but with far fewer troops than expected: only 12,000 men out of the 33,500 that had been anticipated. Venice had fulfilled her part of the bargain: it had made numerous galleys, large transports, and horse transports, enough for three times the assembled army. The Venetians, under their old and blind *doge*, Enrico Dandolo, would not let the Crusaders leave Venice without paying the full amount agreed to, 85,000 silver marks. The Crusader leaders could only pay some 51,000 silver marks, and even that only by selling all their possessions and reducing themselves to poverty. This was disastrous to the Venetians, who had halted their commerce for a great length of time to prepare this expedition.

In addition to this catastrophe 20,000 to 30,000 men (out of Venice's total population of 60,000 people) were needed to man the Crusader fleet, placing further strain on the Venetian economy. (Phillips 2004, p. 57). But the old and blind *doge* Enrico Dandolo and his Venetians succeeded in turning the Crusade to their own purposes as a form of repayment. Following riots and massacres of "Latin foreigners," specifically Venetians, in Constantinople in 1182, the Venetian merchant population had been expelled by the ruling Byzantine Angelos dynasty, with the support of the Greek population. These traumatic events made the Venetians hostile to Byzantium. Enrico Dandolo, who joined the Crusade in a public ceremony in Venice's *Chiesa di San Marco,* proposed that the Crusaders pay their debts by attacking the port of Zara in Dalmatia.

Zara, now the Croatian city of Zadar, then the capital of the Duchy of Dalmatia, was called *Jadera* in Latin documents. The Venetian *Zara* was a later derivation of the contemporary vernacular *Zadra.* Zara had been dominated by Venice throughout the twelfth century, but it had rebelled against Venice in 1181 and allied itself with the kingdom of Hungary and Croatia. Its king at that time was Béla III (died 1196), the King of Hungary and Croatia and former Duke of Croatia and Dalmatia. Béla's son Imre (1174–1204), was crowned in 1182, in his father's lifetime, and became King of Hungary and Croatia (1182–1204), and Duke of Croatia and Dalmatia (1194–1196). Subsequent Venetian attacks on Zara were repulsed by Béla and Imre, and by 1202 the city was economically independent, under the protection of the King of Hungary and Croatia. (Phillips 2004, pp. 110–111).

The Hungarian and Croatian king was Catholic and had himself agreed to join this Fourth Crusade, though this was mostly for political reasons, and he had made no actual preparations to leave for Egypt or the "Holy Land". In view of Pope Innocentius III's ban on attacking Christian lands, many Crusaders were opposed to attacking Zara. Some, including the French nobleman Simon de Montfort (1160–1218), Seigneur de Montfort-l'Amaury (who was also the titular Earl of Leicester), refused to participate and returned home.

While the Papal legate to the Crusade, Pietro Cardinal di Capuano (died 1214), endorsed the move on Zara as necessary to prevent the Crusade's complete failure, Pope Innocentius III was alarmed at this development. He wrote a letter to the Crusading leadership expressing his alarm (Hughes 1934, New edition 1948, p. 371).

Medieval war often involved atrocities like hacking the bodies of enemies into parts, beheadings, mutilating corpses, rape, murdering babies and children, and other unspeakable acts committed by frenzied soldiers in the heat of battle. The survivors, both perpetrators and victims, were traumatized. In his letter of 1202 to the Fourth Crusade leaders, Pope Innocentius III "forbade" the Crusaders of Western Christendom from committing any atrocities on their Christian neighbors, despite his wanting to secure his Papal authority over Byzantium (Hindley 2003, pp. 143, 152). This letter, however, was concealed by the leaders of the Crusade from the bulk of the Crusader army, and the attack on Zara proceeded. The citizens of Zara demonstrated their Catholic Christianity by hanging banners marked with crosses from their windows and the walls of the city, but nevertheless the city fell to the Crusaders after a brief siege. Both the Venetians and the Crusaders were threatened with excommunication by an angry Pope Innocentius III. Nonetheless, they proceeded from Zara to Corfu (now the Greek island of Kerkyra) to attack the Byzantine capital of Constantinople.

Bonifacio del Montferrato, the leader of the Fourth Crusade, had left the fleet before it sailed from Venice, to visit his cousin Philip of Swabia, the rival of the pope's favorite for "German king and Holy Roman Emperor," Otto of Brunswick. The reasons for his visit are a matter of debate; he may have realized the Venetians' plans and left the expedition to avoid excommunication, or he may have wanted to meet with the Byzantine prince Alexios IV Angelos, Philip's brother-in-law and the son of the recently deposed Byzantine emperor Isaakios II Angelos. Alexios had fled to Philip when his father was overthrown by his brother Alexios III Angelos and jailed in 1195, but it is unclear whether or not Bonifacio knew that he was at Philip's court. In Swabia, Alexios IV offered Bonifacio 200,000 silver marks, 10,000 men to help the Crusaders, the maintenance of 500 knights in the "Holy Land", the service of the Byzantine navy to transport the Crusader Army to Egypt, and the placement of the Greek Orthodox Church under the Roman Catholic Church – if they sailed to Byzantium and toppled the reigning emperor, his uncle Alexios III Angelos. It was a very tempting offer for an enterprise that was short on funds and that still owed some 35,000 silver marks to Venice.

Relations between the "Latins" of Western Europe and the "Greeks" of Byzantium were strained for at least two decades. The "Latins" of the First, Second, and Third Crusade had fought Constantinople on their way to the "Holy Land", whereas the Greeks of Byzantium had been accused by the Latins or "Franks" of betraying the Crusaders to the "Saracens." Many Venetian merchants had been attacked and deported during the anti-Latin riots in Constantinople in 1182. The Byzantine prince's proposal to the Crusader leader involved his restoration to the throne, not the sack of his capital city. Bonifacio accepted the proposal. Alexios IV returned with Bonifacio to rejoin the fleet at Corfu after it had sailed from Zara. Some of the other Crusader leaders eventually accepted the plan as well. There were many other leaders, however, of the rank and file, who wanted nothing to do with the proposal, and many deserted.

The fleet of 60 war galleys, 100 horse ships, and 50 large transports (the entire fleet was manned by 8,000 Venetian oarsmen and mariners) arrived at Constantinople in late June 1203. In addition, 300 siege engines were brought along on board the fleet. When the Fourth Crusade arrived at Constantinople, the city had a population of 150,000 people, a garrison of 30,000 men (including 5,000 Varangians), and a fleet of 20 galleys. The "Latins" laid siege to Constantinople for ten months (June 1203 to April 1204). Emperor Isaakios II Angelos (1156–1204), had been Emperor from 1185 to 1195, but had been deposed, blinded and imprisoned for eight years by his own brother, Alexios III Angelos (died 1211), along with his son, Alexios IV Angelos (died 1204). Alexios IV had managed to escape in 1201 with the help of Pisan merchants. Isaakios had been traumatized by his confinement, and the Crusaders placed his son Alexios IV Angelos on the throne as the effective monarch. It was Alexios IV who had promised the Crusaders his complete support in money, men, and ships.

The Byzantine emperor Alexios Doukas Mourzouphlos (died 1205) reigned for only two months (February 5 to April 12, 1204), at the end of the siege of Constantinople by the "Latin Franks." He was from the Doukas family, a rival of the Angelos dynasty. His Greek nickname *Mourzouphlos* either denoted his overhanging eyebrows or his sullen character. A Byzantine nobleman, Alexios had risen to the court position of *protovestarios* by the time the Fourth Crusade arrived in Byzantium in 1203. He had been married twice, but was now the lover of Eudokia Angelina, a daughter of Emperor Alexios III Angelos.

Byzantine politics were, well, Byzantine. In 1200 Alexios Doukas had participated in an attempted usurpation of the throne of Emperor Alexios III Angelos by Johannes Komnenos, a member of the rival Komnenos dynasty. Alexios III had himself deposed his brother Isaakios II five years earlier. Alexios Doukas was imprisoned, until the accession to the throne of Isaakios II Angelos and of his son Alexios IV Angelos in 1204. Fearing imprisonment and execution for his treatment of his brother Isaakios eight years earlier, Alexios III fled Constantinople in July 1203 with some 10,000 pounds of gold and some priceless jewels, leaving the imperial treasury short on funds. Being heavily beholden to the Crusaders for his throne, Isaakios II was briefly restored to the throne, but his son Alexios IV succeeded him shortly thereafter. Alexios could not meet his obligations to them, and his vacillation caused him to lose the support of both his Latin Crusader allies and his Greek subjects.

By the beginning of 1204, the emperors Isaakios II and his son Alexios IV had inspired little confidence among the Greeks of Constantinople in their failed efforts to defend the city from the besieging Latins and Venetians. The Byzantine Greeks became restless and rioted when the money and aid promised by Alexios IV was not forthcoming. Using the riots, Alexios Doukas emerged as a leader of the anti-Latin movement. He personally led some skirmishes against the Crusaders outside the city walls. When the Greek populace rose up against its two emperors in January 1204, the two emperors barricaded themselves in their palace and entrusted Alexios Doukas with a mission to seek help from the Crusaders. Instead, Alexios Doukas took advantage of the Greek riots in the capital to imprison Alexios IV and to seize the throne as Emperor Alexios V. He at once set about eliminating his enemies and fighting the Latins.

Alexios Doukas was crowned Emperor of Byzantium in early February 1204. He began to strengthen the defenses of Constantinople and stopped the negotiations with the invading Latins. After the incompetent acts of his two predecessors, however, it was too late for the new emperor to save Constantinople. The young emperor Alexios IV was murdered in prison, while his old father, Isaakios II, died, a victim of his physical and emotional trauma, or, as was said, dying of fright, sorrow, or foul play.

On April 8–9, 1204, there were very dramatic events in Constantinople. The Crusaders and Venetians, incensed at the murder of their patron, demanded that Alexios Doukas honor the contract which Alexios IV had promised. When the Byzantine emperor refused, the Crusaders assaulted the city once again. Alexios V's army put up a strong resistance, however, which did much to discourage the Crusaders. It was said that the Greeks were so elated at their victory that they "mooned" the Latin by baring their buttocks at them. The Greeks used fire ships and "Greek fire" to set ablaze the siege engines of the Latins.. A serious hindrance to the Crusaders was bad weather conditions. Wind blew from the shore and prevented most of the ships from drawing close enough to the walls to launch an assault. Only five of the Greek towers were actually engaged and none of these could be secured; by mid-afternoon it was evident that the Crusader attack had failed.

The Latin clergy of the Crusaders discussed the situation amongst themselves and settled upon the message they wished to spread through their demoralized army. They tried to convince the men that the events were not God's judgment on a sinful enterprise: the campaign, they argued, was righteous and with proper belief it would succeed. The concept of God testing the determination of the Crusaders through temporary setbacks was a familiar means for the clergy to explain failure in the course of a campaign. Alexios Doukas was not invincible. An attempted Byzantine surprise attack on the Crusaders failed, despite the emperor's personal leadership. During the ensuing fight, he defended the city with courage and tenacity, beating back the

Crusader assault of April 9, 1204. But the Crusaders' second attack on April 12 proved too strong to repel, and during that night, Alexios Doukas fled to Thrakia (Thrace), accompanied by his lover Eudokia Angelina and her mother Euphrosyne Doukaina Kamatera. Constantinople was under "Latin" control on April 13.

Emperor Alexios Doukas and his fellow refugees from Constantinople reached the Thracian city of Messinopolis (now the Bulgarian city of Messinopol), to join the deposed emperor Alexios III Angelos, who had fled Constantinople. They were initially well received, and Alexios Doukas married Eudokia Angelina, the daughter of Alexios III. Later, however, a scheming and vengeful Alexios III arranged for his son-in-law to be ambushed, captured, and blinded, making him ineligible for the imperial throne. Abandoned by his supporters and enemies alike, Alexios Doukas was captured near Mosynopolis by the advancing Latins under Thierry de Loos (died 1208) in November 1204. Brought back to Constantinople, Alexios Doukas was tried and condemned to death for his treason against his predecessor, Alexios IV. He was thrown to his death from the top of the Column of Theodosius, traumatizing both Greeks and Latins.

Alexios Doukas was the last Byzantine emperor to reign in Constantinople before the establishment of the "Latin Empire of Constantinople," which ruled the city for the next 57 years (1204–1261). The sack of Constantinople in 1204 and the creation of the "Latin Empire of Constantinople" were no less bloody and traumatic than the capture of Jerusalem in 1099, even though the Byzantines were "good Christians," not "evil Saracens." The Greek-American historian Speros Vryonis (1928–2019) gave us a vivid account of the sack of Constantinople by the Frankish and Venetian Crusaders from the Greek point of view:

> The Latin soldiery subjected the greatest city in Europe to an indescribable sack. For three days they murdered, raped, looted and destroyed on a scale which even the ancient Vandals and Goths would have found unbelievable. Constantinople had become a veritable museum of ancient and Byzantine art, an emporium of such incredible wealth that the Latins were astounded at the riches they found. Though the Venetians had an appreciation for the art which they discovered (they were themselves semi-Byzantines) and saved much of it, the French and others destroyed indiscriminately, halting to refresh themselves with wine, violation of nuns, and murder of Orthodox clerics. The Crusaders vented their hatred for the Greeks most spectacularly in the desecration of the greatest Church in Christendom. They smashed the silver iconostasis, the icons and the holy books of Hagia Sophia, and seated upon the patriarchal throne a whore who sang coarse songs as they drank wine from the Church's holy vessels. The estrangement of East and West, which had proceeded over the centuries, culminated in the horrible massacre that accompanied the conquest of Constantinople. The Greeks were

convinced that even the Turks, had they taken the city, would not have been as cruel as the Latin Christians. The defeat of Byzantium, already in a state of decline, accelerated political degeneration so that the Byzantines eventually became an easy prey to the Turks. The Crusading movement thus resulted, ultimately, in the victory of Islam, a result which was of course the exact opposite of its original intention.

(Vryonis 1967, p. 152)

In other words, not only did the Fourth Crusade fail to reach the "Holy Land", and to "liberate" Jerusalem and the "Holy Sepulcher", it also greatly weakened the Christian world in its prolonged struggle with the "Saracens."

We have three reliable eyewitness accounts of the Fourth Crusade. One is by Geoffroy de Villehardouin, the French soldier and writer, another by Robert de Clari, a French Crusader knight, and the third by the Byzantine chronicler Niketas Akominatos Choniates (c. 1155–1217). All three were present in Constantinople during the brief reign of Alexios Doukas in 1204, before the city's capture by the Crusaders. Niketas, who did not like Alexios, related his usurpation of the throne of Byzantium from his two predecessors, while the two "Franks" related in detail the Crusader siege of Constantinople and its fall. In fact, however, Alexios Doukas was an able ruler, but he was not supported by all the Greeks. The historian Peter Noble believed that Alexios "almost achieved the impossible, and [that] much of his failure can be attributed to the incompetence of his predecessors" (Noble 2002, p. 178).

In 1185 the Bulgarians had thrown off Byzantine rule and set up their second Bulgarian Empire. After the conquest of the Byzantine Empire by the "Latins" in 1204, the Fourth Crusade was over. Geoffroy de Villehardouin continued to serve as a military leader. In 1205 he fought at the Battle of Adrianopolis (now the Turkish city of Edirne) between the Bulgarians under Tsar Kaloyan "the Greek slayer" (died 1207) and the Crusaders under Emperor Baudouin I (1172–1205), the first Latin emperor of Constantinople, one of the most prominent leaders of the Fourth Crusade. That battle was won by the Bulgarians after a skillful ambush with the help of their Cuman and Greek allies. Around 300 "Latin" knights were killed, including Louis de Blois, the Duke of Nicaea. Emperor Baudouin of Byzantium was captured, blinded, and later died in Bulgarian captivity. The Bulgarians overran much of Thrace and Macedonia and annexed them to their country. Geoffroy de Villehardouin led the retreat of the "Latins" from the Battle of Adrianople in 1205. In recognition of his services, Bonifacio del Montferrato, the leader of the Fourth Crusade, gave Geoffroy the Thracian city of Messinopolis.

The Byzantines had moved their capital to Nicaea (now İznik, Turkey). On August 20, 1205, Emperor Baudouin was succeeded on the throne of Constantinople by his younger brother, Henry de Flandre. Henry had married Agnes de Montferrat, daughter of Bonifacio del Montferrato, the Crusader leader, but she had died (probably in childbirth) before her father's death in 1207. Henry's reign as Emperor of Byzantium was passed in successful battles with Tsar Kaloyan of Bulgaria, and with his Byzantine Greek rival, Theodoros Komnenos Laskaris, the emperor of Nicaea. After the death of Tsar Kaloyan in 1207, Henry briefly fought his successor, Tsar Boril (died 1218), defeating him at the Battle of Plovdiv in 1208. Some contemporary chroniclers wrote that Henry made peace with the Bulgarians after the death of Tsar Kaloyan, and that Pope Innocentius III ordered Henry to marry Kaloyan's only child, his daughter Maria. Henry's first wife, Agnes of Montferrat, died in childbirth with her child in 1207, and this second marriage also left no heirs. In 1216 Henry died, poisoned, it was said, by his Bulgarian wife, Maria.

In 1207, after the death of Tsar Kaloyan of Bulgaria and the possible peace between Byzantium and Bulgaria, Villehardouin began to write his chronicle of the Fourth Crusade, *Sur la conqueste de Constantinople* (Villehardouin 1891, 1915). It was written in French rather than in Latin, making it one of the earliest works of French prose. Villehardouin's account is read alongside that of Robert de Clari, a lowly French knight, that of Niketas Choniates, a high-ranking Byzantine official and historian, who gives an eyewitness account, and that of Gunther von Pairis, an Alsatian Cistercian monk who tells the story from the perspective of his abbot, Martin of Pairis. Pairis was a Cistercian abbey in Alsace, near Orbey, and its abbot, Martin, had taken an active part in the Fourth Crusade. He claimed to have brought with him fragments of the "True Cross" of Jesus Christ from Jerusalem.

Chapter 14

The Fifth Crusade
An Invasion of Egypt that Predictably Fails

Medieval Europeans had no trouble calling several different people by the same name, as well as spelling the same names several different ways. The French knight Geoffroy de Villehardouin (died 1213) was the chronicler of the Fourth Crusade, the author of *De la Conqueste de Constantinople* (Joffroi de Villehardouin & Henri de Valenciennes 1838). Guillaume de Champlitte le Champenois (died 1209) was the first Crusader Prince of Achaea (the Latin name of the Greek Peloponnesus after it was taken from the Byzantines). His principality was a vassal of the short-lived "Latin Empire of Constantinople." Another Geoffroy de Villehardouin (died 1229), a nephew of the chronicler, was a French knight from Champagne who took the cross with his uncle during the knightly tournament at Escry-sur-Aisne in 1199, joined the Fourth Crusade, went to Syria and became the second prince of Achaea in 1209. A third Geoffroy de Villehardouin (c. 1195–1246), the eldest son of the former Geoffroy, became the third Prince of Achaea in 1229.

The tragic Fourth Crusade, in which Christians killed other Christians, was over in 1204, but Christian Europe did not give up. Within thirteen years the Fifth Crusade had begun. Like its predecessors, the Fifth Crusade (1217–1221) was another fantastic attempt by the European Christians, who called themselves "Franks" and "Latins," to take back Jerusalem and the rest of the "Holy Land from the 'Saracens'" by defeating and conquering the powerful Ayyubid state in Egypt. Set up by "Saladin," the Ayyubid dynasty was a Kurdish Muslim dynasty which ruled Egypt, Syria (including Palestine), most of Yemen, Diyar Bakr (now Diarbakır in southeastern Turkey), Mecca, the Hejaz (now in Saudi Arabia), and northern Iraq in the twelfth and thirteenth centuries. Unable to mourn their losses, the traumatized "Latins" and "Franks" made war on the Ayyubids to regain them (Fornari 1975).

The history of the Fifth Crusade can be told in a nutshell, and it can also be told in great detail (Fuller 1639; Röhricht 1891). Perhaps because the Fourth Crusade had ended with the capture of Christian Constantinople and with the creation of the "Latin Empire of Constantinople," against his own wishes, it was not until 1213 that the old pope Innocentius III issued a new papal bull entitled *Quia maior*, calling all Christians to join a new Crusade. As usual, the kings and emperors of Europe were busy fighting each other. Moreover, Pope Innocentius III did not really want their help, because the previous Crusades led by kings had failed, and because kings were as prone to seek conquest in Christian lands as in "Saracen" ones. The pope ordered processions, prayers, and preachings to help organize the Crusade, as these would involve the general population, the lower nobles, and the knights. No Crusade, however, came about in his lifetime.

Pope Innocentius III, who had called the Fourth and Fifth Crusades, died in 1216. By Catholic Church custom, the cardinals who were present at his death assembled at Perugia and elected their colleague Cardinal Cencio (died 1227) as Pope Honorius III. In 1217 Honorius organized Crusading armies, led by Duke Leopold VI of Austria (1176–1230) and King András II of Hungary (died 1235), but their attempt to take Jerusalem left the city in Muslim hands. Neither Leopold nor András could achieve any major military success. András was obliged to issue the Golden Bull confirming the privileges of the noblemen of Hungary and later he was also obliged to confirm the special privileges of the clergy. During his long reign, he had several quarrels with his sons.

In 1218 a German Crusader army led by Oliver of Cologne and a mixed army of Dutch, Flemish, and Frisian soldiers led by Willem, Count of Holland (died 1222), arrived in Egypt. Holland was then a County in the Low Countries or Netherlands. In order to attack the Egyptian port of Damietta, the Crusaders allied themselves with the Seljuk Turkish sultan of "Rum" in Anatolia, who attacked the Ayyubids in Syria in an attempt to free the Crusaders from fighting on two fronts. After occupying the Egyptian port of Damietta in 1221, the Crusaders marched south towards Cairo, but were turned back after their dwindling supplies led to a forced retreat. A nighttime attack by Sultan Al-Kamil resulted in a great number of Crusader losses and eventually in the surrender of the traumatized Crusader army. Al-Kamil agreed to an eight-year peace agreement with the "Franks."

The same history, however, can also be told in detail, revealing its psychological paradoxes, fantasies, and tragedies. Here is the longer version. The main European countries involved in the Fifth Crusade were France, Germany, the Low Countries (now Belgium and the Netherlands), and Hungary (which included Croatia). In France, the message of the Crusade was preached by Robert de Courçon (died 1218), an Anglo-Norman cardinal. Unlike the previous Crusades, where the French were the largest and most important contingent, not many French knights joined the Fifth Crusade, as they were busy fighting the "Albigensian Crusade" against the "heretical" Cathars in southern France, at the pope's behest.

The "Albigensian Crusade" or "Cathar Crusade" (1209–1229), which overlapped with the Fifth and Sixth Crusades, was a military campaign initiated by the Roman Catholic Church to eliminate the "Cathar heresy" in Languedoc. That "heresy" was of a Christian religious sect with dualistic and gnostic elements that rose in the Languedoc region of southern France in the eleventh century and flourished in the twelfth and thirteenth centuries. "Catharism" had "Paulician" and "Bogomile" roots. They had dualist and Manichaean beliefs, seeing the world as a struggle between Good and Bad, Light and Darkness. The Cathars were numerous in what is now southwestern France, which was part of the Kingdom of Aragon. They were called Albigensians, either because of the movement's presence in and around Albi, northeast of Toulouse, or because of the Church Council held near Albi which declared the Cathar doctrine heretical.

Political control in Languedoc had been divided among the local lords and town councils. Before the "Albigensian Crusade," there was little fighting in the area, and a fairly sophisticated and calm polity. After the Crusade was initiated by Pope Innocentius III in 1209, however, it was prosecuted by the French king Louis le Lion (1187–1226), and promptly became a political power struggle, resulting in not only a significant reduction in the number of Cathars but also in a political realignment of southern France, bringing it into the sphere of the French crown and diminishing its distinct regional culture and language and its high level of foreign influence. By the end of the "Cathar Crusade," many of the people of southwest France had become refugees in neighboring countries. King Louis the Lion died of an epidemic that hit his army during his siege of Avignon. While on his way back to Paris, he fell ill with dysentery, and died on November 8, 1226, in the *château* de Montpensier in Auvergne.

In 1215, the year before his death, Pope Innocentius III had called the Fourth Lateran Council, where, along with the "Latin Patriarch of Jerusalem," Raoul de Merencourt (died 1225), and with many of his suffragan bishops, he discussed the recovery of the "Holy Land". Pope Innocent wanted this Crusade to be under the full control of the papacy, as the First Crusade was supposed to have been, in order to avoid the mistakes of the Fourth Crusade, which had been hijacked by the Venetians and diverted to Constantinople. Pope Innocent planned for the Crusaders to meet at the port of Brindisi in 1216, and prohibited trade with the "Saracens" to ensure that the Crusaders would have ships and weapons. Each Crusader would receive a free indulgence from the pope, including those who only helped pay the expenses of a Crusader but did not go on the Crusade themselves. This was a great enticement, as medieval Christians feared the Devil and believed that their sins would lead them to hell, and that an indulgence from the pope would save them from this fate.

Germany and Hungary were different from France. Oliver of Cologne had preached the Crusade in Germany, and Friedrich von Hohenstaufen (1194–1250) half-heartedly attempted to join it in 1215, the year he became King of Germany. Friedrich, however, was not the king whom Pope Innocent wanted to join the Crusade: in the perennial power struggle between the Pope and the

"Holy Roman Emperor," he had challenged the Papacy. Friedrich had claimed the title of *Rex Romanorum* from 1212 and held that title from 1215. As such, he was King of Germany, of Italy, and of Burgundy, and also King of Sicily from his mother's inheritance. But he could not become "Holy Roman Emperor" before being crowned by the pope in Rome, which took another five years.

Pope Innocentius III wanted the Duke of Austria and the King of Hungary, both parts of the "Holy Roman Empire," to take up the leadership of the Crusade. Pope Innocent, however, died in 1216. He was succeeded by Pope Honorius III, who, like his predecessor, at first barred the "rebellious" Friedrich from participating in the Crusade, but instead organized Crusading armies led by Leopold of Austria and András of Hungary. However, the new pope soon realized that Friedrich of Germany was crucial to his undertaking. In 1217 the pope crowned Pierre de Courtenay (died 1219) "Latin Emperor of Constantinople." Before the new emperor could reach his empire, however, he was captured on his eastward journey by Theodoros Komnenos Doukas, the despot of Epiros, and, after an imprisonment of two years, died in prison. Pope Honorius III finally became aware that there was only one man in Europe who could bring about the recovery of the "Holy Land," and that man was his former pupil and rival, King Friedrich II of Germany. Like many other European Christian rulers, Friedrich had taken an oath to embark for "the Holy Land" in 1217. But he procrastinated, waiting for the pope to crown him "Holy Roman Emperor," and Honorius III repeatedly put off the expedition.

The Crusaders, led by Duke Leopold of Austria and King András of Hungary, left Brindisi by sea for Acre in 1217, where they joined Jean de Brienne (died 1237), the "King of Jerusalem," who did not rule Jerusalem, which was in "Saracen" hands, but was still considered the most valorous knight of his time. They were also joined by Hugues de Lusignan (died 1218), the King of Cyprus, and by Prince Bohemond of Antioch (died 1233). All these kings and princes had come to fight against the "Saracen" Ayyubids in Syria. In the city of Jerusalem, however, the "Saracens" had demolished the walls and fortifications of the city, to prevent the Christians from being able to defend the city from their assault, if they should ever reach it and take it. Collective trauma is transmitted to following generations. Fearing the "Franks," the Muslims fled the city, afraid of a bloodbath like that of the First Crusade in 1099. The Ayyubids, however, tried to avoid fighting. The battles were inconclusive. Nothing came of this campaign, and András, Bohemond, and Hugues returned home in 1218, leaving behind King Jean of Jerusalem, Duke Leopold of Austria, and some of the Crusaders. Later in 1218, Oliver of Cologne arrived in Acre with a new German army, and Willem of Holland arrived in Egypt with an army consisting of Dutch, Flemish, and Frisian soldiers.

Willem of Holland, also known as "William the Crazy," was an interesting character. Born around 1167, he had been raised in Scotland, had risen up against his brother, Dirk VII, and became Count of Friesland after a reconciliation. However, the Counts of Holland considered Friesland part of their county. Willem's niece, Ada, married Count Louis of Holland and inherited Holland in 1203, but Willem wanted Friesland and Holland for himself. The civil war that ensued lasted several years. Louis and Ada were supported by the bishops of Liège and of Utrecht and by the count of Flanders. Willem was supported by the duke of Brabant and by the majority of the Hollanders. Willem finally won the civil war, and "Holy Roman Emperor" Otto of Germany recognized Willem as Count of Holland in 1203, because he supported the Welf dynasty in Germany.

In 1214 the Battle of Bouvines took place in a town between Lille and Tournai, then in the County of Flanders. The military alliances of that battle were orchestrated by Pope Innocentius III. In the battle, King Philippe Auguste of France defeated "Holy Roman Emperor" Otto of Germany and Count Ferrand of Flanders. Otto was deposed and replaced as German king by Friedrich von Hohenstaufen. Ferrand was captured and imprisoned. Their ally, King John of England, was forced by his discontented barons to return home and to sign the *Magna Carta*. Philippe Auguste of France took undisputed control of the territories of Anjou, Brittany, Maine, Normandy, and the Touraine, which he had recently seized from Otto's kinsman and ally John of England.

After the battle of Bouvines, Count Willem of Holland and many other noblemen switched their allegiance to King Friedrich von Hohenstaufen of Germany. Willem also took part in a French expedition against king John of England. The pope excommunicated Willem for this. Excommunication was a very grave matter for a medieval Christian. It meant life in hell after death. Possibly to have his excommunication lifted, the traumatized Willem became a fervent Crusader. He campaigned in Prussia with the "Baltic Crusades" and joined in the conquest of Lisbon. In Europe, he came to be called "William the Crazy" for his reckless behavior in battle.

Count Willem of Holland discussed the attack on Damietta with Duke Leopold of Austria, King Jean of Jerusalem, and Oliver of Cologne. They allied themselves with the Seljuk Turkish leader Izzeddin Keykavus (died 1220), the Seljuk Turkish Sultan of "Rum" in Anatolia, against the Ayyubid caliph in Damacus. Now the "Saracens" were fighting one another. As the Ayyubids ruled both Syria and Egypt (and several other territories), the Seljuk Turkish "Rumians" attacked the Ayyubids in Syria, seeking to free the Crusaders from one of their two fronts.

This left the Crusaders free to sail for Egypt and try to take Damietta from the Ayyubids. In June 1218 the Crusaders began their siege of Damietta, and despite resistance from the Ayyubid sultan, al-Malik al-Adil Sayf al-Din Abu-Bakr ibn Ayyub (1145–1218), the tower outside the city was taken on August 25. The Crusaders could not gain Damietta itself, however, and in the ensuing months diseases killed many of them, including Robert Cardinal de Courçon, who had preached the Crusade in France. Sultan Al-Adil also died that year and was succeeded by Sultan al-Malik al-Kamil Naser al-Din Abu al-Ma'ali Muhammed (1180–1238).

In 1219 Pope Honorius III sent Pelagius of Albano (Pelagio Galvani, 1165–1230), a Portuguese-born Benedictine monk, cardinal, and canon lawyer, as his legate to lead the Fifth Crusade (Donovan 1950, p. 115; Maleczek 1984, p. 169; Linehan 2023) Sultan Al-Kamil of Egypt tried to negotiate peace with the Crusaders. He offered to trade Damietta for Jerusalem, but Cardinal Pelagius turned him down, confident that the Crusaders would defeat Egypt. After hearing this, Count Willem of Holland left the Crusade and sailed home. In August or September, Francesco d'Assisi, a future saint of the Roman Catholic Church, arrived in the Crusader camp and crossed over to preach to Sultan Al-Kamil. By November, the Crusaders had worn out the sultan's forces, and were finally able to occupy the port of Damietta.

As soon as they had occupied Damietta, the papal and secular powers fought for control of the town. Jean de Brienne, the "Latin King of Jerusalem," claimed it for himself. Cardinal Pelagius would not hear of it, and an angry Jean de Brienne returned to his capital of Acre later that year. Cardinal Pelagius had hoped that the German king Friedrich von Hohenstaufen would arrive from Germany with a fresh army, so that the Crusaders could take Egypt, but Friedrich never did, as part of his struggle with Pope Honorius. In April 1220, after a five-year wait, Friedrich was elected *Imperator Romanorum* and on November 22 he was crowned "Holy Roman Emperor" in Rome by Pope Honorius. Yet, despite the insistence of the pope, Friedrich delayed sending his army to Egypt, and the Egyptian campaign failed miserably.

After a year of inactivity in Syria and Egypt, Jean de Brienne, the nominal "King of Jerusalem," returned from Acre to Damietta, and the Crusaders marched south towards Cairo in July 1221. By now Sultan Al-Kamil of Egypt was able to ally with his fellow Ayyubids in Syria, who had defeated the Seljuk Turkish leader Keykavus in 1220. The Crusader march to Cairo was disastrous; the river Nile flooded ahead of them, stopping the Crusader advance. A dry canal that was previously crossed by the Crusaders also flooded, blocking the Crusader army's retreat. With supplies dwindling, a forced retreat began, culminating in a nighttime attack by Al-Kamil, which resulted in a great number of Crusader losses and eventually in the surrender of the traumatized army under Pelagius. Pelagius relinquished Damietta to Al-Kamil in exchange for the release of the Crusader prisoners. Al-Kamil agreed to an eight-year peace agreement with the "Franks" and to the return of a piece of "the True Cross" of Jesus Christ, which, in reality, of course, he did not possess. "Holy Roman Emperor" Friedrich von Hohenstaufen of Germany failed to arrive in Egypt, and the failure of the Crusade was blamed on him.

The failure of the Fifth Crusade, and the machinations of Pope Innocentius III and Pope Honorius III that preceded and accompanied it, were a disaster for the pope. They caused an outpouring of anti-papal sentiment from many

Western European Christians, including the Provençal poet Guilhem Figueira, a southern French *jongleur* and *troubadour* from Toulouse, who was active at the court of "Holy Roman Emperor" Friedrich von Hohenstaufen, the pope's rival, in the 1230s, after the Sixth Crusade. Figueira was a close associate of Aimery de Pégulhan and Guillem Augier Novella, and was popular with the lower classes.

Figueira was the son of a Toulouse tailor and himself also a tailor by trade. As a result of the "Albigensian Crusade," he was exiled from his homeland and took refuge in Lombardy, whence he eventually made his way to Friedrich's court in Germany. In Italy he and his fellow exile Aimery de Pégulhan, who were bitter about their exile, helped found a *troubadour* tradition of lamentation for the "good old days" of pre-Crusade Languedoc. Their Lombard successors continued to employ the Provençal language, and it was not until the time of Dante Alighieri in the fourteenth century that the Italian language got a significant vernacular literature of its own.

A precursor of the revolt of Martin Luther three centuries later, in 1228 Guilhem Figueira angrily and publicly denounced the papal "indulgences" given to the Crusaders and blamed the death of the "good" King Louis VIII of France, who died of dysentery at the siege of Avignon, on the false indulgence which had drawn him out of the safety of Paris. His most famous work, *D'un sirventes far*, or the *Sirventes contra Roma*, was a powerful reprimand of the papacy. Its violence had to do with the circumstances of its composition: Guilhem wrote it while he was in Toulouse, besieged by the Crusaders in 1229. It was set to the tune of a famous hymn about the Virgin Mary, and was thus easily sung by the masses. Figueira's *D'un sirventes far* was a venomous diatribe against Rome:

> Treacherous Rome, avarice ensnares you, So that you shear, too much wool from your sheep; May the Holy Ghost, who takes on human flesh, Hear my prayers, And break your beaks, O Rome! You will never have truce with me, Because you are false and perfidious, With us and with the Greeks! ... Rome, to the Saracens, you do little damage, But to the Greeks and Latins, massacre and carnage; In the bottom of the abyss, Rome, you have your seat, In hell."
>
> (Throop 1938)

The third-century pro-papal Occitan poetess Gormonda de Monpeslier was a *troubadresse* from Montpellier in Languedoc. Her only surviving work, *A sirventes*, while written in the Provençal dialect, has been called "the first French political poem by a woman." Gormonda de Monpeslier responded to Figueira's attack on the pope in *D'un sirventes far* with a poem of her own, *Greu m'es a durar*. Instead of blaming Pelagius or the Papacy, she laid the blame for the horrors of the crusades on the "foolishness of the wicked."

The tragedy of the Fifth Crusade, however, was neither the "wickedness of the pope" nor the "foolishness of the wicked." It was the denial of reality, the inability to mourn, and a life in fantasy. Most of those who left on it were either killed, defeated, or returned home traumatized and empty-handed. The religious fanaticism and political ambition that drove it were based on pure fantasy. "Holy wars," whether in the name of Christ, God or Allah, are always disastrous.

Chapter 15

The Sixth Crusade
Winning Jerusalem Peacefully

The Sixth Crusade was unique among the nine major Crusades, as well as among the minor Crusades in Europe, in that it was the only one whose goal was achieved peacefully. The "Holy City" of Jerusalem was bought peacefully from the "Saracens," even though they also considered it a holy place and called it *Al-Quds* (the holy one). The chief protagonist of the Sixth Crusade was the German king and "Holy Roman Emperor" Friedrich von Hohenstaufen (1194–1250), who had refused to play a serious military role in the Fifth Crusade, and who was excommunicated by Pope Honorius III for it. It was none other than Friedrich who negotiated with the "Saracens" for Jerusalem, and it was he who crowned himself King of Jerusalem in 1225, after marrying its teen-age queen, Isabella II (1212–1228), who three years later died of complications following her second childbirth, aged sixteen.

The old pope Honorius III, who had played a major role in the Fifth Crusade, died in 1227. He was succeeded by Pope Gregorius IX (Ugolini di Conti, died 1241). In 1228, seven years after the failure of the Fifth Crusade, the European Christians worked themselves into another Crusading frenzy. Once again, the Crusade was born out of Europe's internal conflicts, above all the perennial power struggle between the old Pope and the young "Holy Roman Emperor," with all the earmarks of an Oedipal battle: the pope was an old man and was called *Papa* (father) in Latin, whereas the "Holy Roman Emperor," who was also "king of the Romans," was a much younger man. In 1228, Pope Gregorius IX was anywhere from fifty-eight to eighty-three years old, while Emperor Friedrich was only thirty-four.

Despite the opposition of Pope Innocentius III and the initial reluctance of Pope Honorius III, "Holy Roman Emperor" Friedrich von Hohenstaufen partially involved himself in the Fifth Crusade, sending troops from Germany, but he had not accompanied the army personally, and had failed to send it to Egypt, where it was badly needed, despite the encouragement of Honorius III and Gregorius IX. Friedrich wished to consolidate his position in Germany and Italy before embarking on a dangerous Crusade. Friedrich had promised to go on a Crusade after his coronation as emperor in 1220 by Pope Honorius

III, but did not leave for Egypt, and the Fifth Crusade failed miserably in 1221.

In 1210, Jean de Brienne had married the heiress Maria del Monferrato, daughter of Isabella and Conrad of Montferrat, assuming the title of "King of Jerusalem" in right of his wife. In 1211 he concluded a six years' truce with Sultan Malik-el-Adil of Egypt, but in 1212 he lost his beloved wife, Maria del Monferrato. She had given him a daughter, Isabella but Maria died shortly thereafter, probably from puerperal fever. Jean de Brienne became Regent of Jerusalem for his daughter Isabella, now the baby Queen of Jerusalem. Soon afterwards Jean married Princess Stephanie, a daughter of King Leo of Armenia. But Jean de Brienne had trouble mourning the loss of his first wife. He was a prominent figure during the Fifth Crusade, but the papal legate Pelagius of Albano claimed the command; insisting on the advance from Damietta to Cairo, in spite of Jean's warnings, Cardinal Pelagius refused to accept the favorable terms of the sultan of Egypt, as Jean de Brienne advised, until it was too late.

After the failure of the Fifth Crusade in 1221, Jean de Brienne, the "King of Jerusalem" and future "Latin Emperor of Constantinople," came to Europe to obtain help for his kingdom. He became a tragic victim of the ambitions of "Holy Roman Emperor" Friedrich von Hohenstaufen. In 1223 Jean met Pope Honorius and Emperor Friedrich at Ferentino, southeast of Rome, where, in order to have closer ties to the "Holy Land," against Jean's wishes, the twenty-nine-year-old Friedrich was betrothed to Jean's *eleven-year-old* daughter Isabella (1212–1228), the heiress of the "Latin Kingdom of Jerusalem". A disconsolate Jean de Brienne then went to France and England, then to Santiago de Compostela, a famous place of pilgrimage in northwest Spain, where King Alfonso IX of León offered him the hand of one of his daughters and the promise of his kingdom. Jean de Brienne passed over Alfonso's eldest daughter and heiress in favor of a younger daughter, Berenguela de León (1204–1237).

In 1225 the thirty-one-year-old "Holy Roman Emperor" Friedrich von Hohenstaufen of Germany married Jean de Brienne's daughter, the *thirteen-year-old* Isabella, who was known as "Queen Isabella II of Jerusalem." Friedrich now had a claim to the truncated "Kingdom of Jerusalem," and a reason to attempt to restore Jerusalem to Christian rule. After the wedding of Friedrich and Isabella, she was kept in seclusion by her husband in his harem in Sicily. In November 1226, the fourteen-year-old Isabella gave birth to her first child, a daughter (called Marguerite or Margareta), but this baby girl died in August 1227. Friedrich and his army had set sail from Brindisi for Acre, but an epidemic at Otranto had forced him to turn back. Gregorius took this opportunity to excommunicate Friedrich for breaking his Crusading vow, though this was a pretext. Friedrich had been trying to consolidate his imperial power in Italy at the expense of the papacy.

In 1225, after a visit to Germany, Jean de Brienne, "King of Jerusalem," had returned to Rome, where he received a demand from his son-in-law Emperor Friedrich von Hohenstaufen that Jean abandon his title and dignity of king, which, so Friedrich claimed, had passed to himself along with the heiress of the kingdom, Jean's daughter Isabella. This was "an offer that could not be refused," and the "King of Jerusalem" abdicated in favor of his daughter – and in effect, in favor of Friedrich. Jean de Brienne, "the most valorous knight of his time," avenged himself on Friedrich three years later, after his daughter's death, by commanding the papal troops that attacked Friedrich's domains in southern Italy during the emperor's absence on the Sixth Crusade (1228–1229). Once again, we can see here a confirmation of Franco Fornari's theory that those who cannot mourn their losses must make war (Fornari 1975). In 1229 Jean de Brienne became the "Latin Emperor of Constantinople."

Pope Gregorius IX had stated in 1227 that the reason for the excommunication of Emperor Friedrich was Friedrich's failure to honor his Crusading oath, dating back to the Fifth Crusade. As we have seen, for Gregorius the Crusade was a pretext to excommunicate the emperor, whose Italian ambitions he feared, just as his predecessors had feared all "Holy Roman Emperors." Friedrich attempted to negotiate with the stubborn old pope, but eventually decided to ignore him, and on 8 September 1227 Friedrich von Hohenstaufen of Germany sailed from Brindisi for Jerusalem. However, as we have seen, he fell ill at Otranto, where the young Landgrave Ludwig of Thuringia (1200–1227), who had joined the Sixth Crusade, had been put ashore, and Friedrich postponed his journey while he and Ludwig tried to recover. Ludwig had fallen ill with the fever after reaching Brindisi and Otranto. He received "Extreme Unction" from the Patriarch of Jerusalem and the Bishop of Santa Croce and died in Otranto. A few days after his death, his daughter Gertrud was born. Ludwig's remains were buried in Germany in 1228. Emperor Friedrich's sixteen-year-old wife Isabella died on 25 April 1228 in Andria, Bari, Italy, after giving birth to her second child, a son, Corrado (Conrad). She was buried in the Cathedral of Bari.

Some contemporary chroniclers, who were sympathetic to the pope, doubted the sincerity of Friedrich's illness, stating that he had deliberately delayed sailing for selfish reasons, using his "illness" as a pretext. Roger of Wendover (died 1236), an English chronicler, wrote:

> ... he went to the Mediterranean sea, and embarked with a small retinue; but after pretending to make for the holy land for three days, he said that he was seized with a sudden illness [...] this conduct of the emperor redounded much to his disgrace, and to the injury of the whole business of the Crusade.
>
> (Peters 1971)

In fact, Emperor Friedrich was forced to return home after an epidemic broke out in his camp before departing for Acre, and took the life of Ludwig of

Thuringia. The fourth Grand Master of the Teutonic Knights, Hermann von Salza (died 1239), who had come on the Crusade with his Knights, recommended that Friedrich return to the mainland to recuperate.

A skilled diplomat with ties to both the "Holy Roman Emperor" and the Pope, Hermann von Salza oversaw the expansion of his order into Prussia. He was also a chief figure in the Baltic Crusades. Hermann was a friend and councilor of Emperor Friedrich von Hohenstaufen, whom he represented as a mediator in the Papal Curia from 1222 onwards. Pope Honorius III recognized Hermann's capabilities and granted the Teutonic Knights an equal status with the Knights Hospitaller and with the Knights Templar, after the Teutonic order had gone into decline under previous Grand Masters. This was a major coup for Hermann. His order became important, and in 1291 it defended Acre, where it had been created in 1190, along with the older orders.

Hermann von Salza's visits to the Pope and the Emperor brought new privileges and donations to the Order of the Teutonic Knights. In 1237 he obtained the incorporation of the Livonian Knights into the Teutonic Order. The importance of Hermann's role as mediator between the popes and the emperor can be seen by the fact that all communication between the two broke off with Hermann's death. Yet, within his own Teutonic Order, the knights were unhappy with the absence of their Grand Master, like children with an absent father. They recalled him, and he had to withdraw from political life. Being less successful as a religious leader, he soon retired to Salerno in 1238, where he died in 1239.

After recuperating from his illness, in 1228, the thirty-four-year-old "Holy Roman Emperor" Friedrich of Germany embarked again for Jerusalem, arriving at Acre in September. Pope Gregorius saw this as another provocation, since Friedrich gave the Church no part in the "honor" of the Crusade. Gregorius once more excommunicated Friedrich. By this time the army of the Sixth Crusade had dwindled. Knowing that he could not take Jerusalem by force of arms, Friedrich negotiated with the Ayyubid ruler for peace, along the lines of a previous agreement he had intended to broker with Al-Kamil. The Ayyubid ruler of the region, who feared a possible war with his relatives in Syria and Iraq, wished to avoid trouble from the Christians, at least until his domestic rivals were subdued. The treaty he signed in 1229 resulted in the peaceful restitution of Jerusalem, Nazareth, and Bethlehem to the "Kingdom of Jerusalem," for the first time since 1187, though historians disagree as to the extent of the territory returned. The Sixth Crusade ended in a truce and in Friedrich's coronation by himself as "Latin King of Jerusalem", in the "Holy Sepulcher" of Jerusalem itself, on March 18, 1229.

In 1228 the 16-year-old Queen Isabella of Jerusalem had died. Pope Honorius III and Isabella's father Jean de Brienne used Friedrich's absence to attack Friedrich's territories in southern Italy Friedrich's teen-age wife, Isabella, the true heiress of the throne of Jerusalem from her father Jean de

Brienne, had died, leaving their infant son Corrado (Conrad) as the rightful heir to the kingdom. Friedrich ruled Jerusalem as regent on behalf of his son, Conrad, settling a truce with the "Saracens." *This was the first and last time Jerusalem was taken peacefully by the Crusaders from the Muslims.*

Nor did Jerusalem remain in Christian hands for a long time. In 1244 the "Saracens" once more took Jerusalem from the Crusaders. This time the "Saracens" were the Khwarezmians, recently displaced by the advance of the Mongols from Central Asia westward. They took Jerusalem on their way to ally with the Egyptian Mamluks. They had come from the Khwarezm, a series of states centered on the Amu Darya river delta of the former Aral Sea, in Greater Iran (now in Uzbekistan and Turkmenistan). Soon the Mamluks would be the masters of Jerusalem.

Chapter 16

The Seventh Crusade
The Unhappy War of "Saint Louis"

The Seventh Crusade (1248–1254) followed the recapture of Jerusalem by the "Saracens" of Egypt and was led by King Louis IX of France (1214–1270). This king, who ruled France from the age of twelve until his death at the age of fifty-six, was pious, ascetic, deeply religious, and deeply hostile to the Jews. Indeed, from a Jewish viewpoint, this French king, whom the Christians later canonized and called "Saint Louis," was more a devil than a saint. He actively and cruelly persecuted the Jews. As money lending was one of the few professions allowed the Jews in France, and as high rates of interest were their only insurance against the very high rate of non-repayment of debts by Christians, the Jewish money lenders were considered greedy and usurious. In order to finance his Crusade, Louis ordered the expulsion of all the Jews of France engaged in usury. This action enabled Louis to confiscate the property of the expelled Jews for use in his Crusade (Joinville 1617).

Louis IX did not forgive all the debts incurred by Christians to Jews, however. One-third of the debt was forgiven, but the other two-thirds was remitted to his royal treasury. Louis also ordered the burning of some 12,000 handwritten copies of the Jewish *Talmud* in Paris in 1242, on the pretext that they contained anti-Christian statements. Legislation against the Talmud, which was not uncommon in the history of European Christendom, was due to medieval courts' concerns that its production and circulation might weaken the faith of Christian individuals and threaten the Christian basis of society, whose protection was the duty of any Christian monarch. (Joinville 1617).

In 1248 two Christian envoys from the Mongols, whom the Crusaders named "David and Marc," visited King Louis IX of France in Cyprus seeking an alliance against the Muslim Ayyubids (Joinville 1617). "David and Marc" were two Arabized Eastern Christians. "David" was known by his Arabic name of Saif al-Din Muzaffar Dawoud. "David and Marc" had met three years earlier, in 1245, with André de Longjumeau, a thirteenth-century French Dominican missionary and diplomat, one of the most active diplomats of his time, in the Persian city of Tabriz, during his Papal mission to the Mongols (1245–1247). Louis sent Logjumeau to the Great Khan Güyük, who died that year.

DOI: 10.4324/9781003527367-16

In 1249, the army of the Seventh Crusade under King Louis IX of France, numbering tens of thousands of men, landed in Egypt and took the port city of Damietta from the "Saracens." The Egyptian troops retreated inland. King Louis sent an arrogant letter to the Egyptian sultan, as-Salih Ayyub (1205–1249), threatening him with destruction. The Egyptian Muslim historian Taqi al-Din Ahmad ibn 'Ali ibn 'Abd al-Qadir ibn Muhammad al-Maqrizi (1364–1442) quoted the letter of King Louis to the Egyptian sultan:

> As you know that I am the ruler of the Christian nation. I know you are the ruler of the Muhammadan nation. The people of Andalusia give me money and gifts while we drive them like cattle. We kill their men and we make their women widows. We take the boys and the girls as prisoners and we make houses empty. I have told you enough and I have advised you to the end, so now if you make the strongest oath to me and if you go to Christian priests and monks and if you carry kindles before my eyes as a sign of obeying the cross, all these will not persuade me from reaching you and killing you at your dearest spot on earth. If the land will be mine then it is a gift to me. If the land will be yours and you defeat me then you will have the upper hand. I have told you and I have warned you about my soldiers who obey me. They can fill open fields and mountains, their number like pebbles. They will be sent to you with swords of destruction.
>
> (Al-Maqrizi 1969, p. 436)

The Egyptian Ayyubid sultan, As-Salih Najm al-Din Ayyub, died soon after receiving Louis' letter, without answering it, and power temporarily passed to Sultan as-Salih's son, Turanshah (died 1250), and to Sultan as-Salih's widow, Shajar al-Durr (died 1257), a former concubine in the Abbasid caliph's harem in Baghdad, who took control of Egypt with Mamluk support and launched a counterattack on the invading "Franks."

Fearful of the "Franks," however, the Egyptian sultan's widow did not announce the death of her husband for some time. The news of the death of Sultan as-Salih Ayyub reached the Crusaders in Damietta, however. Encouraged by the news of the death of the Sultan, and by the arrival of "Frankish" reinforcements led by Alphonse de Poitiers, a brother of Louis IX, the French Crusaders decided to march on Cairo. In 1250 a Crusader force led by Louis IX's other brother, Robert d'Artois, crossed the canal of Ashmum (now the Albahr Alsaghir) and attacked the Egyptian camp at Gideila, near Al Mansurah. The Egyptian Emir Fakhr ad-Din ibn al-Shaykh was killed during the sudden attack. The Crusader force advanced toward Al Mansurah, where Robert d'Artois was killed, and the army of Louis IX was annihilated by an Egyptian military force led by the Mamluk leaders, who were about to establish the state that would dominate the entire southern Mediterranean: Izz ad-Din Aybak (died 1257), Saif ad-Din Qutuz (died 1260), Baybars al-Bunduqdari (died 1277), and Qalawun al-Alfi (died 1290).

The year 1250 was a dramatic one in Egypt. Al-Muazzam Turanshah, the son of the dead Sultan as-Salih Ayyub, was enthroned Sultan of Egypt at as-Salhiyah, having no time to go to Cairo, due to his war on the "Franks." Feeling relieved by the arrival of the new Sultan, her son, the dead sultan's widow Shajar al-Durr finally announced the death of her husband, Sultan as-Salih Ayyub. Turanshah went to Al Mansurah to fight the Crusaders. The Egyptian "Saracens" began to turn back the "Franks." An overconfident Louis IX, however, delayed his retreat from Egypt. He had 15,000 to 25,000 men, but the "Saracen" troops of Turanshah, along with those of the Mamluk commanders Baybars, Qutuz, Aybak, and Qalawun, outnumbered and defeated the French troops at Fariskur near Damietta, in the Nile Delta region.

In March 1250 the rigid, arrogant and self-righteous King Louis IX of France finally realized his hopeless position and tried to return to the port of Damietta, but on April 6 he was defeated and taken captive at Fariskur and his army was annihilated. Sultan Turanshah was assassinated at Fariskur by the Mamluks, who felt that he was discriminating against them. King Louis fell ill with dysentery, and was cured by an Arab physician, but the "Saracens" demanded 800,000 gold bezants, or 400,00 French *livres d'or* (more than the entire annual revenue of the Kingdom of France) as his ransom.

The Knights Templar lent Louis IX the money for his ransom, and in May 1250 Louis IX was ransomed for 250,000 *livres d'or* (the remaining 150,000 *livres* of this ransom were never paid). He was set free, and immediately left Egypt for Acre, the capital of the "Latin Kingdom of Jerusalem" and one of the few remaining Crusader possessions in the "Holy Land." Louis spent four years in the "Latin Kingdom of Jerusalem" fortifying Acre, Caesarea, and Jaffa (now in Israel). He helped the Crusaders build their defenses and sent diplomats to the sultans of Syria and Egypt. In 1254 Louis and his few remaining and traumatized troops returned to France. During those four years Louis fortified the Crusader strongholds along the Eastern Mediterranean coast.

Meanwhile, in Egypt, one political assassination followed another. After Turanshah's murder in 1250, political pressure for a male Sultan in Egypt made the widow Shajar al-Durr marry the Mamluk commander, Izz ad-Din Aybak, but he was murdered in his bath in 1257. Shajar al-Durr was beaten to death. In the power struggle that ensued, the vice-regent, Saif ad-Din Qutuz, became Sultan. In 1260 the Mamluks defeated a Mongol army commanded by Kitbuqa at Ain Jalut (now in northern Israel) and forced the Mongols to retreat to what is now Iraq. The defeat of the "invincible" Mongols by the Mamluks enhanced their reputation and their position in the southern Mediterranean basin. Later that year, after the assassination of Qutuz on his way home to Cairo, Baybars, one of the Mamluk leaders at the battle, became Sultan of Egypt. Baybars was the fifth Mamluk sultan in ten years, and he belonged to the Bahri dynasty, named after its *Bahriya* or River Island regiment, which was based in al-Manial Island in the River Nile. This regiment consisted mainly of Kipchak Turks.

After the Mamluks had killed Turanshah, toppled the Ayyubids, and created the Bahri dynasty in Egypt, King Louis of France negotiated both with the Mongols and with the Mamluks, and from his new base in Acre began to rebuild the other Crusader cities in the "Holy Land." Although the Kingdom of Cyprus claimed authority over the "Holy Land," Louis IX was its *de facto* ruler. The myth of Prester John, which was popular in Europe from the twelfth century, told of a Christian patriarch and king said to rule over a Christian nation lost amid the Muslims and "pagans" in the "Orient." The superstitious Louis, who believed in this myth, negotiated with the Mongols, who had begun to appear in the "Orient." The Christians, encouraged by legends of a Nestorian kingdom among them, hoped that the Mongols might help them fight the Muslims and restore the Crusader States. Some Crusaders even believed that the Mongols were the subjects of Prester John.

Tragically, both the Christians and the Muslims, each of which tried to make an alliance with the Mongols against the other, failed to realize that the Mongols were not interested in helping either side, and that they would eventually conquer both. The Mongols were in the midst of the greatest expansion in their history. In 1227 their leader Temüjin Chinggis Khan (died 1227) had been succeeded by his son, Ögödei Khan (1185–1241). In 1241, Ögödei's widow Töregene Khatun became the Regent of the Mongol Empire and ruled the empire until 1246, when her son Güyük Khan (1206–1248) was elected the new Khagan (Great Khan) by all the Mongol khans.

In 1249, in response to the Mongol offer of alliance against the Muslim Ayyubid rulers of Syria, King Louis of France had sent André de Longjumeau to Güyük Khan, who had died and had been succeeded by Möngke Khan (1209–1259). In 1253 he also sent the Flemish Franciscan missionary Willem van Rubroeck, who had accompanied Louis on his Seventh Crusade, to Batu Khan, the Mongol ruler of the Kipchak Khanate (the Golden Horde). Batu Khan rejected Louis' invitation to convert to Christianity, sending the ambassadors to his boss, Möngke Khan. In early 1254 Willem van Rubroeck was given an audience by Möngke Khan. He returned to Tripoli in 1255. Möngke Khan had turned down Louis's offer of conversion and instead suggested that Louis submit to him.

By 1254 Louis' money had run out, and his presence was badly needed in France, where his mother and regent, Blanche de Castille (1188–1252), had died. Louis returned to Paris. The Crusade of "Saint Louis" was a dismal failure and he also badly persecuted the Jews, but was nonetheless considered a saint by many of his subjects, and his fame gave him greater authority in Europe than that of the "Holy Roman Emperor." The history of the Seventh Crusade was written by Matthew Paris (died 1259), a friend of King Louis who also participated in the Crusade, by Jehan de Joinville (1224–1317), and by many Muslim historians. Like Ambroise in the Third

Crusade, Joinville labeled all Muslims *Sarrasins*, the French form of "Saracens," and described them as evil, mean, and murderous. The Europeans Christians saw the "Saracens" (and the Jews) as children of the Devil, and this was expressed in their art, which depicted them as such (Strickland 2005).

Chapter 17

The Eighth Crusade
The Tragic Death of "Saint Louis"

Unable to accept his humiliating defeat in Egypt, Louis IX of France attempted another Crusade. Louis was disturbed by events in Syria, where the Mamluk sultan Baybars had been attacking the remnants of *Outremer*. Baybars had taken advantage of the war between the Italian republics of Venice and Genoa in 1256–1260, which had exhausted the Syrian ports that these cities controlled. By 1265 Baybars had captured Nazareth, Haifa, La Torón (now the monastery of Latrun), and Arsuf (all of them now in Israel).

King Hugues III of Cyprus (died 1284), the nominal "king of Jerusalem", landed in Acre to defend that city, while Baybars marched his army as far north as Armenia, which was at that time under Mongol rule. In 1266 Charles d'Anjou (died 1285) had conquered Sicily from King Manfred von Hohenstaufen (1232–1266) and made himself its King. Louis IX's confessor, Geoffroy de Beaulieu, claimed that Louis IX was convinced that the sultan of *Ifriqiya* was ready to be converted to Christianity (Geoffroy de Beaulieu & Guillaume de Chartres 2014). By now Louis was delusional. This sultan, al-Mustansir, actually declared himself the Caliph of all the Muslims. The thirteenth-century Italian historian Saba Malaspina wrote that the king's brother Charles d'Anjou who was now the king of Sicily had persuaded Louis IX to attack Tunis because he wanted to secure the payment of the tribute that their rulers had paid to the former Sicilian monarchs (Saba Malaspina 1999; Dunbabin 2000).

These events led Louis IX of France to call a new Crusade, although there was little popular support for a Crusade by this time. Jehan de Joinville, the chronicler who accompanied Louis on the Seventh Crusade, refused to go on the Eighth. Louis was convinced by his brother, Charles d'Anjou (1226–1285), to attack Tunis in North Africa, which would give them a strong base for attacking Egypt, the focus of Louis's previous Crusade.

Charles d'Anjou, who was the King of Sicily, had his own interests in this area of the Mediterranean. The Caliph of Tunis, Muhammad al-Mustansir (died 1277), had connections with Christian Spain and was considered a good candidate for conversion to Christianity. Louis landed on the North African coast in the summer of 1270, a bad season for such an invasion. Much of the

DOI: 10.4324/9781003527367-17

army became sick due to poor drinking water, and on August 25 Louis himself died from a "flux in the stomach," a day after the arrival of Charles. According to Joinville, his last word was "Jerusalem." Louis IX himself had caused his own defeat and his own death.

Charles d'Anjou, the dead king's brother, proclaimed Louis's son, Philippe (Philippe III, 1245–1285), the new king of France, but due to Philippe's youth Charles became the Regent and the leader of the Eighth Crusade. Due to further diseases, the siege of Tunis was abandoned on October 30, 1270, by an agreement with the sultan. In this peace treaty, the Christians gained free trade with Tunis, and residence for monks and priests in the city was guaranteed, so the Crusade could be proclaimed a success. Not so for "Saint Louis," whose Crusading zeal had led him to his death.

Chapter 18

The Ninth Crusade
The End of a Two-Century Fantasy

The Ninth Crusade was the weakest of them all, and one of the hardest to explain. In 1271 Charles d'Anjou (1226–1285), who had conquered Sicily and become its king in 1266, as well as being King of Naples, allied himself with Edward Longshanks of England (1239–1307), the duke of Gascony and Prince of Wales. Edward had pledged himself in 1268 to undertake a Crusade, and had arrived in Tunis in 1270 with fewer than 1000 men, including some 225 knights, only to find that King Louis IX of France had died. Charles d'Anjou called off the attack on Tunis, and Edward sailed on to Acre, the last Crusader outpost in "the Holy Land," in an attempt to restore the "Latin Kingdom of Jerusalem".

Edward's military activities in Acre against the Mamluks (1271–1272) are called the Ninth Crusade. A chronicler erroneously named *Le Templier de Tyr* claimed that during Edward's stay there, Sultan Baybars tried to have him assassinated (Crawford 2003). This Crusade was the last Crusade to "the Holy Land." Like its predecessors, the Ninth Crusade failed because the "crusading spirit" was extinct in Europe, and because of the growing military power of the Mamluks in Egypt. It also foreshadowed the imminent collapse of Acre and of the last few remaining Crusader strongholds along the Mediterranean coast.

Prince Edward of England and King Charles d'Anjou of Sicily decided to take their armies to Acre, the capital of the remnant of the "Latin Kingdom of Jerusalem" and the final objective of the military campaign of the Mamluk sultan Baybars. The small armies of Edward and Charles arrived in Acre in 1271, just as Baybars was besieging the city of Tripoli, which, as the last remaining Christian outpost of the County of Tripoli, harbored tens of thousands of Christian refugees. From their bases in Cyprus and Acre, Edward and Charles managed to attack Baybars' interior lines and break the siege of Tripoli. This was the first Crusader victory in many years. The Crusaders had won the battle, but they would lose the war.

When Edward arrived in Acre in 1271, he sent an embassy to the Mongol ruler of Persia, Ilkhan Abaqa (1234–1282), an enemy of Baybars, offering to join him in an alliance against Baybars. The Mongols had sacked Muslim

Baghdad in 1258, and Edward believed that they would ally themselves with the Christians against the Muslims. Edward's embassy to the Mongols was led by Reginald Rossel, Godefroi de Waus, and John of Parker (Grousset 1934, vol. 3, p. 652). Abaqa Khan was busy with other wars in Turkestan. On September 4, 1271, Abaqa Khan sent Edward 10,000 Mongol horsemen, along with some Seljuk Turks, commanded by a Mongol general named Cemakar or Samaghar. Abaqa wrote Edward:

> After talking over the matter, we have on our [own] account resolved to send to your aid Cemakar at the head of a mighty force; thus, when you discuss among yourselves the other plans involving the aforementioned Cemakar be sure to make explicit arrangements as to the exact month and day on which you will engage the enemy.
> (Paviot 2009)

Abaqa Khan, a great-grandson of Chinggis Khan and a son of Hülegü Khan, had not consulted his uncle, the Mongol khagan (chief khan) at that time, Khubilai Khan. Khubilai was a Mongol emperor of China whose temple name was Emperor Shizu of Yuan, and whose regal name was Setsen Khan, and who would become the protagonist of Samuel Taylor Coleridge's poem *Kubla Khan*. The Mongols, along with some Seljuk Turks, ravaged the land from Aleppo to Cairo. The Muslim population fled, remembering the atrocities of the Mongols under Kitbuqa. Baybars mounted a counter-attack and the Mongols retreated east of the Euphrates River.

The arrival in Acre of the forces of King Hugues of Cyprus (died 1284), the nominal king of the "Latin Kingdom of Jerusalem", temporarily emboldened Edward, whose small army raided the "Saracen" town of Qaqun (northwest of what is now the Palestinian town of Tulkarm). Baybars suspected that there would be a combined land-and-sea attack on Egypt by the "Franks." He endeavored to head off such an assault by building a fleet of his own. Having finished the construction of the fleet, rather than attack the Crusader army directly, in 1271 Baybars attempted to land in Cyprus, hoping to draw King Hugues and his fleet out of Acre, with the objective of conquering the island and leaving Edward and the Crusader army isolated in the "Holy Land." However, in the ensuing naval battle the Egyptian fleet was destroyed and Baybars' armies were temporarily forced back.

The Crusader states in *Outremer* and Cyprus were fighting one another. Following his temporary victory over the "Saracens," Prince Edward of England realized that it was necessary to end the internal rivalry within the Christian camp. He at first mediated the conflict between Hugues and the Ibelin knights of Cyprus. Prince Edward of England then began negotiating a truce with Sultan Baybars, even though the latter's spies had assassinated Philippe de Montfort, the Lord of Tyre (died 1270). According to the misnamed "Templar of Tyre" this negotiation almost ended when Baybars sent a spy to assassinate Edward as well (Crawford 2003, Konieczny 2011). Edward and his knights personally killed the assassins and began preparations for a direct attack on Jerusalem. However, in late 1272 news arrived that Edward's father, Henry III (1207–1272), had died in England. Prince Edward signed a peace treaty with Sultan Baybars, allowing Edward to return home and to be crowned King of England. Hugues returned to Cyprus and Charle d'Anjou to Sicily. The Ninth Crusade had ended with none of its goals, above all the recapture of Jerusalem, being realized.

Chapter 19

Trauma in the Crusades

The American historian Dominick LaCapra (born 1939) wrote poignantly:

> Despite notable exceptions (such as Saul Friedländer) [2009] it is astonishing how little historians recognize the significance of individual and collective trauma even when they write of events and processes in which it is prevalent, such as genocides, wars, rape, and various forms of victimization and abuse both of humans and of other animals.
> (LaCapra 2014, pp. ix–x)

Individual and collective trauma were an essential part of the Crusades. Post-traumatic stress disorder was common among the Teutonic Knights (Eickman 2017) and quite possibly among other Crusaders as well. The transgenerational transmission of trauma (Volkan 2001) made the children and grandchildren of traumatized Crusaders and Muslims experience the trauma of their parents and repeat their traumatic experiences in the endless violence of the Crusader wars.

LaCapra's younger colleague Kathleen Biddick (born 1959) thought that medieval European history could not be understood without exploring the trauma of the endless wars, massacres, persecutions, and other violent acts that were part of everyday life in medieval Europe (Biddick 1997, 2014). The Crusades were born out of collective trauma, beginning with the Byzantine defeats by the Seljuk Turks and continuing with the fiery preachings of Pope Urban II and Bernard de Clairvaux in 1095 that incited the Christians to march on the "Holy Land." (Rowan 2023).

The "people's Crusade" of 1096 that preceded the Crusades of the European kings and noblemen can be seen as a collective traumatic reaction to the intolerable living conditions of the masses of poor peasants and other exploited populations in feudal Europe. Unable to rise up against their feudal overlords, who would have killed them had they tried, the "people" unconsciously displaced their rage and vented their murderous fury on the Jews along the River Rhine. The religious fervor that was whipped up by Pope Urban II was a reaction to the trauma of his conflict with Emperor Heinrich

DOI: 10.4324/9781003527367-19

IV. The religious and political frenzy of the French *pastoureaux* who led a Crusade of their own in 1251, during the Seventh Crusade of King Louis IX, was also a reaction to trauma (Dickson 1988).

The Greek word "trauma" originally denoted a physical wound or injury. It was only in modern times that the word was used to denote psychic trauma, an injury to the soul. The British physician, anthropologist, and archaeologist Piers Mitchell studied physical trauma and surgery in the Crusades, in particular in the port city of Caesarea, built by Herod the Great (died 4CE) more than eleven centuries before the First Crusade, as well as the prevalence of violence, war injuries, and torture in the medieval Middle East (Mitchell 2002, 2006, 2013). It is hard to imagine the extreme violence experienced by both the "Franks" and the "Saracens" without the attendant psychic trauma, both individual and collective, produced both by inflicting and by suffering this violence. The First Crusaders who massacred thousands of people in Jerusalem in 1099 heard the terrible screams of their victims and the writhing of their dying bodies. They waded in rivers of blood, and many of them were deeply traumatized by the infernal scene. The few survivors, needless to say, were even more deeply traumatized. Mitchell's findings reinforce the view of the Crusades both as a reaction to collective trauma and as the producers of further trauma, in a seemingly vicious circle.

The Australian medievalist Megan Cassidy-Welch studied the collective medieval European memory of the Crusades. She believed that the theory of collective trauma could be applied to medieval history. Cassidy-Welch thought that "trauma theory can expose [the] links between representation, memory and violence during the period of the Crusades." She chose as an example "one case study of 'collective trauma' – the capture of a relic of the True Cross by the army of 'Saladin' at the battle of Hattin in 1187" (Cassidy-Welch 2017). Cassidy-Welch pointed out that:

> ... the battle of Hattin was particularly brutal and its effects were long-lasting. Yet it was not the battle itself that was recorded by [European] commentators as particularly damaging. Rather, it was the capture during the battle of a piece of the True Cross, one of the holy land's most precious relics, that was recorded by eyewitnesses, later chroniclers, artists and preachers as the most shattering aspect of this event.
>
> (Cassidy-Welch 2017)

Cassidy-Welch thought that the loss in 1187 of what the "Franks" believed to be "the True Cross" was "a moment of significant ontological rupture," or collective trauma, for the European Christians (Cassidy-Welch 2017).

Cassidy-Welch wove together individual and collective psychology, writing that the relationship between individual experience and collective identifications that lay at the heart of Crusading culture can be illuminated by paying attention to contemporaneous theories of cognition, memory, experience and suffering.

She explored

> ... how past peoples tried subjectively and collectively to make sense of devastating experiences and how modern historians of the Middle Ages might usefully integrate trauma theory into historical method.
> (Cassidy Welch 2017)

The American journalist, lawyer and scholar Spencer Ford Rowan, Jr., is the grandson of a native American Choctaw woman whose tribe was forced out of its native land in Mississippi into the Trail of Tears that led to an "Indian" reservation in Oklahoma. The Choctaw were one of five tribes (or nations) to be driven out of their homeland: the others were the Cherokee, the Muskogee, the Chickasaw, and the Seminole (Akers 2004). The survivors were deeply traumatized. Rowan spent a lifetime as a journalist and then as a lawyer before taking up the subject of collective trauma as a scholar.

Rowan wrote his master's thesis about collective trauma in the First Crusade (Rowan 2019). Citing Richard Fidler's characterization of Pope Urban's call for a Crusade as "one of the most incendiary speeches in the history of the world" (Fidler 2017), Rowan focused on large-group psychology and on collective trauma in analyzing the First Crusade. Ignoring the key importance of the Byzantine Emperor's conflict with the Seljuk Turks and his plea to the Pope in 1095 to help him drive away the "Saracens," Rowan focused on the inflammatory speeches of Pope Urban II and the other instigators of the First Crusade to illustrate the power of the "Us and Them" psychology and of collective trauma in producing the Crusades.

Using the terms and theories of the psychoanalyst Vamık Volkan, Rowan believed that the extreme violence of the First Crusade was instigated in part by "exaggerated claims" and "provocative statements" made by political and religious leaders who "tapped into shared memories of traumatic warfare between Muslims, Jews, and Christians." Each group saw its own collective traumatic past and its historical context differently. "The different recollections of wrongdoing by these large, religious [and] ethnic groups were fuel for renewing violence" (Rowan 2019, 2023; Volkan 1997, 2000, 2001, 2004, 2006, 2013, 2014, 2017).

Rowan pointed out that the First Crusade "was launched after exaggerated claims were made [by Church leaders] that Roman Catholics had been persecuted by Muslims in the Holy Land and mistreated by Eastern Orthodox Christians." Using the psychological terms of Vamık Volkan, Rowan wrote,

The vastly different large-group identities made it possible for differing religious traditions to view "the other" as an enemy, even after they had lived peacefully together for many years. The perceived trauma of past encounters became fuel for violence – and a phenomenon that has continued long after the Crusades ended.

(Rowan 2019; Volkan 2000)

Typically, each group tended to see itself as the victim and the others as the perpetrators of violent oppression. Rowan wrote,

> As each of these [religious] traditions evolved, they brought with them stories of oppression and violence, often contained in holy scripture. Jews heard ancient accounts of enslavement and warfare with other tribes. Christians were oppressed for three centuries by Romans and blamed Jews for the killing of Jesus. Muslims quarreled among themselves in Sunni and Shia warfare—and in armed conflict with Christians. The retelling of ancient stories often resulted in what some psychologists describe as the transmission of trauma across generations.

(Rowan 2019; cf. Volkan 2001)

Like Dominick LaCapra, Rowan thought that,

> Psychological insights about trauma can [illuminate] historical accounts of religious violence. A psychological perspective does not refute the findings of historians, but it may help understand how thousands of Christians were persuaded to leave their homes and travel more than a thousand miles to battle with Muslims in the Holy Land. Not only does psychology shed light on past events, it can provide lessons from violent episodes like the Crusades that may help prevent trauma from triggering conflicts in the future.

(Rowan 2019, 2023)

He argued that,

> Psychological insights increase our understanding of how those who feel their ancestors (and themselves) have been victims can themselves become victimizers and oppressors. Lessons from past violence can inform contemporary efforts at peacemaking and interfaith cooperation.

(Rowan 2019)

Dropping his first name of Spencer, Ford Rowan, a co-founder of the International Dialogue Initiative, published his master's thesis in an edited book on large-group identity, societal conflict and collective trauma (Rowan 2023).

The Canadian historian Donna Trembinski compared the medieval terms "melancholy" and "mania" with the modern notion of "trauma." She tried to assess the prevalence of combat trauma in the Middle Ages, suggesting that the modern term of "psychic trauma" could be used to describe the emotional states that appear in pre-modern sources as "melancholy" and "mania." Trembinski based her argument on Guibert de Nogent's account of his nightmares, Jehan Froissart's account of the Hundred Years War (1337–1453), and Francesco Petrarca's grief-laden writing in the wake of the Black Death (1348–1349) (Trembinski 2011).

The collective trauma that precipitated the First Crusade was the Byzantine Empire's loss of territory to the Seljuk Turks. The Byzantine emperor Alexios Komnenos (1048–1118) had requested military support from the Church Council of Piacenza (1095) in the Byzantine empire's conflict with the Turks. Pope Urban II supported the Byzantine request for military assistance and urged faithful Christians to undertake an armed pilgrimage to Jerusalem. This call was met with an enthusiastic popular response across all social classes in western Europe.

During the "people's Crusade," mobs of predominantly poor Christians numbering in the tens of thousands, led by Pierre l'Hermite, the French priest, were the first to respond. The mobs of the "people's Crusade" passed through Germany and began their wide-ranging anti-Jewish activities, including the Rhineland massacres. On leaving Byzantine-controlled territory in Anatolia, another collective trauma hit the Christians, when they were annihilated in a Seljuk Turkish ambush led by Kilij Arslan (1079–1107) at the Battle of Civetot (now the Turkish town of Altınova in the province of Yalova) in October 1096.

Following the riots of the "people's Crusade," the First Crusade was led by members of the French high nobility and their followers, who embarked in late-summer 1096 and arrived at Constantinople between November 1096 and April 1097. This was a large feudal host led by notable Western European princes: southern French forces under Raymond de Toulouse and Adhemar du Puy; men from Upper and Lower Lorraine led by Godefroy de Bouillon and by his brother Baudouin de Boulogne; Italo-Norman forces led by Bohemond de Taranto and his nephew Tancred; as well as various contingents of northern French and Flemish forces under Robert Courteheuse de Normandie, Estienne de Blois, Hugues de Vermandois, and Robert de Flanders. In total and including non-combatants, the forces are estimated to have numbered as many as one hundred thousand.

The rational causes of the Crusades included the Byzantine Empire wanting to regain lost territory from the Seljuk Turks, the Pope wanting to strengthen his own position through a prestigious and "glorious" "holy war," merchants wanting access to Middle East trade, and devoutly religious knights wishing to defend Christianity and its sacred sites. The extensive *irrational* collective fantasies involved in the Crusades, however, were those of the "Holy Land," of the "Holy Roman Empire," of the Latin Kingdom of Jerusalem, of the "Saracens," of the "holy war" to recover the "holy sepulcher," and of the Crusaders themselves as "Franks" and "Latins." These cannot be explained without taking into account the collective traumas of the eleventh century in Europe (Audergon 2004, 2006).

The Frankish (and later German) fantasy of *"translatio imperii"* that was acted out with the coronation in 962 of the "King of the Romans" (in reality the German king) Otto the Great as "Holy Roman Emperor" was the beginning of the collective acting out of psychogeographical fantasies on a hitherto unheard-of scale. Thinking of Germany as a "Holy Roman Empire" was a collective fantasy that would eventually lead to the "holy wars" of the Crusades.

The "Saracen" conquests of Iberia and their wars with the "Franks" during the eighth, ninth, tenth, and eleventh centuries engraved the "Saracen" enemy in the European mind. The Norman conquest of England in 1066 was yet another collective trauma on a massive scale. It not only traumatized the Angles and Saxons, it also changed the way Europeans perceived their continent and their way of life and took away the sense of security they had in their feudal political institutions. The "pagan" Slavic people in Eastern Europe threatened the Roman Catholic Church and its control of the European Christian mind. The "Wendish Crusade" and the other Crusades to force baptize the "pagan" Slavs went on for centuries.

The wars in eleventh-century Europe boggle the mind, and they produced collective traumas on a large scale. There were also religious wars. Take, for instance, the Great Schism of 1054, the splitting of the Roman Catholic Church from the Greek Orthodox Church of Byzantium. A series of ecclesiastical differences, theological disputes, and political power struggles had preceded the formal split. These included theological disputes over how the "Holy Ghost" proceeded from the Father to the Son, whether leavened or unleavened bread should be used in the Eucharist, the Roman Pope's claim to universal jurisdiction over all Christians, and the place of the "Holy See" of Constantinople in relation to the Pentarchy. The latter was the organization of the Christian Church by the Roman Emperor Justinian (482–565) under which the Church was governed by the "patriarchs" of the five chief episcopal sees of the Roman Empire (Rome, Constantinople, Alexandria, Antioch, and Jerusalem), with the "patriarch" of Rome being the *primus inter pares*.

There were great military, social, and political upheavals in eleventh-century Europe. In Germany, the century was marked by the political and military ascendancy of the "Holy Roman Emperors" over the local kings, dukes, counts, barons, and bishops. In Britain, it saw the transformation of Scotland into a single, unified and centralized kingdom, and the Norman conquest of England. The social upheavals in these countries brought them into the orbit of European feudal politics. Needless to say, none of these changes occurred without bloody wars and the attendant collective trauma of the people involved. In fact, trauma was almost part of everyday life.

In France, the military, political, and social upheavals were just as great. The eleventh century saw wars that weakened the monarchy and strengthened the local lords, especially the dukes of Aquitaine and Normandy. These rulers fostered collective fantasies about their lands, such as that of "the pious warrior" Guillaume *le conquerant* who conquered Britain, Italy, and the East, and that of the "impious peace lover," the troubadour, who crafted out of the the spoken French vernacular its first great literary themes. These fantasies created the *chansons de geste*.

The eleventh century saw the birth of scholasticism, which would develop until it gradually came to dominate European education in the twelfth century. Scholasticism was a school of philosophy that employed a critical organic method of philosophical analysis predicated upon the ten Aristotelian Categories. Christian scholasticism emerged within the monastic schools that translated scholastic "Judeo-Islamic" philosophies into Church Latin, and thereby "rediscovered" the collected works of Aristotle. Scholasticism emphasized dialectic arguments in disputes of Christian theology as well as classical philosophy. This was the "intellectualization" of internal conflict. The first scholastic scholars were Archbishop Lafranc of Canterbury (died 1089), Archbishop Anslem of Canterbury (1033–1109), and the French monk Pierre Abélard (died 1142).

In Italy, the eleventh century began with the military integration of the kingdom of Italy into the "Holy Roman Empire." Emperor Heinrich II (973–1024), who had fought three wars against the Poles, was crowned "King of Italy" in the royal Lombard city of Pavia in 1004, where he re-asserted his claim to the throne of Italy in 1014 and again in 1024. In southern Italy, Lombard and Byzantine rule was usurped by the invading Normans and the power of the territorial magnates was replaced by that of the citizens. In northern Italy, a growth of population in urban centers gave rise to an early organized capitalism and more sophisticated, commercialized culture, most notably in Venice.

In Spain, most of which had been conquered by the Muslims, there were endless wars as well. The Christians tried to push the Muslims out of Spain. The century opened with the gradual downfall of the last Muslim caliphs of Córdoba (1009–1031) and ended in the rule of the Almoravids, a "Berber" Muslim dynasty centered in the territory of present-day Morocco. In the 1050s it established an empire that stretched over the western Maghreb and "al-Andalus" and lasted throughout the century until its fall to the Almohads in 1147.

There were three Christian kingdoms in Iberia during the eleventh century: Navarra, Aragon, and León-Castilla. While often fighting among themselves, they occasionally formed an alliance under Navarrese hegemony and saw the temporary success of the *Reconquista* against the Muslim *ta'ifa* kingdoms and principalities that had replaced the fallen caliphate. The *tawa'if* were small, independent Muslim kingdoms in *"al-Andalus"* that emerged after the fall of the Umayyad Caliphate of Córdoba in 1031. They were a recurring feature of *"al-Andalus"* history.

In an oblique reference to a popular film, *Apocalypse Now*, the Danish historian Thomas Kristian Heebøll-Holm called the traumas of war in the eleventh century *Apocalypse Then?* (Heebøll-Holm 2014). He highlighted the traumatic and violent role played by Thomas de Marle (1073–1130), the French *Sire* de Coucy et de Boves, and the owner of the castle of Marle, north of Reims. Thomas de Marle was notorious for his aggressive and brutal war tactics, for his atrocities, and for his bloody revolt against King Louis *le Gros* (Louis VI, 1081–1137), which cost Thomas his life. During most of his adult life Thomas de Marle acted like a traumatized man who had no control over his murderous rage.

Before leaving for "the Holy Land" in 1096, Thomas de Marle married Ide de Hainault, who bore him two daughters. During his first marriage he was away on Crusade for four or five years. Ide died in 1101, having been abandoned by her husband for several years while he was on the Crusade. She died after his return to France, but he did not spend much time mourning his loss of her. In 1102 Thomas de Marle married his second wife, a daughter of Roger de Montaigu and of his wife Ermengarde. This marriage was annulled two years later due to consanguinity. In 1104 Thomas married his third wife, Mélisende de Crécy, who bore him four children and died in 1114.

The majority of the noblemen who led the First Crusade were French. Thomas de Marle and his father Enguerrand de Boves were among them. At first, they joined the army of Count Emicho, who led the murderous attacks on the Jews along the Rhine. Father and son took part in the battles against the "Saracens" on their way to the "Holy Land." In 1099 they were among the besiegers of Jerusalem, and Thomas de Marle was among the first Crusaders who entered the "Holy City." He took part in the bloodbath that followed. Traumatized by this experience, he and his father returned to France with little to show for their pilgrimage.

An obviously troubled man, Thomas de Marle settled in his second wife's hereditary fortress of Montaigu, northeast of Paris, and began raiding, ravaging and devastating the surrounding countryside, including Laon, Amiens, and Reims. Thomas de Marle's atrocities enraged his father, Enguerrand, the Count of Amiens, whose army besieged his son's fortress of Montaigu along with those of several other French noblemen. Thomas de Marle escaped, joined Crown Prince Louis *le gros*, and with his aid was able to lift the siege. He lost the fortress of Montaigu, however, after his marriage to its heiress was annulled in 1104. In 1108 Louis *le gros* succeeded his father Philippe as King Louis VI of France.

In 1113 the people of Amiens formed a commune and asked Thomas de Marle to help them fight Adam, the castellan who guarded the castle and tower of Chastillon for Thomas's father Enguerrand, the Count of Amiens.

Instead, Thomas made peace with his father and fought against the people of Amiens. In late 1114 a church synod excommunicated Gautier, the archdeacon of Laon and the half-brother of Sibylle de Chasteau-Porcien (died 1116), the adulterous wife of Thomas's father Enguerrand, whose marriage Gautier had sanctioned.

Thomas de Marle continued to commit atrocities. His stepmother Sibylle, in whom Thomas confided his warlike plans, betrayed Thomas by warning the Picard prelate and future patriarch of Jerusalem, Guermond de Picquigny (died 1128), of his designs. Guermond set up an ambush for Thomas, wounding him gravely. Thomas escaped to his castle of Marle. Exploiting Thomas de Marle's weakness, Guermond de Picquigny attacked the castle commanded by Adam for Enguerrand, winning the support of King Louis *le gros*, who sent him reinforcements, and entering Amiens in 1115.

Thomas slowly recovered in his castle of Marle, planning revenge against Sibylle and executed her half-brother Gautier. Thomas continued his barbaric acts, and King Louis *le gros* punished him by taking away his castles of Crécy and of Nouvion and by destroying the forts built by Thomas on the lands belonging to the abbey of Saint-Jean de Laon. The king's army besieged the tower of Chastillon, and, after two years of siege, razed it to the ground. Thomas was able to buy his peace with the king by paying him a huge sum of money and by promising to repair all the damages he had done to the Church.

In 1116 Thomas's father Enguerrand, the Count of Amiens, died, as did his wife Sibylle. In 1117 King Louis VI took the county of Amiens away from its lawful heir, Thomas de Marle, and gave it to Adélaïde de Vermandois (c. 1065–1124), who gave it as a dowry to her daughter, Marguerite de Clermont, the wife of Charles of Flanders, who thus became the Count of Amiens. Thomas de Marle was beside himself with rage. He allied himself with Baudouin, the count of Hainaut, and with Hugues, the count of Saint-Pol, against the king. In 1130 Thomas killed Henri de Vermandois, a son of Adèle de Vermandois. King Louis *le gros* ordered a siege of Coucy, and later that year Thomas was mortally wounded by Raoul de Vermandois, an older brother of Henri de Vermandois, whom Thomas had killed. He died soon thereafter (Heebøll-Holm 2014).

The American historian Patrick Eickman studied traumatic reactions among the Teutonic Knights, one of the key groups that fought both in "the Holy Land" and in the Baltic countries, where they tried to force-Christianize the "heathen" Letts and Latvians (Eickman 2017). Eickman pointed out that most historians ignored the emotional aspects of medieval warfare, describing the Teutonic Knights either as heroic ascetics who lived by a strict military and religious code, or as war criminals who committed atrocities during their Baltic Crusades.

Eickman cited the studies Heebøll-Holm, who had shown that many of the survivors of the brutal and bloody First Crusade suffered from post-traumatic stress disorder (Heebøll-Holm 2014). Eickman cited the fourteenth-century chronicle of Nicolaus von Jeroschin (died 1341), a chaplain of the Grand Masters of the Teutonic Knights (Nicolaus von Jeroschin 1331–1341, 2010). Eickman focused on the thirteenth-century Prussian uprisings which were "the centerpiece of the chronicle's narrative." Eickman thought that the miracles, visions, and apparitions of the Virgin Mary reported by Nicolaus of Jeroschin as prevalent among the Teutonic Knights were symptoms of PTSD and "helped to treat the knights' mental wounds" (Eickman 2017, p. 52).

The British historian Kathryn Hurlock introduced the concept of "moral injury," defined as "the psychological impact [on a person] of having one's moral expectations and beliefs violated" (Shay 2014). "Moral injury" is not identical with psychic trauma, nor with the psychiatric diagnosis of post-traumatic stress disorder, but it occurs in the context of military combat and warfare. Hurlock thought that in addition to "combat trauma" the notion of "moral injury" was a useful way of looking into medieval history. Hurlock called moral injury

> ... a condition influenced by cultural and moral expectation, rather than a diagnosis with specific criteria [...] which changes depending on the moral expectations of individuals or their societies, and thus offers a useful critical framework for studying 'combat trauma' in historical conflict.

As she put it,

> There is no doubt that many participants in medieval conflict suffered psychological consequences of the violence they saw, endured, or carried out, and that this fact was widely recognised by writers throughout the Middle Ages.
>
> (Hurlock 2022, p. 145)

Hurlock thought that the study of combat trauma had received little attention from medieval historians, who used the term "psychological impact" very loosely. Recent works had examined trauma in the First Crusade (Rowan 2019) and the mental impact of military service during the Hundred Years War (1337–1453), but Hurlock complained that existing studies did not engage with psychological theory in depth, and tended to cherry-pick diagnostic criteria. She thought that part of the reason for the comparative lack of study in this field was the primary sources, as medieval writers tended to glorify war and rarely reflected on the impact of trauma. The literary genre in which many [of them] wrote (the *chanson de geste*) meant they lacked the necessary vocabulary to express their [traumatic] experiences (Hurlock 2022, pp. 123–124).

Hurlock argued that

> combat trauma, the psychological impact of conflict, did exist in the Middle Ages, but that current approaches to its study, and in particular the desire to define psychological experiences using the diagnosis of Post-Traumatic Stress Disorder (PTSD) have constrained our ability to recognize and understand this aspect of the medieval experience.
>
> (Hurlock 2022)

Hurlock thought that "historians of the Middle Ages [...] should move away from the emphasis on historical PTSD and instead read historical sources in light of the psychological theory of moral injury."

We can see from all of the above studies the vital importance of individual and collective trauma to our understanding of the Crusades. Whether or not Jesus was as he is described in the gospels and whether he was really buried in the "Holy Sepulcher" in Jerusalem was immaterial. The First Crusade was a religious war initiated by the Roman Catholic Church with the objective of recovering the "Holy Sepulcher" from "Saracen" rule. The cost in lost lives and in traumatized people was not a consideration. The medieval awareness of the crucial emotional side of life was very limited, as we can see from the chronicles of the Crusades. All the Crusades that followed either had the same objective or were attempts to force Christianized "pagan" people. The quest for lands to rule as kings and princes was a secondary, if powerful, motive for the leaders of the Crusades.

The prevalence of psychic trauma and of moral injury among the Crusaders highlights the vicious circle of the collective traumas they both inflicted and suffered. The Crusades can be seen as a series of reactions to collective trauma that lasted two centuries and which in their turn inflicted additional collective trauma upon the Christians of Europe, upon the Byzantines, upon the Muslims of the Middle East, and upon the Crusaders themselves. Dominick La Capra's dictum that writing history is writing trauma finds a very clear expression in the Crusades.

Chapter 20

Aftermath
The End of a Two-Century Fantasy

After the Ninth Crusade (1271–1272), the Mamluks, who ruled in Egypt, repeatedly tried to take Acre from the "Franks." It took them another twenty years. Edward of England had been accompanied on his Crusade by Theobaldo Cardinal Visconti (1210–1276), who in 1271 became Pope Gregorius X. At the Church Council of Lyon in 1274, Gregory called for a new Crusade, but nothing came of this. Europe's "Crusading spirit" had died. New fissures arose within the Christian states of *Outremer* when Charles d'Anjou took advantage of a dispute between Hugues of Cyprus (the "Latin King of Jerusalem"), the Knights Templar, and Venice in order to bring the remaining Christian states under his control. Having bought Princess Mary of Antioch's claims to the "Latin Kingdom of Jerusalem", Charles attacked Hugues, causing a civil war within the rump kingdom. In 1277 Hugo of San Severino captured Acre for Charles d'Anjou. In that year Sultan Baybars of Egypt died, as did Sultan Muhammad al-Mustansir of *Ifriqiya*, who claimed to be the *khalifa* of all the Muslims. Al-Mustansir had been a vassal of the King of Sicily, but had shaken off this yoke after King Manfred of Sicily was overthrown by Charles d'Anjou in 1266.

Although the civil war within the Crusader ranks had weakened them badly, it also gave the opportunity for a single commander to take control of the Crusade. That commander was Charles d'Anjou, King of Sicily. However, this new Crusader hope too was dashed when the *Doge* of Venice again suggested that a Crusade be called not against the "Saracens" but against the Byzantine "Greeks" of Constantinople, where in 1261 the Byzantine Emperor Michaelis Palaeologos (1224–1282) had taken Constantinople from the "Latins" and ended the "Latin Empire of Constantinople," which had existed since the Crusader conquest of Constantinople in 1204.

Michaelis Palaeologos re-established the Byzantine Greek Empire, and drove out the Venetians as well. Pope Gregory X would not have supported an attack by Western Christians on Eastern Christians, but in 1281 his successor Pope Martin IV (died 1285) did so. This led in 1282 to the twenty-year-long "War of the Sicilian Vespers" (1282–1302). The war began as a popular Sicilian uprising against the foreign King Charles d'Anjou, who had conquered Sicily in 1266. The war was instigated by Emperor Michaelis Palaeologos of Byzantium. Charles d'Anjou was driven from Sicily, and the French and Norman population of Sicily was massacred. Charles d'Anjou died in 1285 in Italy and was buried in Naples. His heart was cut out, taken to France and placed in the *Couvent Saint-Jacques* in Paris.

In 1285 King Henri of Cyprus (1270–1324) captured Acre from the Angevins and in 1286 Henri was crowned "Latin King of Jerusalem," even though Jerusalem had not been part of this "kingdom" since 1187. Henri returned to Cyprus, appointing Philippe of Ibelin as Bailiff in his absence. By 1289 the Mamluks had captured the coastal cities north of Tyre, Beirut, and Tripoli, preparing to besiege. The Ninth Crusade was the last Christian expedition launched either against the Byzantines in Europe or the "Saracens" in the "Holy Land." During the last nine years of the "Latin Kingdom of Jerusalem" (1282–1291) the Mamluks demanded ever increasing tribute from the "Franks," who were mainly in Acre, and also persecuted the Christian pilgrims to Jerusalem, breaking their truce with King Edward of England.

In 1289 the Mamluk sultan Qalawun al-Alfi of Egypt gathered a large army and attacked the remnants of the Christian County of Tripoli, laying siege to the capital of Tripoli, and finally taking it after a bloody assault. Their attack on Tripoli was terrible for the Mamluks themselves as well, however, as the desperate and frenzied Christian resistance to the siege reached fanatical proportions. Qalawun lost his eldest and ablest son in the Tripoli campaign. Qalawun died in 1290, but in 1291 the Mamluks under his son Al-Ashraf Khalil (1262–1293) finally took Acre from the Crusades.

Following the fall of Tripoli to the Mamluks in 1289, the French king Henri of Cyprus (1270–1324), had sent his seneschal Jehan de Grailly (died 1303) to Europe to warn the European monarchs about the critical situation in the "Levant." In Rome, Jean de Grailly met Pope Nicolaus IV (Girolamo Masci, 1227–1291) who promptly wrote to all the European princes urging them to do something about the "Holy Land." Most of them, however, were too preoccupied by the "War of the Sicilian Vespers" to organize a Crusade, and King Edward of England was busy handling his own troubles at home. Only a small army of Italian peasants and unemployed Italians from Tuscany and Lombardy could be raised. They sailed in 1290. The Italians were transported in 20 Venetian galleys, led by Nicolò Tiepolo, the son of Lorenzi Tiepolo, the *Doge* of Venice, and assisted by Jean de Grailly. As they sailed eastward, the fleet was joined by five Spanish galleys sent by the Catalan king Jaume of Aragon (1267–1327), who was also the King of Sicily from 1285 to 1295, and who wished to help despite his conflict with the Pope and Venice.

The fall of Acre was tragic and bloody. It was also the end of the "Latin Kingdom of Jerusalem", and it was preceded by a tragic massacre of Muslims by Christians. The inexperienced and poorly controlled peasants from Italy had killed Muslim merchants and peasants in and around Acre without the permission of Acre's rulers. These killings gave the Mamluk Sultan Qalawun a pretext to attack Acre. Although a ten-year truce had been signed between the Mamluks and the Crusaders in 1289, Qalawun declared the truce null and void following the killings of the Muslims. Qalawun first asked the Crusaders that the men guilty of the massacre be handed over to him so that he could apply justice to them.

Guillaume de Beaujeu, the Grand Master of the Knights Templar who died in the fighting with the Mamluks, proposed handing over to Qalawun the Christian criminals from Acre's jails, but the Council of Acre refused to hand over anybody to Qalawun, and instead tried to argue that the Muslims had died through their own fault. At one point during the siege, Guillaume de Beaujeu dramatically dropped his sword and walked away from the walls. When his Knights Templar remonstrated with him, Beaujeu reportedly replied, *Je ne m'enfuis pas; je suis mort. Voici le coup* (I am not running away; I am dead. Here is the blow). He then raised his arm to show the mortal wound he had received from the Muslim archers (Barber 2001; Crawford 2003).

After the Council of Acre refused to hand over the culprits for the massacre of the "Saracens," Sultan Qalawun ordered a general mobilization of the Mamluk armies of Egypt. Though he died in late 1290, he was at once succeeded by his son Al-Ashraf Khalil, who led the forces attacking Acre. The island of Cyprus at that time was the base of operations for the three major Crusader military orders: the Knights Templar, the Teutonic Knights, and the Knights Hospitaller. These orders sent their knights to Acre, which was well fortified, and now had these three groups of defenders.

The population of Acre at the time was some 40,000 souls, its troops numbering around 15,000, and an additional 2,000 troops coming on May 6, 1291, with King Henri from Cyprus. There are no reliable figures for the Mamluk army besieging Acre, though it was certainly much larger than the Crusader one, with most of the force being volunteer siege workers. The siege itself lasted six weeks, beginning on April 6 and ending with the fall of the city on May 18. The Grand Master of the Knights Hospitaller, Guillaume de Villaret (died 1305), and the *maréchal des Hospitaliers,* Mathieu de Clermont (who died at Acre), were among the last defenders of Acre. The Knights Templar, however, held out in their fortified headquarters in Acre until May 28.

After the Mamluks took Acre, they utterly destroyed it, so as to prevent the "Franks" from ever taking it again and reestablishing their "kingdom of Jerusalem." Within months, the remaining Crusader cities in "the Holy Land" fell easily, including Sidon (July 14, 1291), Haifa (July 30), Beirut (July 31), Tartus (August 3), and Atlit (August 14). The small Mediterranean island of Arados off the Syrian coast held out until 1302 or 1303. For the European Christians, this was the tragic end of the fantasy of the "Kingdom of

Jerusalem," which had been a fascinating combination of psychohistorical and psychogeographical fantasies from its very outset.

The "Baltic Crusades," however, continued well into the fifteenth or even sixteenth century. Paying no heed to Roger Bacon, the thirteenth-century *Doctor Mirabilis*, the Franciscan monk who wrote that religion can only be acquired by preaching, not imposed by war, the European Christians continued to try to impose their religion on the "heathen Saracens" of the Baltic region by the sword. Those who are unsure of their own faith try to force others to believe as they do. Those who are strong and calm in their faith let others believe as they wish.

Epilogue
"The New Crusaders"

The memory of the Crusades among the groups whose ancestors took part in them is a fascinating subject (Paul & Yeager 2012). The term "new Crusaders" has been used in a variety of political and other contexts (Siberry 2016, Koch 2017, Den Uyl 2020). Arab politicians and scholars have compared the Crusader "Latin Kingdom of Jerusalem" with Israel, calling the Zionists "the new Crusaders" (Ochsenwald 1976). The tragic Arab-Israeli conflict began in the nineteenth century, led to the creation of Israel in 1948, and has continued with great fury into the twenty-first century (Falk 2004). It culminated with the *Hamas* massacre of 1,200 Israelis and its atrocities on October 7, 2023, with the taking of 250 others hostage, and with the tragic war in Gaza that has killed tens of thousands of people.

Following their own chroniclers of the Crusades, the Arabs have come to regard the Israeli Jews as "the new Crusaders." This was formally expressed by the Egyptian Arab diplomat and politician Abdulrahman Hassan al-Azzam (1893–1976), also known as Azzam Pasha, the first secretary-general of the Arab League, which was founded in Cairo in 1945, and which Azzam led until 1952. In 1947 Azzam Pasha met in Cairo with Abba Eban (1915–2002) and with David Horowitz (1899–1979), the representatives of the Jewish Agency for Palestine, who had come to seek an accommodation between the Palestinian Jews and the Arabs. Azzam Pasha told them that the Jews of Palestine were "not a fact" but only "a temporary phenomenon," like the medieval Crusaders. Just as they had driven out the Crusaders, said Azzam, even if it took two centuries, the Arabs would drive the Jews away from Palestine. Azzam Pasha told Eban and Horowitz that:

> Were a war to take place with the proposed establishment of a Jewish state, it would lead to a war of extermination and [a] momentous massacre which will be spoken of like the Mongolian massacre [of the thirteenth century] and the Crusades.
>
> (Horowitz 1953; Barnett & Karsh 2011)

It is dangerous to see the present with the eyes of the past. History does not repeat itself. Historical events may seem similar while being very different. Living at a time of colonial expansion by the great powers, the early political Zionists called their Jewish settlement in Palestine *yishuv* (colonization) and their early settlements *moshavot* (colonies). This made the Arabs think of them as imperialist colonizers and compare them to the medieval Crusaders.

The Muslims had not accepted the Crusaders, and had driven them away from Palestine after two centuries of warfare. Many Arabs still think of Israel as a colonial European outpost, like the "Latin Kingdom of Jerusalem", that will not last any longer than did that kingdom. In view of Israel's military might and of the determination of its people to stay put, however, and of the Israeli Jews having no other "homeland" to go back to, this is a collective denial of reality by the Arabs, which, not accidentally, is also shared by the Iranian ayatollahs and mullahs, whose supreme leader and president openly declare their intention of destroying Israel. Israel is powerful militarily, however, and, "according to foreign sources" it also has nuclear weapons, which Israel's leaders intend to use if they are ever convinced that Israel's very existence is at stake. The Arab leaders knew this, yet for many decades they denied this reality and continued to think of the Israelis as "the new Crusaders." After the "Abraham Accords" several Arab countries are at peace with Israel, but fanatical Islamic groups like *Hamas, Hizballah,* and *Islamic Jihad* still think this way.

Large groups have their "chosen glory." The Arabs and Muslims have lived in their "glorious" medieval past for a long time, just as the Jews lived in their own "glorious" ancient past for fifteen centuries, after their loss of their sovereignty, country, holy city, and temple in 70 CE (Yerushalmi 1982, Falk 1996). To live in the present, and in reality, one must first mourn one's losses, come to terms with them, and give them up. The failure of the medieval Crusaders to mourn their losses cost them countless lives and untold tragedy. If the Israeli Jews and the Palestinian Arabs can mourn their own losses, perhaps the latter will no longer confuse the former with the Crusaders, nor will the fanatical Israeli Jews confuse the Arabs with their past enemies, like Amalek or the German Nazis. Then, perhaps, peace can be achieved between these two hostile groups which have been locked in an intractable conflict for so long.

Bibliography

Abels, Richard P. & Bachrach, Bernard S. (Eds.). (2001). *The Normans and Their Adversaries at War*. Woodbridge, UK and Rochester, NY: Boydell Press.
Académie des inscriptions et belles-lettres (1841). *Recueil des historiens des croisades*. Fifteen volumes. Paris: Académie des inscriptions et belles-lettres. Abridged edition (1967) Farnborough, UK: Gregg Press. [French].
Akers, Donna L. (2004). *Living in the Land of Death: The Choctaw Nation, 1830–1860*. East Lansing, MI: Michigan State University Press.
Al-Isfahani, Imad ad-din (1972). *La Conquête de la Syrie et de la Palestine par Saladin ... Documents relatifs à l'histoire des Croisades publiés par l'Académie des Inscriptions et Belles-Lettres*. Tr. Henri Massé. Paris, FR: Paul Guethner. [French].
Al-Maqrizi, Taqi al-Din Ahmad ibn 'Ali ibn 'Abd al-Qadir ibn Muhammad (1969). The Road to Knowledge of the Return of Kings. In Bohn, Henry George (Ed.) *Chronicles of the Crusades*. New York, NY: AMS Press.
Alfonsi, Petrus (2006). *Dialogue against the Jews*. Tr. Irven M. Resnick. Washington, DC: Catholic University of America Press.
Alighieri, Dante (1996). *Dante Alighieri's Divine Comedy. Vol. 1. Inferno*. Ed. & Tr. Mark Musa. Bloomington and Indianapolis, IN: Indiana University Press.
Ambroise (1897). *L'Estoire de la Guerre sainte: histoire en vers de la troisième croisade (1190–1192). par Ambroise; publiée et traduite d'après le manuscrit unique du Vatican [c. 1195] et accompagnée d'une introduction, d'un glossaire et d'une table des noms propres par Gaston Paris*. Paris, FR: Imprimerie Nationale.
Ambroise (1941). *The "Crusade" of Richard Lion-Heart*. Tr. Merton Jerome Hubert. New York, NY: Columbia University Press.
Ambroise (2003). *The History of the Holy War*. Tr. Marianne Ailes. New York, NY: Boydell Press.
Ammianus Marcellinus (1911). *The Roman History of Ammianus Marcellinus*. Tr. C. D. Yonge. London, UK: G. Bell & Sons.
Andrea, Alfred J. (1987). Conrad von Krosigk, Bishop of Halberstadt, Crusader, and Monk of Sittichenbach: His Ecclesiastical Career, 1184–1225. *Analecta Cisterciensia*, vol. 43, pp. 11–91.
Andrea, Alfred J. (Ed.) (2000). *Contemporary Sources for the Fourth Crusade*. Leiden, NL and Boston, MA: Brill.
Angold, Michael (2003). *The Fourth "Crusade": Event and Context*. Harlow, NY: Longman.

Audergon, Arlene (2004). *The War Hotel: Psychological Dynamics in Violent Conflict.* New York, NY: Wiley.
Audergon, Arlene (2006). Collective Trauma: The Nightmare of History? *Psychotherapy and Politics International*, vol. 2, no. 1, pp. 16–31.
Bachrach, Bernard S. (Ed.) (1971). *The Medieval Church: Success or Failure?* New York, NY: Holt, Rinehart and Winston.
Bachrach, Bernard S. (2002). *Warfare and Military Organization in Pre-"Crusade" Europe.* Aldershot, UK and Burlington, VT: Ashgate Publishing Company.
Bacon, Roger (1877–1900). *The Opus Majus of Roger Bacon.* Three volumes. Ed. John Henry Bridges. Oxford, the Clarendon Press and London, Williams & Norgate [Latin].
Ball, Eve (1970). *In the Days of Victorio: Recollections of a Warm Springs Apache.* Tucson, AZ: University of Arizona Press.
Ball, Eve *et al.* (1980). *Indeh: An Apache Odyssey.* Provo, UT: Brigham Young University Press. New edition (1988). Oklahoma City, OK: University of Oklahoma Press.
Barber, Malcolm (1994). *The New Knighthood: A History of the Order of the Temple.* Cambridge, UK and New York, NY: Cambridge University Press.
Barber, Malcolm (2001). *The Trial of the Templars.* Second edition. Cambridge, UK and New York: Cambridge University Press.
Barber, Malcolm *et al.* (Eds.) (1996–2021). Crusades Texts in Translation. Farnham, UK: Ashgate. Burlington, VT: University of Vermont Press. London, UK: Routledge.
Barnett, David & Karsh, Efraim (2011). Azzam's Genocidal Threat. *Middle East Quarterly*, vol. 18, no. 4, pp. 85–88.
Bartlett, W. B. (2000). *An Ungodly War: The Sack of Constantinople and the Fourth Crusade.* Stroud, UK: Sutton Publishing.
Baudric de Dol (Baldric of Bourgueil) (2014). Steven Biddlecombe (Ed.), *Historia Ierosolimitana.* Woodbridge, UK: Boydell & Brewer.
Bédier, Joseph (Ed. & Tr.) (1988). *La Chanson de Roland. Publié et traduit d'après le manuscrit d'Oxford.* Paris, FR: Union générale d'éditions. [French].
Biddick, Kathleen (1997). *The Shock of Medievalism.* Durham, NC: Duke University Press.
Biddick, Kathleen (2014). Trauma. In Elizabeth Emery & Richard Utz (Eds.), *Medievalism: Key Critical Terms*, pp. 247–254. Cambridge, UK: D. S. Brewer.
Biran, Michal (2016). The Islamization of Hülegü: Imaginary Conversion in the Ilkhanate. *Journal of the Royal Asiatic Society*, vol. 26, no. 1, pp. 1–10.
Bizumic, Boris (2018). *Ethnocentrism: Integrated Perspectives.* Abingdon, UK: Routledge.
Bohn, Henry George (Ed.) (1848). *Chronicles of the Crusades, Being Contemporary Narratives of the "Crusade" of Richard Coeur de Lion / by Richard of Devizes and Geoffrey de Vinsauf; and of the "Crusade" of St. Louis, by Lord John de Joinville.* London, UK: Henry George Bohn. New edition (1892) London, UK and New York, NY: G. Bell & Sons. Reprinted (1969). New York, NY: AMS Press.
Boia, Lucian (2001). *History and Myth in Romanian Consciousness.* Budapest, HU and New York, NY: Central European University Press.

Bossong, Georg. (2002). Der Name Al-Andalus: Neue Überlegungen zu einem alten Problem. In David Restle and Dietmar Zaefferer (Eds.), *Sounds and Systems: Studies in Structure and Change*, pp. 149–164. Berlin, DE and New York, NY: Mouton de Gruyter. [German].

Bradford, Alfred S. (2001). *With Arrow, Sword, and Spear: A History of Warfare in the Ancient World*. Westport, CT: Praeger.

Brand, Charles M. (1968). *Byzantium Confronts the West, 1180–1204*. Cambridge, MA: Harvard University Press.

Braudel, Fernand (1989–1990). *The Identity of France*. Two volumes. Tr. Siân Reynolds. London, UK: Fontana Press.

Brett, Michael & Fentress, Elizabeth W. B. (1996). *The Berbers*. Oxford, UK and Cambridge, MA: Basil Blackwell.

Bridges, John Henry(Ed.) (1877–1900). *The Opus Majus of Roger Bacon*. Three volumes. Oxford, UK: PNU. Reprinted (1964). Frankfurt, DE: PNU. [Latin].

Brundage, James A. (Ed. & Tr.) (1962). *The Crusades: A Documentary Survey*. Milwaukee, WI: Marquette University Press. [Latin and English].

Burchard von Ursberg (1916). *Die Chronik des Propstes Burchard von Ursberg*. Oswald Holder-Egger & Bernhard von Simson (Eds.). Hannover, DE: Hahn. [Latin and German].

Callahan, Tim (2014). Did Jesus Exist? What the Evidence Reveals. *Skeptic Magazine*, vol. 19, no. 1, pp. 10 ff.

Canter, David (2006). The Samson Syndrome: Is There a Kamikaze Psychology? *Twenty-First Century Society*, vol. 1, no. 2, pp. 107–127.

Caruth, Cathy (1996). *Unclaimed Experience: Trauma, Narrative and History*. Baltimore, MD: Johns Hopkins University Press.

Cassidy-Welch, Megan (2017). Before Trauma: The Crusades, Medieval Memory and Violence. *Journal of Media & Cultural Studies*, vol. 31, no. 5, pp. 619–627.

Charny, Israel W. (Ed.). (1999). *Encyclopedia of Genocide*. Forewords by Desmond M. Tutu and Simon Wiesenthal. Santa Barbara, CA: ABC-CLIO.

Claudius Claudianus (1979). *De bello gothico. Critical Edition*. Giovanni Garuti (Ed.). Bologna, IT: Pàtron Editore. [Latin & Italian].

Cobb, Paul M. (2005). *Usama ibn Munqidh: Warrior-Poet in the Age of Crusades*. Oxford, UK: Oneworld.

Cohen, Chapman (1936). *Did Jesus Christ Exist?*London: Pioneer Press.

Cole, Juan Ricardo (2002). *Sacred Space and Holy War: The Politics, Culture and History of Shi'ite Islam*. London, UK: I. B. Tauris.

Comfort, William Wistar (1940). The Literary Role of the Saracens in the French Epic. *PMLA*, vol. 55, no. 3, pp. 628–659.

Comnena, Anna (2003). *The Alexiad of the Princess Anna Comnena: Being the History of the Reign of her Father, Alexius I, Emperor of the Romans, 1081-1118 A.D.* Tr. Elizabeth A.S. Dawes. New York, NY: Kegan Paul.

Crawford, Paul (Ed.) (2003). *The "Templar of Tyre": Part III of the "Deeds of the Cypriots."* Aldershot, UK and Burlington, VT: Ashgate Publishing Co. New edition (2016). London, UK: Routledge.

David, Charles Wendell (Ed. & Tr.) (2000). *De expugnatione Lyxbonensi*. [On the conquest of Lisbon]. With a foreword and bibliography by Jonathan Philipps. New York, NY: Columbia University Press. [English & Latin].
Dawkins, Clinton Richard (2006). *The God Delusion*. Boston, MA: Houghton Mifflin Co.
De Mente, Boyé Lafayette (2003). Ichiban To Biri: Feeling Superior and Inferior. In Boyé Lafayette De Mente, *Japanese Etiquette & Ethics in Business*. New edition. Lincolnwood, IL: Contemporary Publishing Company.
De Mente, Boye Lafayette (2005). *Japan Unmasked: The Character and Culture of the Japanese*. Tokyo, Japan and Rutland, VT: Tuttle Publishing.
Den Uyl, Douglas (2020). *The New Crusaders*. London, UK and New York, NY: Routledge.
Dickson, Gary (1988). The Advent of the *Pastores* (1251)." *Revue belge de Philologie et d'Histoire*, vol. 66, no. 2, pp. 249–267.
Donovan, Joseph P. (1950). *Pelagius and the Fifth Crusade*. Philadelphia, PA: University of Pennsylvania Press.
Duby, Georges (1984). *Guillaume le Maréchal, ou, Le meilleur chevalier du monde*. Paris, FR: Fayard.
Duby, Georges (1985). *William Marshal: The Flower of Chivalry*. Tr. Richard Howard. New York, NY: Pantheon Books.
Dunbabin, Jean (2000). Die Chronik des Saba Malaspina. *The English Historical Review*, vol. 115, no. 462, pp. 693 ff.
Edbury, Peter W. (1996) *The Conquest of Jerusalem and the Third "Crusade": Sources in Translation*. Aldershot, UK and Brookfield, VT: Ashgate Publishing Company.
Edbury, Peter W. (2015). Ernoul, Eracles and the Beginnings of Frankish Rule in Cyprus, 1191–1232. In Sabine Rogge & Michael Grünbart (Eds.) *Medieval Cyprus: A Place of Cultural Encounter*. Munster, DE: Waxmann, pp. 29–52.
Edbury, Peter W. (2016). New Perspectives on the Old French Continuations of William of Tyre. *Crusades*, vol. 9, pp. 119–126.
Edbury, Peter W. (2017). Ernoul, Eracles and the Fifth Crusade. In E. J. Mylod *et al.* (Eds.). *The Fifth Crusade in Context: The Crusading Movement in the Early Thirteenth Century*. London, UK: Routledge, pp. 163–199.
Ehrman, Bart D. (2012). *Did Jesus Exist? The Historical Argument for Jesus of Nazareth*. New York, NY: HarperOne.
Eickman, Patrick (2017). Miracles, Visions, and St. Barbara's Head: Teutonic Knights and PTSD. *Medieval Warfare*, vol. 7, no. 4, pp. 52–55.
Einhard (1998). *Charlemagne's Courtier: The Complete Einhard*. Ed. & Tr. Paul Edward Dutton. Peterborough, Ontario: Broadview Press.
Eliade, Mircea (1987). *The Sacred and the Profane: The Nature of Religion*. Tr. William R. Trask. New York, NY: Harcourt Brace Jovanovich.
Ellenblum, Ronnie (1998). *Frankish Rural Settlement in the Latin Kingdom of Jerusalem*. Cambridge, UK and New York, NY: Cambridge University Press.
Ellenblum, Ronnie (2007). *Crusader Castles and Modern Histories*. Cambridge, UK and New York, NY: Cambridge University Press.
Epstein, Isidore (Ed.) (1935–1948). *The Babylonian Talmud: Translated into English with Notes, Glossary, and Indices under the Editorship of I. Epstein*. London, UK: Soncino Press.
Ernoul (1973). *The Chronicle of Ernoul and the Continuations of William of Tyre*. Margaret Ruth Morgan (Ed.). Oxford, UK and New York, NY: Oxford University Press.

Ernoul (1982). *La Continuation de Guillaume de Tyr (1184–1197)*. Margaret Ruth Morgan (Ed.). Paris, FR: L'Académie des Inscriptions et Belles-Lettres. [French].
Esposito, John L. (Ed.) (2003). *The Oxford Dictionary of Islam*. Oxford, UK and New York, NY: Oxford University Press.
Falk, Avner (1987). The Meaning of Jerusalem: A Psychohistorical Inquiry. *The Psychohistory Review*, vol. 16, no. 1, pp. 99–113. Expanded version (1989) in Howard F. Stein & William G. Niederland (Eds.), *Maps from the Mind: Readings in Psychogeography*. Norman, OK: University of Oklahoma Press.
Falk, Avner (1996). *A Psychoanalytic History of the Jews*. Madison and Teaneck, NY: Fairleigh Dickinson University Press.
Falk, Avner (2001). Osama Bin Laden and America: A Psychobiographical Study. *Mind and Human Interaction*, vol. 12, no. 3, pp. 161–172.
Falk, Avner (2004). *Fratricide in the Holy Land: A Psychoanalytic View of the Arab-Israeli Conflict*. Madison, WI: University of Wisconsin Press.
Falk, Avner (2008). *Anti-Semitism: The History and Psychoanalysis of Contemporary Hatred*. Westport, CT and London, UK: Praeger.
Falk, Avner (2008a). *Islamic Terror: Unconscious and Unconscious Motives*. Westport, CT and London, UK: Praeger Security International.
Feldner, Yotam (2000). "Honor" Murders – Why the Perps Get off Easy. *Middle East Quarterly*, vol. 7, no. 4, pp. 41–50.
Fidler, Richard (2017). *Ghost Empire: A Journey to Legendary Constantinople*. New York, NY: Penguin.
Flori, Jean (1999). *Richard Cœur de lion: le roi-chevalier*. Paris, FR: Editions Payot. [French].
Flori, Jean (2001). *La guerre sainte: la formation de l'idée de croisade dans l'Occident chrétien*. Paris, FR: Editions Aubier-Flammarion. [French].
Flori, Jean (2001a). *Les croisades*. Paris, FR: Editions Gisserot. [French].
Flori, Jean (2002). *Guerre sainte, jihad, croisade: violence et religion dans le christianisme et l'islam*. Paris, FR: Editions du Seuil. [French].
Flori, Jean (2006). *Pierre l'Ermite et la première croisade*. Paris, FR: Editions Fayard. [French].
Flori, Jean (2007). *L'Islam et la fin des Temps: l'interprétation prophétique des invasions musulmanes dans la chrétienté médiévale*. Paris, FR: Editions du Seuil. [French].
Flori, Jean (2007a). *Bohémond d'Antioche: chevalier d'aventure*. Paris, FR: Editions Payot. [French].
Flori, Jean (2008). *La fin du monde au Moyen Age*. Paris, FR: Editions Gisserot. [French].
Fornari, Franco (1975). *The Psychoanalysis of War*. Bloomington, IN: Indiana University Press.
France, John & Zajac, William G. (Eds.) (1998). *The Crusades and Their Sources: Essays Presented to Bernard Hamilton*. Aldershot, UK and Brookfield, VT: Ashgate Publishing Company.
Fredegar *et al.* (1960). *The Fourth Book of the Chronicle of Fredegar; With its Continuations*. Tr., Ed. & Intr. J. M. Wallace-Hadrill. London, UK and New York, NY: Nelson. New edition (1981) Westport, CT: Greenwood Press.
Fredriksen, Paula (1988). *From Jesus to Christ: The Origins of the New Testament Images of Jesus*. New Haven, CT: Yale University Press. Second edition (2000). New Haven, CT: Yale University Press.

Friedländer, Saul (2009). *Nazi Germany and the Jews.* Abridged by Orna Kenan. New York, NY: Harper Collins.
Fulcher of Chartres (Foucher de Chartres) (1998). *The First Crusade: The Chronicle of Fulcher of Chartres and Other Source Materials.* Edward Peters (Ed.), second edition. Philadelphia, PA: University of Pennsylvania Press.
Fuller, Thomas (1639). *The historie of the holy warre.* Cambridge, UK: Thomas Buck & John Williams.
Gabriele, Matthew (2016). Debating the "Crusade" in Contemporary America. *The Mediaeval Journal*, vol. 6, no. 1, pp. 73–92.
Gabrieli, Francesco (Ed.) (1969). *Arab Historians of the Crusades.* Selected and translated from the Arabic sources into Italian by Francesco Gabrieli. Tr. E. J. Costello. Berkeley, CA: University of California Press. London, UK: Routledge & Kegan Paul.
Geary, Patrick J. (Ed.) (2003). *Readings in Medieval History.* Third edition. Peterborough, Ontario: Broadview Press.
Gibb, Hamilton Alexander Rosskeen & Kramers, Johannes Hendrik (Eds.) (2001). *Concise Encyclopedia of Islam.* Edited on behalf of the Royal Netherlands Academy. Leiden, NL and Boston, MA: Brill Academic Publishers.
Geoffroy de Beaulieu & Guillaume de Chartres (2014). *The Sanctity of Louis IX: Early Lives of Saint Louis by Geoffrey of Beaulieu and William of Chartres.* Ed. & Intr. M. Cecilia Gaposchkin & Sean L. Field. Ithaca, NY and London, UK: Cornell University Press.
Given, John (2014). *The Fragmentary History of Priscus.* Merchantville, NJ, Evolution Publishing.
Godfrey, John (1980). *1204: The Unholy Crusade.* Oxford, UK: Oxford University Press.
Goitein, S. D. (Ed.) (1974). *Religion in a Religious Age.* Cambridge, MA: Association for Jewish Studies.
Graves, Robert & Patai, Raphael (1964). *Hebrew Myths: The Book of Genesis.* New York, NY: Doubleday. New edition (1983). New York: Greenwich House.
Gregorius IX (1896–1955). *Les registres de Pope Grégoire IX.* Four volumes. L. Auvray (Ed.). Paris, FR: PNU. [Latin and French].
Gregory of Tours (1976) (Gregorius de Turones, 1976). *The History of the Franks.* Tr. & Intr. Lewis Thorpe, Betty Radice (Ed.). New York, NY: Penguin Classics.
Grousset, René (1934). *Histoire des Croisades et du royaume franc de Jérusalem.* Three volumes. Paris, FR: Quadrige / Presses Universitaires de France.
Hagenmeyer, Heinrich (Ed.) (1892). [Originally written around 1100]. *De Gesta francorum et aliorum Hierosolymytanorum.* Ten Books. Heidelberg, DE: Verlag Carl Winter. New edition (2003) with an Italian translation. Luigi Rosso (Ed.). Alessandria, Piemonte, IT: Edizioni dell'Orso. [Latin].
Haley, James L. (1981). *Apaches: A History and Culture Portrait.* New York, NY: Doubleday.
Halm, Heinz (1989). Al-Andalus und Gothica Sors. *Der Islam*, vol. 66, pp. 252–263. [German].
Handyside, Philip D. (2015). *The Old French William of Tyre.* Leiden, NL: Brill.
Harris, Jonathan (2003). *Byzantium and the Crusades.* London, UK and New York, NY: Hambledon Press.
Heebøll-Holm, Thomas Kristian (2014). Apocalypse Then? The First Crusade, Traumas of War and Thomas de Marle. In Kerstin Hundahl *et al.* (Eds.), *Denmark and Europe in the Middle Ages, c. 1000–1525: Essays in Honour of Professor Michael H. Gelting*, chapter 14. London, UK: Routledge.

Heer, Friedrich (1968). *The Holy Roman Empire.* Tr. Janet Sondheimer. London, UK: Weidenfeld & Nicolson. New York, NY: Praeger.
Hillenbrand, Carole (1991). Jihad Poetry in the Age of the Crusades. In Thomas F. Madden*et al.* (Eds.) *Crusades – Medieval Worlds in Conflict.* London, UK: Routledge.
Hillenbrand, Carole (1999). *The Crusades: Islamic Perspectives.* Edinburgh, UK: Edinburgh University Press. Chicago, IL: Fitzroy Dearborn Publishers.
Hindley, Geoffrey (2003). *The Crusades: A History of Armed Pilgrimage and Holy War.* New York, NY: Carroll & Graf.
Hindley, Geoffrey (2004). *The Crusades: Islam and Christianity in the Struggle for World Supremacy.* New York, NY: Carroll and Graf.
Hirschfeld, Ariel (2008). Armida: A Review of Haydn's Opera Directed by Nicolaus Harnoncourt. *Haaretz Weekly Supplement*, June 20.
Holt, Andrew & Muldoon, James (2008). *Competing Voices From the Crusades: Fighting Words.* Westport, CT and Oxford, UK: Greenwood World Publishing.
Horowitz, David (1953). Abdulrahman Azzam Pasha Rejects Any Compromise with the Zionists. In David Horowitz, *State in the Making*, pp. 233–235. New York, NY: Alfred Knopf.
Houghton, Robert & Peters, Damien (2017). *A Macat Analysis: Carole Hillenbrand's The Crusades Islamic Perspectives.* London, UK: Macat Library.
Houtsma, Martijn Theodoor*et al.* (Eds.). (1913–1936). *The Encyclopaedia of Islam: A Dictionary of the Geography, Ethnography and Biography of the Muhammadan Peoples, Prepared by a Number of Leading Orientalists. Published under the Patronage of the International Association of the Academies.* Five volumes. Leiden, NL: E. J. Brill. London, UK: Luzac & Co. [English, German and French editions].
Houtsma, Martijn Theodoor*et al.* (Eds.). (1954–2007). *The Encyclopaedia of Islam: A Dictionary of the Geography, Ethnography and Biography of the Muhammadan Peoples, Prepared by a Number of Leading Orientalists. Published under the Patronage of the International Association of the Academies.* Second edition. Twelve volumes. P. J. Bearman*et al.* (Eds.). Leiden, NL: E. J. Brill. [English and French editions].
Hughes, Philip (1934). *A History of the Church: An Introductory Study.* New York, NY: Sheed & Ward. New edition (1935–1947) Three volumes. New York, NY: Sheed & Ward. New edition (1947). *A History of the Church.* New York, NY: Sheed & Ward. New edition (1948). New York, NY: Sheed & Ward. New edition (1976). *A History of the Church: To the Eve of the Reformation.* London, UK: Sheed & Ward.
Huillard-Bréholles, J.-L.A. (Ed.) (1852–1861). *Historia diplomatica Friderici secundi.* Six volumes in eleven. Paris, FR: PNU. Reprinted (1963). Turin, IT: PNU. [Latin].
Hurlock, Kathryn (2011). *Wales and the Crusades: c. 1095–1291.* Aberystwyth, UK: University of Wales Press.
Hurlock, Kathryn (2022). Was There Combat Trauma in the Middle Ages? A Case for Moral Injury in Pre-modern Conflict. In Owen Rees*et al.* (Eds.), *Combat Stress in Pre-modern Europe*, pp. 123–150. Cham, CH: Palgrave Macmillan and Springer Nature Switzerland.
Ibn al-Qalanisi, Abu Ya'ala Hamzah ibn Asad (1932). *The Damascus Chronicle of the Crusades*, extracted and translated from the chronicle of Ibn al-Qalanisi by Hamilton Alexander Rosskeen Gibb. London, UK: Luzac. New edition (1992). Mineola, New York: Dover Publications.
Ibn Munqidh, Usamah (1929). *An Arab-Syrian Gentleman and Warrior in the Period of the Crusades: Memoirs of Usamah ibn-Munqidh (Kitab al i'tibar).* Arabic text

edited from the unique manuscript in the Escorial Library, Spain, by Philip K. Hitti. New York, NY: PU. Reprinted (1930) as *Usamah's memoirs, entitled Kitab al-i'tibar, by Usamah ibn Munqidh.* Princeton, NJ: Princeton University Press. New edition (2000). with a new foreword by Richard W. Bulliet. New York, NY: Columbia University Press.

Ibn Shaddad, Baha al-Din Yusuf ibn Rafi' (2001). *The Rare and Excellent History of Saladin, or al-Nawadir al-Sultaniyya wa'l-Mahasin al-Yusufiyya.* Tr. D. S. Richards. Aldershot, UK and Burlington, VT: Ashgate Publishing Company.

Ireland, William W. (1906–1907). On the Psychology of the Crusades. Part I, *Journal of Mental Science*, vol. 52, no. 219, pp. 745–755.

Ireland, William W. (1906–1907). On the Psychology of the Crusades. Part II, *Journal of Mental Science*, vol. 53, no. 221, pp. 322–341.

Irwin, Robert (1998). Usama ibn Munqidh: An Arab-Syrian Gentleman at the Time of the Crusades Reconsidered. In John France & William G. Zajac, (Eds.), *The Crusades and Their Sources: Essays Presented to Bernard Hamilton.* Aldershot, UK and Brookfield, VT: Ashgate Publishing Company.

Jackson, Peter (Ed.) (2007). *The Seventh Crusade, 1244–1254: Sources and Documents.* London, UK: Routledge.

Jacques de Vitry (1997). *Histoire occidentale: Historia occidentalis: tableau de l'Occident au XIIIe siècle.* Tr. Gaston Duchet-Suchaux. Ed. & Intr. Jean Longère. Paris, FR: Editions du Cerf. [French].

Jean de Joinville (1617). *Histoire de S. Loys IX. du nom, roy de France.* Paris, FR: En la boutique de Nivelle, chez Sebastien Cramoisy.

Joffroi de Villehardouin & Henri de Valenciennes (1838). *De la Conqueste de Constantinople.* Paris, FR: Jules Renouard.

John of Damascus (1958). *Writings.* Translated by Frederic H. Chase, Jr. New York, NY: Fathers of the Church. Reprinted (1970). Washington, DC: Catholic University of America Press. New edition (1999). Washington, DC: Catholic University of America Press.

Kamola, Stefan (2019). *Making Mongol History: Rashid al-Din and the Jami'al-Tawarikh.* Edinburgh, UK: Edinburgh University Press.

Kazhdan, Alexander (2001). Latins and Franks in Byzantium: Perception and Reality from the Eleventh to the Twelfth Century. In Angeliki E. Laiou & Roy Parviz Mottahedeh (Eds.), *The Crusades from the Perspective of Byzantium and the Muslim World.* Washington, DC: Dumbarton Oaks.

Kedar, Benjamin Ze'ev (1984). *"Crusade" and Mission: European Approaches Toward the Muslims.* Princeton, NJ: Princeton University Press.

Kedar, Benjamin Ze'ev*et al.* (Eds.). (1982). *Outremer: Studies in the History of the Crusading Kingdom of Jerusalem Presented to Joshua Prawer.* Jerusalem, IL: Yad Izhak Ben-Zvi Institute.

Kehew, Robert (Ed.) (2005). *Lark in the Morning: The Verses of the Troubadours.* Tr. Ezra Pound, W.D. Snodgrass, & Robert Kehew. Bilingual edition. Chicago, IL: The University of Chicago Press.

Killebrew, Ann E. (2003). Biblical Jerusalem: An Archaeological Assessment. In Andrew G. Vaughn & Ann E. Killebrew (Eds.), *Jerusalem in Bible and Archaeology: The First Temple Period.* Leiden, Netherlands and Boston, MA: E. J. Brill. Atlanta, GA: Society of Biblical Literature.

Killebrew, Ann E. (2005). *Biblical Peoples and Ethnicity: An Archaeological Study of Egyptians, Canaanites, Philistines, and Early Israel, 1300–1100 B.C.E.* Leiden, Netherlands and Boston, MA: E. J. Brill. Atlanta, GA: Society of Biblical Literature.

Koch, Ariel (2017). The New Crusaders: Contemporary Extreme Right Symbolism and Rhetoric. *Perspectives on Terrorism*, vol. 11, no. 5, pp. 13–24.

Kolbaba, Tia M. (2001). Byzantine Perceptions of Latin Religious Errors: Themes and Changes from 850 to 1350. In Angeliki E. Laiou & Roy Parviz Mottahedeh (Eds.), *The Crusades from the Perspective of Byzantium and the Muslim World.* Washington, DC: Dumbarton Oaks.

Konieczny, Peter (2011). The Prince, the Assassin and the Mongols. Paper delivered at the session of *De Re Militari: High Medieval Warfare* at the 46th International Congress on Medieval Studies. Online article on Medievalists.net.

Krämer, Ulrike (1996). *Translatio imperii et studii: zum Geschichts - und Kulturverständnis in der französischen Literatur des Mittelalters und der frühen Neuzeit.* Bonn, DE: Romanistischer Verlag. [German].

LaCapra, Dominick (2014). *Writing History, Writing Trauma.* With a New Preface. Baltimore, MD: Johns Hopkins University Press.

Laroui, Abdallah (1976). *The Crisis of the Arab Intellectual: Traditionalism or Historicism?* Berkeley, CA: University of California Press.

Levron, Jacques (1963). *Le château fort et la vie au moyen âge.* Paris, FR: Fayard.

Levron, Jacques (1976). *Louis IX and Absolutism.* London, UK: Palgrave Macmillan.

Lewis, Bernard (1950). *The Arabs in History.* London, UK and New York: Hutchinson's University Library.

Lilie, Ralph-Johannes (1988). *Byzantium and the Crusader States, 1096–1204.* Tr. J. C. Morris and Jean E. Ridings. Oxford, UK: Clarendon Press. Revised edition (1993). Oxford, UK and New York, NY: Oxford University Press.

Linehan, Peter (2023). *The Spanish Church and the Papacy in the 13th Century*, The Library of Iberian Resources Online, Ch. 12.

Littell, Jonathan (2006). *Les Bienveillantes: Roman.* Paris, FR: Gallimard [French].

Locke, John L. & Bogin, Barry (2006). Language and Life History: A New Perspective on the Development and Evolution of Human Language. *Behavioral and Brain Sciences*, vol. 29, no. 3, pp. 259–280.

López Pereira, José Eduardo (Ed. & Tr.) (1980). *Epitoma imperatorum: Crónica mozárabe de 754.* Zaragoza, ES: Anubar. [Spanish & Latin].

Maalouf, Amin (1983). *The Crusades Through Arab Eyes.* Tr. Jon Rothschild. New York, NY: Schocken Books. Reprinted (1984). London, UK: Al Saqui Books. Reprinted (1985). New York, NY: Schocken Books.

Madden, Thomas F. (2003). *Enrico Dandolo and the Rise of Venice.* Baltimore, MD: Johns Hopkins University Press.

Maleczek, Werner (1984). *Papst und Kardinalskolleg von 1191 bis 1216: Die Kardinäle unter Coelestin III. und Innocenz III.* Vienna, AT: Verlag der Österreichischen Akademie der Wissenschaften.

Maqsood, Ruqaiyyah Waris (2001). *A Basic Dictionary of Islam.* New Delhi, IN: Good Word Books. Lahore, IN: Talha Publication.

Marin, Serban (2000). A Humanist Vision regarding the Fourth "Crusade" and the State of the Assenides. The Chronicle of Paul Ramusio (Paulus Rhamnusius). *Annuario del Istituto Romano di Cultura e Ricerca Umanistica*, vol. 2, pp. 51–57.

Martin, Sean (2004). *The Knights Templar: The History & Myths of the Legendary Military Order.* New York, NY: Thunder's Mouth Press.
Martini, Raimundo (1968). *Pugio fidei adversus Mauros et Judaeous.* Farnborough, UK: Gregg Press. [Latin].
McNeal, Edgar & Wolff, Robert Lee (1962). The Fourth "Crusade". In Kenneth M. Setton*et al.* (Eds), *A History of the Crusades, vol. 2.* Philadelphia, PA: University of Pennsylvania Press.
Michaud, Joseph-François (1853). *The History of the Crusades.* Three volumes. Tr. W. Robson. Illustr. Gustave Doré. New York, NY: Redfield. New edition (1973) New York, NY: AMS Press.
Migne, Jacques-Paul (Ed.) (1844–1864). Liber registrorum sive epistolarum. In *Patrologiae cursus completus, sive biblioteca universalis, integra, uniformis, commoda, oeconomica, omnium SS. Patrum, doctorum scriptorumque eccelesiasticorum qui ab aevo apostolico ad usque Innocentii III tempora floruerunt ... [Series Latina, in qua prodeunt Patres, doctores scriptoresque Ecclesiae Latinae, a Tertulliano ad Innocentium III] Accurante J.-P. Migne.* Three volumes. Paris, FR: PNU. [Latin].
Migne, Jacques-Paul (Ed.) (1965). Liber registrorum sive epistolarum. In *Index alphabeticus omnium doctorum, patrum, scriptorumque ecclesiasticorum quorum opera scriptaque vel minima in Patrologia Latina reperiuntur. J. B. Pearson: Conspectus auctorum quorum nomina indicibus Patrologiae Graeco-Latinae a J. P. Migne editae continentur.* Three volumes. Farnborough, UK and Ridgewood, NJ: Gregg Press. [Latin].
Mijolla, Alain de (Ed.) (2005). *International Dictionary of Psychoanalysis.* Three volumes. Detroit, MI: Macmillan Reference USA.
Milger, Peter (2000) *Die Kreuzzüge: Krieg im Namen Gottes,* Munich, Orbis Verlag.
Mitchell, Piers D. (2002). *Trauma and Surgery in the Crusades to the Medieval Eastern Mediterranean.* M.D. Thesis, Welcome Centre for the History of Medicine at University College London. London, UK: University of London.
Mitchell, Piers D. (2006). Trauma in the Crusader Period City of Caesarea: A Major Port in the Medieval Eastern Mediterranean. *International Journal of Osteoarchaeology,* vol. 16, no. 6, pp. 493–505.
Mitchell, Piers D. (2013). *Violence and the Crusades: Warfare, Injuries and Torture in the Medieval Middle East.* London, UK: Routledge.
Mitscherlich, Alexander & Mitscherlich, Margarethe (1975). *The Inability to Mourn: Principles of Collective Behavior.* Pref. Robert Jay Lifton. Tr. Beverley R. Placzek. New York, NY: Grove Press.
Molinier, Auguste (1902) *Les sources de l'histoire de France des origines aux guerres d'Italie (1494),* Paris, Alphonse Picard et fils.
Morris, Colin (1968). Geoffroy de Villehardouin and the Conquest of Constantinople. *History,* vol. 53, no. 177, pp. 24–34.
Muir, William (1883). *Annals of the Early Caliphate, From Original Sources, by Sir William Muir.* London, UK: Smith, Elder & Co.
Murray, Alan V. (Ed.) (2006). *The Crusades: An Encyclopedia.* Four volumes. Santa Barbara, CA: ABC-CLIO.
Mylod, E. J.*et al.* (Eds.) (2017). *The Fifth Crusade in Context: The Crusading Movement in the Early Thirteenth Century.* London, UK: Routledge.
Mynors, R. A. B. (Ed.) (1964). *XII Panegyrici Latini.* Oxford, UK: Clarendon Press.

Nahon, Gérard (1996). Adversus Judaeus: sources hébraïques et latines sur la Première Croisade. In Alain Dierkens (Ed.), *Le penseur, la violence, la religion*, pp. 83–95. Bruxelles, BE: Editions de l'Université de Bruxelles.
Nicholson, Helen J. (2005). *God's Warriors: Knights Templar, Saracens and the Battle for Jerusalem*. Oxford, UK and New York, NY: Osprey Publications.
Nicol, Donald (1993). *The Last Centuries of Byzantium, 1261–1453*. Cambridge, UK and New York, NY: Cambridge University Press.
Nicol, Donald MacGillivray (1988). *Byzantium and Venice: A Study in Diplomatic and Cultural Relations*. Cambridge, UK and New York, NY: Cambridge University Press.
Nicolaus von Jeroschin (1331–1341). *Di Kronike von Pruzinlant*.
Nicolaus von Jeroschin (2010). Mary Fischer (Ed.). *The Chronicle of Prussia by Nicolaus von Jeroschin: A History of the Teutonic Knights in Prussia*. Burlington, VT: Ashgate Publishing.
Noble, Peter S. (1999). Eyewitnesses of the Fourth "Crusade": The War against Alexius III. *Reading Medieval Studies: Annual Proceedings of the Graduate Centre for Medieval Studies in the University of Reading*, vol. 25, pp. 75–89. Reading, UK: University of Reading.
Noble, Peter S. (2002). Eyewitnesses of the Fourth "Crusade": The Reign of Alexius V. In Erik Kooper (Ed.), *The Medieval Chronicle II: Proceedings of the 2nd International Conference on the Medieval Chronicle Driebergen/Utrceht 16–21 July 1999*. pp. 178–189. Leiden, NL: Brill.
Ochsenwald, William L. (1976). The Crusader Kingdom of Jerusalem and Israel: An Historical Comparison. *Middle East Journal*, vol. 30, no. 2, pp. 221–226.
Olster, David M. (1994). *Roman Defeat, Christian Response and the Literary Construction of the Jew*. Philadelphia, PA: University of Pennsylvania Press.
Önal, Ayse (2008). *Honour Killing: Stories of Men Who Killed*. London, UK: Saqi Books.
Partner, Peter (1997). *God of Battles: Holy Wars of Christianity and Islam*. Princeton, NJ: Princeton University Press.
Patai, Raphael (1974). *The Arab Mind*. New York, NY: Charles Scribner's Sons.
Patai, Raphael (1976). Ethnohistory and Inner History. *The Jewish Quarterly Review*, vol. 67, pp. 1–15. Reprinted (1977) in Raphael Patai, *The Jewish Mind*, pp. 28–37. New York, NY: Charles Scribner's Sons.
Paul, Nicholas & Yeager, Suzanne (Eds.) (2012). *Remembering the Crusades: Myth, Image, and Identity*. Baltimore, MD: Johns Hopkins University Press.
Paviot, Jacques (2009). England and the Mongols (c.1260–1330). *Journal of the Royal Asiatic Society*, vol. 10, no. 3, pp. 305–318.
Peters, Damien (2017). *A Macat Analysis: Jonathan Riley-Smith's The First Crusade and the Idea of Crusading*. London, UK: Macat Library.
Peters, Edward (Ed.) (1971). *Christian Society and the Crusades: 1198–1229: Sources in Translation, Including "The Capture of Damietta" by Oliver of Paderborn, Translated with Notes by John J. Gavigan*. Philadelphia, PA: University of Pennsylvania Press.
Peutinger, Conrad (2003). *Tabula Peutingeriana: le antiche vie del mondo*. Ed. Francesco Prontera. Firenze (Florence): Leo Samuele Olschki. [Italian].
Phillips, A. *et al.* (Eds.) (1882–1886). *Preußisches Urkundenbuch*. Six volumes. Königsberg: Aalen & Marburg.
Phillips, Jonathan P. (2002). *The Crusades, 1095–1197*. London, UK: Pearson Education.

Phillips, Jonathan P. (2004). *The Fourth "Crusade" and the Sack of Constantinople.* London, UK: Jonathan Cape. New York, NY: Viking. Reprinted (2005). London, UK: Pimlico.
Powell, James (1986). *Anatomy of a Crusade, 1213-1221.* Philadelphia, PA: University of Pennsylvania Press.
Prawer, Joshua (1972). *The Crusades' Kingdom; European Colonialism in the Middle Ages.* New York, NY: Praeger. New edition (2001). London, UK: Phoenix.
Prawer, Joshua (1980). *Crusader Institutions.* Oxford, UK: Clarendon Press. New York, NY: Oxford University Press.
Procopius of Caesarea (1653). *The History of the Warres of the Emperour Justinian in Eight Books.* Tr. Henry Holcroft. London, UK: Henry Moseley.
Pryor, John H. (Ed.) (2006). *Logistics of Warfare in the Age of the Crusades: Proceedings of a Workshop Held at the Centre for Medieval Studies, University of Sydney, 30 September to 4 October 2002.* Aldershot, UK and Burlington, VT: Ashgate Publishing Company.
Queller, Donald E. (1971). *The Latin Conquest of Constantinople.* New York, London, Sydney, and Toronto: John Wiley and Sons.
Queller, Donald E. & Madden, Thomas F. (1977). *The Fourth "Crusade": The Conquest of Constantinople, 1201-1204.* Philadelphia, PA: University of Pennsylvania Press.
Queller, Donald E. & Stratton, Susan J. (1969). A Century of Controversy on the Fourth Crusade. *Studies in Medieval and Renaissance History*, vol. 6, pp. 237-277. Reprinted (1980) in Donald E. Queller, *Medieval Diplomacy and the Fourth Crusade.* London, UK: Variorum Reprints.
Raoul de Caen (2005). *Gesta Tancredi. The Gesta Tancredi of Ralph of Caen: A History of the Normans on the First Crusade.* Tr. & Intr. Bernard S. Bachrach and David S. Bachrach. Aldershot, UK and Burlington, VT: Ashgate Publishing Company.
Raymond d'Aguilers (1611). Historia Francorum qui ceperunt Iherusalem. In Jacques Bongars (Ed.), *Gesta Dei per Francos, siue Orientalivm expeditionvm, et regni Francorvm hierosolimitani historia a variis, sed illius æui scriptoribus, litteris commendata: nunc primu?m aut editis, aut ad libros veteres emendatis. Auctores præfatio ad lectorem exhibet. Orientalis historiae tomus primus [et secundus]*, vol. I, pp. 139-183. Hanoviæ: typis Wechelianis, apud heredes I. Aubrii. [Latin].
Raymond d'Aguilers (1824). Histoire des Francs qui prirent Jérusalem. In François Guizot, (Ed. & Tr.) *Mémoires sur l'histoire de France*, vol. XXI, pp. 227-397. [French].
Raymond d'Aguilers (1968). *Historia Francorum qui ceperunt Iherusalem.* Intr. Ed. & Tr. John Hugh Hill and Laurita L. Hill. Philadelphia, PA: American Philosophical Society. [Latin and English].
Reiter, Yitzhak (2008). *Jerusalem and Its Role in Islamic Solidarity.* New York, NY: Palgrave Macmillan.
Reston, James, Jr. (2001). *Warriors of God.* New York, NY: Doubleday.
Ricardus Canonicus Sanctae Trinitatis Londoniensis [Richard Canon of Saint Trinity Church London] (1997). *Chronicle of the Third Crusade [A Translation of the Itinerarium Peregrinorum et Gesta Regis Ricardi].* Tr. Helen J. Nicholson. Aldershot, UK and Brookfield, VT: Ashgate Publishing Co.
Richard of Devizes*et al.* (1892). *Chronicles of the Crusades: Contemporary Narratives of the "Crusade" of Richard Coeur de Lion, by Richard of Devizes and Geoffery de Vinsauf; and of the "Crusade" of Saint Louis, by Lord John de Joinville.* With illustrative notes and an index. London, UK and New York, NY: G. Bell & Sons.

Riley-Smith, Jonathan Simon Christopher (1973). *The Feudal Nobility and the Kingdom of Jerusalem, 1174–1277*. London, UK: Macmillan.
Riley-Smith, Jonathan Simon Christopher (1977). *What Were the Crusades?* Totowa, NJ: Rowman and Littlefield. Third edition (2002). San Francisco, CA: Ignatius Press.
Riley-Smith, Jonathan Simon Christopher (1986). *The First "Crusade" and the Idea of Crusading*. Philadelphia, PA: University of Pennsylvania Press.
Riley-Smith, Jonathan Simon Christopher (1987). *The Crusades: A Short History*. New Haven, CT: Yale University Press.
Riley-Smith, Jonathan Simon Christopher (1991). *The Atlas of the Crusades*. New York, NY: Facts on File.
Riley-Smith, Jonathan Simon Christopher (Ed.) (1995). *The Oxford Illustrated History of the Crusades*. New York, NY: Oxford University Press. New edition (1997). New York, NY: Oxford University Press.
Riley-Smith, Jonathan Simon Christopher (1997). *The First Crusade and the Idea of Crusading*. Philadelphia, PA: University of Pennsylvania Press.
Riley-Smith, Jonathan Simon Christopher (1997). *The First Crusades, 1095–1131*. Cambridge, UK and New York, NY: Cambridge University Press.
Riley-Smith, Jonathan Simon Christopher (1997a). Families, Crusades and Settlement in the Latin East, 1102–1131. In Eberhard Mayer (Ed.), *Die Kreuzfahrerstaaten als multikulturelle Gesellschaft: Einwanderer und Minderheiten im 12. und 13. Jahrhundert*. Berlin, DE: De Gruyter Oldenbourg.
Riley-Smith, Jonathan Simon Christopher (1999). *Hospitallers: The History of the Order of St. John*. London, UK and Rio Grande, OH: Hambledon Press.
Riley-Smith, Jonathan Simon Christopher (2005). *The Crusades: A History*. 2nd edition. London, UK and New York, NY: Continuum.
Riley-Smith, Jonathan Simon Christopher (2008). *The Crusades, Christianity, and Islam*. New York, NY: Columbia University Press.
Riley-Smith, Louise & Riley-Smith, Jonathan Simon Christopher (1981). *The Crusades: Idea and Reality, 1095–1274*. London, UK: E. Arnold.
Robert de Rheims (Robertus Monachus, or Robert the Monk) (1866), Historia Hierosolymitana. In *Recueil des historiens des croisades, publié par les soins de l'Académie des inscriptions et belles-lettres, 16 volumes*. Paris, FR: Imprimerie royale, vol. 3, Part IX.
Robinson, Grace Reade & Robinson, James Harvey (Eds.) (1894). *Translations and Reprints from the Original Sources of European History*. Philadelphia, PA: University of Pennsylvania Department of History. New edition (1895–1907). Philadelphia, PA: University of Pennsylvania Department of History. New edition (1898–1912). Six volumes. Philadelphia, PA: University of Pennsylvania Department of History. Reprinted (1902). Six volumes. London, UK and New York, NY: Longmans, Green & Co.
Röhricht, Reinhold (1891). *Studien zur Geschichte des fünften Kreuzzuges*. Innsbruck, AT: Wagner.
Rowan, Spencer Ford (2019). *Reimagined History: Trauma as Provocation for the First Crusade*. Master's Thesis, Harvard Extension School.
Rowan, Spencer Ford (2023). Religious Identity and Shared Trauma: The First Crusade. In Vamık Volkan, Regine Scholz & Gerlad M. Fromm (Eds.), *We Don't Speak of Fear: Group Identity, Societal Conflict and Collective Trauma*, pp. 227–244. Bicester, UK: Phoenix Publishing House.
Runciman, Steven (1951–1955). *A History of the Crusades*. Three volumes. *Vol. 1. The First "Crusade" and the Foundation of the Kingdom of Jerusalem. Vol. 2. The*

Kingdom of Jerusalem and the Frankish East, 1100–1187. Vol. 3. The Kingdom of Acre, and the Later Crusades. Cambridge, UK: Cambridge University Press.
Saba Malaspina (1999). *Die Chronik des Saba Malaspina*. Eds. Walter Koller & August Nitschke. Hannover, DE: Hahnsche Buchhandlung.
Saroglou, Vassilis (2021) *The Psychology of Religion*, London, Routledge.
Schleifer, Abdullah (1972). *The Fall of Jerusalem*. New York, NY: Monthly Review Press.
Setton, Kenneth Meyer*et al.* (Ed.) (1955–1962). *A History of the Crusades*. Two volumes. Philadelphia, PA: University of Pennsylvania Press. Second edition (1969–1989). Six volumes. Madison, WI: University of Wisconsin Press.
Shagrir, Iris et al. (Eds.) (2007). *In Laudem Hierosolymitani: Studies in Crusades and Medieval Culture in Honour of Benjamin Z. Kedar*. Aldershot, UK and Burlington, VT: Ashgate Publishing Company.
Shay, Jonathan (2014). Moral Injury. *Psychoanalytic Psychology*, vol. 31, no. 2, pp. 186–187.
Siberry, Elizabeth (1985). *Criticism of Crusading: 1095–1274*. Oxford, UK: The Clarendon Press. New York, NY: Oxford University Press.
Siberry, Elizabeth (2000). *The New Crusades: Images of the Crusades in the 19th and Early 20th Centuries*. Aldershot, UK and Burlington, VT: Ashgate Publishing Co.
Siberry, Elizabeth (2016). *The New Crusaders: Images of the Crusades in the 19th and Early 20th Centuries*, London, UK: Routledge.
Sidonius Apollinaris (1887). *Gai Sollii Apollinaris Sidonii Epistulae et Carmina*. Christian Lütjohann*et al.* (Eds.). Berlin, DE: Weidmann. [Latin].
Sidonius Apollinaris (2024). *Complete Poems*. Tr. & Intr. Roger Green. Liverpool, UK: Liverpool University Press.
Sintobin, Nikolaas (2023). *Did Jesus Really Exist? and 51 Other Faith Questions*. Waterford, CT: Twenty-Third Publications.
Spencer, Stephen J. (2021). The Third Crusade in Historiographical Perspective. *History Compass*, vo. 19, no. 7, open access (no page numbers).
Spicer, Andrew & Hamilton, Sarah (Eds.) (2005). *Defining the Holy: Sacred Space in Medieval and Early Modern Europe*. Aldershot, UK and Burlington, VT: Ashgate Publishing Co.
Stein, Howard F. & Niederland, William G. (Eds.) (1989). *Maps for the Mind: Readings in Psychogeography*. Norman, Ok: University of Oklahoma Press.
Stein, Samuel M. (Ed.) (1999). *Beyond Belief: Psychotherapy and Religion*. Foreword by Robert D. Hinshelwood. London, UK: Karnac Books.
Stevenson, William Henry (1899). The Beginnings of Wessex. *The English Historical Review*, vol. 14, no. 53, pp. 32–46.
Strehlke, Ernst (Ed.) (1975). *Tabulae ordinis Theutonici ex tabularii regii Berolinensis codice potissimum*. New edition. Toronto, CA: PNU. [Latin].
Strickland, Debra Higgs (2003). *Saracens, Demons & Jews: Making Monsters in Medieval Art*. Princeton, NJ: Princeton University Press.
Suetonius, Gaius Tranquillus (2003). *The Twelve Caesars*. Tr. Robert Graves. Ed. Michael Grant. New York: Penguin Books. New edition (2008). *The Twelve Caesars: The Lives of the Roman Emperors*. Tr. J. C. Rolfe. St. Petersburg, FL: Red and Black Publications.
Tacitus, Cornelius (1999). *Germania*. Tr. and Intr. J. B. Rives. Oxford, UK: The Clarendon Press. New York, NY: Oxford University Press.
Terman, David (1984). Anti-Semitism: A Study in Group Vulnerability and the Vicissitudes of Group Ideals. *The Psychohistory Review*, vol. 12, no. 4, pp. 18–24.

Theophanes the Confessor (1982). *The Chronicle of Theophanes: An English Translation of Anni Mundi 6095–6305 (A.D. 602–813)*. Ed. & Intr. Harry Turtledove. Philadelphia, PA: University of Pennsylvania Press.

Theophanes the Confessor (1997). *The Chronicle of Theophanes Confessor: Byzantine and Near Eastern History, AD 284–813*. Ed., Tr. & Intr. Cyril Mango and Roger Scott, with the assistance of Geoffrey Greatrex. Oxford, UK and New York, NY: Oxford University Press.

Theopylaktos Simokattes (1986). *The History of Theophylact Simocatta: An English Translation with Introduction*. Tr. & Intr. Michael Whitby and Mary Whitby. Oxford, UK and New York, NY: Oxford University Press.

Throop, Palmer A. (1938). Criticism of Papal "Crusade" Policy in Old French and Provençal. *Speculum*, vol. 13, no. 4, pp. 379–412.

Tolan, John Victor (2002). *Saracens: Islam in the Medieval European Imagination*. New York, NY: Columbia University Press.

Tolan, John Victor (2008). *Sons of Ishmael: Muslims Through European Eyes in the Middle Ages*. Gainesville, FL: University Press of Florida.

Tolan, John Victor (Ed.) (1996). *Medieval Christian Perceptions of Islam: A Book of Essays*. New York, NY: Garland Publications.

Treadgold, Warren (1997). *A History of the Byzantine State and Society*. Stanford, CA: Stanford University Press.

Trembinski, Donna (2011). Comparing Premodern Melancholy/Mania and Modern Trauma: An Argument in Favour of Historical Experience of Trauma. *History of Psychology*, vol. 14, pp. 80–99.

Tubb, Jonathan N. (1998). *Canaanites*. British Museum People of the Past. Norman, Ok: University of Oklahoma Press.

Tyerman, Christopher (1998). *The Invention of the Crusades*. Toronto, CA and Buffalo, NY: University of Toronto Press.

Tyerman, Christopher (2004). *Fighting for Christendom: Holy War and the Crusades*. Oxford, UK and New York, NY: Oxford University Press.

Tyerman, Christopher (2005). *The Crusades: A Very Short Introduction*. Oxford, UK and New York, NY: Oxford University Press.

Tyerman, Christopher (2005a). *Interview with Sheila Kast on National Public Radio*, February 27. NPR.org website.

Tyerman, Christopher (2006). *God's War: A New History of the Crusades*. Cambridge, MA: Belknap Press of Harvard University Press.

Tyerman, Christopher (2009). Review of *The Seventh Crusade, 1244–1254: Sources and Documents*. *The English Historical Review*, vol. 124, no. 508, pp. 680–681.

Vallvé Bermejo, Joaquín (1986). *The Territorial Divisions of Muslim Spain*. Madrid, ES: Consejo Superior de Investigaciones Científicas.

Villehardouin, Geoffroy de (1891). *La conquête de Constantinople. Texte et traduction nouvelle, avec notice, notes et glossaire par Emile Bouchet*. Paris, FR: A. Lemerre. [French].

Villehardouin, Geoffroy de (1915). *Memoirs of the Crusades*. London, UK: J. M. Dent & sons. New York, NY: E.P. Dutton.

Villehardouin, Geoffroy de & Joinville, Jehan de (1983). *Memoirs of the Crusades*. Tr. Sir Frank Marzials. Westport, CT: Greenwood Press. New edition (2007). *Chronicles of the Crusades*. Mineola, NY: Dover Publications.

Volkan, Vamık D. (1997). *Blood Lines: From Ethnic Pride to Ethnic Violence*. Boulder, CO: Westview Press.

Volkan, Vamık D. (2000). Large Group Identity and Chosen Trauma. *Psyche*, vol. 54, no. 9, pp. 931–953.
Volkan, Vamık D. (2001). Transgenerational Transmissions and Chosen Traumas: An Aspect of Large-Group Identity. *Group Analysis*, vol. 34, no. 1, pp. 79–97.
Volkan, Vamık D. (2004). *Blind Trust: Large Groups and Their Leaders in Times of Crisis and Terror.* Charlottesville, VA: Pitchstone Publishing.
Volkan, Vamık D. (2006). *Killing in the Name of Identity: A Study of Bloody Conflicts.* Charlottesville, VA: Pitchstone Publishing.
Volkan, Vamık D. (2013). *Enemies on the Couch: A Psychopolitical Journey through War and Peace.* Durham, NC: Pitchstone Publishing.
Volkan, Vamık D. (2013a). Large-Group-Psychology in Its Own Right: Large-Group Identity and Peace-making. *International Journal of Applied Psychoanalytic Studies*, vol. 10, no. 3, pp. 210–246.
Volkan, Vamık D. (2014). *Psychoanalysis, International Relations, and Diplomacy: A Sourcebook on Large-Group Psychology.* London, UK: Karnac.
Volkan, Vamık D. (2017). *Gods Do Not Negotiate: A Psychohistorical Look at Terrorism.* Address given at Margaret Mahler Symposium, Philadelphia, PA, April 15, 2017.
Volkan, Vamık D.*et al.* (Eds.) (2023). *We Don't Speak of Fear: Group Identity, Societal Conflict and Collective Trauma.* Bicester, UK: Phoenix Publishing House.
Vryonis, Speros (1967). *Byzantium and Europe.* London, UK: Thames & Hudson.
Waite, Robert George Leeson (1977). *The Psychopathic God: Adolf Hitler.* New York: Basic Books. Reprinted (1993). New York, NY: Da Capo Press.
Walker, Mack (1981). *Johann Jakob Moser and the Holy Roman Empire of the German Nation.* Chapel Hill, NC: University of North Carolina Press.
Waller, James (2002). *Becoming Evil: How Ordinary People Commit Genocide and Mass Killing.* Oxford, UK and New York, NY: Oxford University Press.
Wells, George Albert (1975). *Did Jesus Exist?*London, UK: Elek. Buffalo, NY: Prometheus Books.
Wheatcroft, Andrew (2004). *Infidels: A History of the Conflict Between Christendom and Islam.* New York, NY: Random House.
Wilkinson, Tony J.*et al.* (2004). *On the Margin of the Euphrates: Settlement and Land Use at Tell Es-Sweyhat and in the Upper Lake Assad Area, Syria.* Chicago, IL: Oriental Institute of the University of Chicago.
William of Tyre (1893). *Godeffroy of Boloyne; or, The siege and conqueste of Jerusalem, by William, Archbishop of Tyre.* Tr. William Caxton. Ed. Mary Noyes Colvin. London, UK: K. Paul, Trench, Trübner & Co.
William of Tyre (1943). *A History of Deeds Done Beyond the Sea, by William, Archbishop of Tyre.* Tr. Emily Atwater Babcock and A. C. Krey. New York, NY: Columbia University Press. Reprinted (1976). New York, NY: Octagon Books.
William of Tyre (1986). *The Conquest of Jerusalem and the Third "Crusade": Sources in Translation.* Ed. & Tr. Peter W. Edbury. Brookfield, VT: Scholar Press.
Yerushalmi, Yosef Hayim (1982). *Zakhor: Jewish History and Jewish Memory.* Seattle, WA and London, UK: University of Washington Press.
Zindler, Frank R. & Price, Robert M. (Eds.) (2013). *Bart Ehrman and the Quest of the Historical Jesus of Nazareth: An Evaluation of Ehrman's Did Jesus exist?*Cranford, NJ: American Atheist Press.
Zosimus (2017). *New History [Historia Nova].* Ronald T. Ridley (Ed.). Leiden, NL: Brill.

Index

Abbasid Caliphate 8–9, 15, 53–54, 58–59, 96, 108–109, 146
Abd ar-Rahman al-Ghafiqi 27, 34, 53, 86
Abdulrahman Hassan al-Azzam 170
Abélard, Pierre 95, 161
Abraham Accords 171
Absolution 66
Abu-Ali al-Mansur al-Hakim bi-Amr Allah 57
Abu-Ja'afar Muhammad Abdallah al-Mansur (Abbasid caliph) 53
Abu-l-Abbas Ahmad ibn Mohammed al-Maqqari (historian) 38
Abu Mansur al-Nizar (al-Mustafa ad-din-illah) 79
Abu Sa'id Bahadur Khan 10
Acre: army attack 152; attack, pretext 168; capture 88, 166, 167; Crusader siege 120; Emperor Friedrich approach 142–143; fall 167–168; Friedrich II sailing 141; "Latin Kingdom of Jerusalem," capital 118; Oliver of Cologne arrival 135
Acre, Council of 168
Adalbert, Archbishop of Bremen (Crusade missions) 98
adam (human) 3
Adam of Ebrach, preaching 97–98
Adelaide del Vasto, Baudouin marriage 88
Africa pronsonsularis (Roman province) 14
Aguilers, Raymond d' 72–73, 75–76; 78, 82–83
Aharon ben Moshe ben Asher *(Masorete)* 14
Ahmed Tegülder 9
Ajuja (Khitan concubine) 9
Aphrodite 52
Akkadian *kinahhu* (Canaan) 11

al-Afdal, caliph 74, 78–80
Alamanni (Allemanni) (Alemanni) (Germanic tribes) 30, 47; battle, victory 38
Al-Amir bi-Ahkam Allah (al-Amir Bi-Ahkamillah) 80
al-Amir Mu'in-al-Din 110
al-Andalus 34, 48–49, 53, 162; army, landing 38–39; capital (Córdoba) 53; Moorish conquest 38–40; mystery 14–16; Umayyad rule 54
Alans (Germanic tribe) 23
Ala-uddin Hussain (Ghor) 58
Albert of Aachen 80
Albigensian Crusade 133–134, 138
Alexander II (pope) 59
Alexander III, Pope (Crusade authorization) 88
Alexandria 15
Alexios Doukas, Byzantine Emperor 127, 129–130
Alexios Angelos, Byzantine Emperor 81–82, 124, 127–129
Alexios Komnenos, Byzantine Emperor 59–60, 65; ally 62–63; military assistance request 71; negotiation 72; unhappiness 70
Alfonsi, Petrus (baptism) 89
al-franj (ifranj) (franji) (Arabic name for Franks) 24, 26–27, 49, 54–55, 91, 104
Al-Hakim (historian) 39
al-Harawi: mission (Baghdad) 109
Ali ibn Abi-Talib 54
Aliso (Roman fort), siege 16
al-jahiliyya (ignorance/darkness) 52
Al-Kamil (sultan of Egypt) 133, 137, 143
alle Männer (all men) 30, 47
Allemanni see Alamanni

al-Malik al-Adil Nur ad-Din Abu al-Qasim Mahmud Ibn Imad ad-Din Zengi (Josselin defeat/capture) 96–97
al-Malik al-Adl Sayf al-Din Abu-Bakr ibn Ayyub, resistance 136–137
al-Malik al-Kamil Naser al-Din Abu al-Ma'ali Muhammed, succession 137
Al Mansurah 146–147
Al-Muazzam Turanshah: assassination 8, 147, 148
al-Musta'li 80
Al-Mustansir 166
al-Mustasim 8
al-Mustazhir Billah 109
Alp Tigin 58
Al-Qa-im, Toğrül (caliph) 58–59
al-Ra'is (head ruler) 112
Al-Walid 39
Amalfitan hospital (Jerusalem) 103
Amalric (Count) 97
Amiens, Count of 124, 162–163
Ammianus Marcellinus 29
Anatolia, Crusader army 72, 119
"Ancient Arabs," tribes 51
Angevin Empire 85, 118, 120; Norman conquest 160
Anglo-Norman (French language) 48
An-Nahar 107
Anjou (royal dynasty) 106, 110, 119, 150–152
Anselme de Ribemont, Count (letter) 90
anti-Latin riots (Constantinople) 126–127
Antioch (Latin principality) 67, 71–73, 80
antipope 62
Apache, endonym 3
"apocalypse then" 162
Aqaba Khan 8–9, 153
Aquae Sextiae (Aix-en-Provence) 18
Aquitaine (Aquitania), duchy 27–28, 33–34, 93, 119, 161
Aquitani 18
Arabs and Ishmaelites (comparison) 50–55
Archbishop Anselm of Canterbury (Anselmo d'Aosta) 161
Archbishop Lafranc of Canterbury 161
Archbishop Manasses II of Reims 90
Archbishop of Cologne (prince-elector) 70
Arghun Khan 9
Aristotelian Categories 161
Armenian Orthodox Christians (Antioch) 72
Arnulf of Chocques 75

Arpa Ke'Un 10
Arp-Arslan (Seljuk Turk leader) 59
ar-Rum (Byzantium) 55
Arslan, Kilij 81, 82, 159
Arya-nam (land of the noble people) 3–4
Aryan-invasion theory 4
Ascalon (Ashkelon) 78–79
Ashkenaz (Germany) 15
Asia Minor, First Crusade 71
as-Salih Ayyub 146–147
Atabeg (Atabek) (Atabey) of Mosul 93; stabbing 96
Atlantis (Arabic name conversion) 15
Augusta Treverorum (Trier, Germany) 17
Aurelian, Emperor 30–31
Austrasia 33–34
Auxerre, Count of (King of the Franks) 41
Avesta language, 14
Ayyubid dynasty 133; toppling 148
Azzam Pasha (Abdulrahman Hassan al-Azzam) 170

Bacon, Roger 100–101, 169
Badr al-Jamali (Armenian Mamluk vizier) 79
Baghdad Khan 10
Baghdad Khatun (Queen Baghdad) 10
Baghdad (caliphate capital) 53
Baha ad-Din ibn Shaddad 113
Bahram Shah 58
Bahri dynasty 147
Balazuc, Pons de 72
Baldwin of Exeter (archbishop of Canterbury) 119
Balian of Ibelin 114
Balkan Turks 26
Baltic Crusades 84, 88, 98–100, 136, 169; atrocities 163
Baltic "heathen," 98
Baltic "Saracens" 98–102
Baltic tribes, Christianization 99
Barbaria (land, designation) 25–26
Barbarian Invasions 29
Barbarians 23–29
Barbarossa, Friedrich 119–120
Bari 62
Barthelemy, Pierre 72–73
Basques 48, 83–85
Batinis (Isma'ili Naziris) 80
Battle of Adrianople (Adrianopolis) 130
battle of *Ager Sanguinis* (Field of Blood) 89

Battle of Arausio, Roman army destruction 18
battle of Ascalon 73
Battle of Azaz, Josselin prisoner 95
Battle of Bouvines 47, 136
Battle of Charlemagne 83
Battle of Civetot 159
Battle of Court of The Martyrs *see ma'arakat bala ash-Shuhada*
Battle of Dandanaqan 58
Battle of Dorylaeum 72
Battle of Guadalete River 38
Battle of Hastings (1066) 46
battle of Hattin 39, 104, 114–116, 156; defeat 118
battle of Kosovo 49
Battle of Manzikert 59
Battle of Melitene 81
Battle of Naissus 23
Battle of Plovdiv 131
Battle of Ramia 79
battle of Roncevaux Pass 48, 83–86; French legend 85–86; historical account (Einhard) 84
Battle of the Elster River 62
Battle of the Teutoburg Forest 16
battle of Tours-Poitiers 27–28, 34, 37, 40, 53, 68; European Christians, defeat 54–55
battle of Volta Mantovana 61
Battle of Zama 13
Batu Khan 7, 10, 148
Baudouin de Boulogne (Baldwin of Boulogne) (Count of Edessa) 74, 81, 87–88
Baudouin de Flandre, Count 123
Baudouin, Emperor (succession) 131
Baudouin IV (Leper King of Jerusalem) 97
Baudouin V, Crusade leader 97
Baybars al-Bunduqdari 147–150, 166
Baybars (al-Malik az-Zahir Rukn al-Din Baybars al-Bunduqdari) 8, 78; attack 152; counterattack 153; dynasty establishment 78; executions 10; war advantage 150
Beaujeu, Guillaume de, 168
Beirut, capture 88
Béla III (Hungarian king) 125
Berber Muslim conquerors 26
Berbers (indigenous North Africans, Imazighen) 25–26
Beringia (land-covered Bering Straits) 3
Bernardo del Carpio (Iberian legend) 85

Bernard of Clairvaux 94–98
Bertha of Maurienne 60
Biblical Hazor, coalition 12
Biblical Hebrew, Jewish names 49
Biddick, Kathleen 155
bigotry 2
Biran, Michal 8
Bishop of Milan, chaplain installation 61
Black Death 159
Bodel, Jehan 27
Bohemond of Taranto (Norman Prince of Antioch) 71–81
Book of Jubilees 51
Bossong, Georg 15
Boulogne, Baudoin de 159
Bourgogne see Burgundy
Boves, Enguerrand de 162
Breton March (border region) 84
Brienne, Jean de ("King of Jerusalem") 137, 141–142; attack, absence 143–144; marriage 123
Britain, conquest by Normans 161
Bronze Age (Andronovo culture) 4
Bructeri (Germanic tribe) 29
Bulgars 7
Burgundy (Bourgogne) 27, 33–34, 37–38, 40–42, 44–45, 57, 65, 93–94, 124, 135
Bury, Richard de 42
Byzantine Empire 35, 57–63, 67–68, 122–131

Caen, Raoul de 77
Cairo (*al-Qāhirat*) 54; Al-Afdal exit 79; Azzam Pasha 170; envoy arrival 9; Crusaders march 133, 137, 146; Fatimid caliphs 79; Fatimid presence 15, 53–54, 58; Fatimid Caliphate 77; Mongol attack 153; Saracen caravan 114; Saracen Fatimid Cairo 124
Caliphate (s) 8–9, 14–15, 34, 52–54, 58, 74, 77, 79, 108–109, 161–162
Caliph of Tunis 150–151
Canaan 11–13
Canaanites (Phoenicians) 12–13, 31
Cannae (battle) 13
Capuano, Pietro Cardinal di 124
Carolingians Franks 35–44
Carolus (Martellus) (Charles Martel) 27, 34
Carpio, Bernardo del 85
Carthage 13–14, 23, 31, 33
Caspian Bagi Seian (emir of Antioch) 91
Cassidy-Welch, Megan 116, 156–157

Cassiodorus 22
Castel Sant'Angelo 62
Castile (Christian kingdom) 47–48
Cathar Crusade 133–134
Celestinus III, Pope: Crusade authorization 88, 98–100; death 121
Celtae (Celts) 18–19
Celtes, Conrad 31
Cemakar (Mongol general) 153
Centenera de Andaluz 16
Chalcedon, Council of 21
Chamavi (Germanic tribe) 17, 29–31
Champlitte le Champenois, Guillaume de 132
Chanson de Roland (poem) 48, 83–85
Chanson de Saisnes (Jehan Bodel) 27, 83
Chaoui (Imazighen, indigenous North Africans). 25
Charlemagne (Charles the Great) 28, 35–36, 40, 46, 48, 83–86
Charles the Simple 45–46
Chasteau-Porcien, Sibylle de 163
Chastellain, Georges 57
Chastillon, Reynauld de 113–116
Chatti (Germanic tribe) 29
Chattuarii (Germanic tribe) 29
Cherusci 16
Chiesa di San Marco (Venetian church) 125
children 1, 18, 46, 50, 52, 78, 97
Chinggis Khan 7–11, 153
Chlodovech (Chlodovechus) 37
chosen glory/trauma 1
Chosen People 3, 32
Christianization 99, 101
Christian nobility (ideal) 94
Christians: antisemitism 4–5; holy war, form 64; massacre 76; territory, reconquest 94; universal jurisdiction 160
Chronique d'Ernoul 114–115
Chroniques de Chastellain (Chastellain) 57
Chronographia (Theophanes) 21
Church Latin 37, 68, 161
Cilician Gates 80–81
Cimbri 18
Cistercian order 94, 124, 131
Clairvaux, Bernard de 93–94; "Doctor of the Church" title 95
Clari, Robert de 131
Claudius Claudianus (chronicles) 29
Clement III (anti-pope) 60
Clermont, Council of 66
Clorinda (Torquato Tasso) 77

Clovis (Chlodovech) 30, 37–38, 42, 45
Coleridge, Samuel Taylor 153
collective group narcissism 25
collective ideology 4–5
collective mourning 1
collective trauma 156–160
Column of Theodosius (Constantinople), Alexios 129
Combattimento di Tancredi e Clorinda (Monteverdi) 77
common language, speech 47
communities, cross-fertilization 89
Conqueste de Constantinople, De la (de Villehardouin) 132
Conrad II, Emperor (impact) 45
Conrad III of Germany 93–95
consanguinity (incest) 97
Constantinople (Byzantine capital) 21, 57–58, 88; Fourth Crusade 122–131
Constantine, Emperor (control) 21
Constantinople, First Council of (Roman primacy) 21
Constantius (praetorian prefect) 17
Córdoba, Umayyad Caliphate 15, 53–54, 161–162
Corpus Juris Canonici 123
Corrado del Montferrato (King Conrad of Jerusalem) *see* King Corrado del Monferrato
Coeur-de-Lion see Richard the Lion Heart
Count Louis de Blois 123
County of Burgundy 44
County of Tripoli 82, 88, 93, 117, 152, 167
Courçon, Robert de 136–137
Courtenay *see* Count Josselin de Courtenay
Courtenay, Agnes de (engagement) 97
Courtenay, Pierre de 135
Courtheuse, Robert (Robert of Normandy) 71
Couvent Saint-Jacques (Paris) 167
Crónica Mozárabe (Mozarab Chronicle) 27–28
Crusade of Richard (*Coeur-de-Lion*) see Richard the Lion Heart
"Crusade of the Faint-Hearted" 81
"Latin Kingdom of Jerusalem" 97, 170
Crusaders: army, transport 126; betrayal 126–127; castle, building 114; Holy Land, European Christian Crusader invasion 28; impact 10–11; Kingdom

of Hungary fight 69–74; Latin clery, discussions 128–129; leadership 133; Seljuk defeat 82; tribe naming 26–27
Crusades 37; barbaric assault, myth 63–64; Eighth Crusade 150; Fifth Crusade 132; First Crusade 41, 49, 56, 63; Fourth Crusade 114, 121; Franks-*versus*-Saracens story 65; homogenous movement, relationship 64; invention, question 63–69; leadership, Pope Innocentius III (relationship) 135; losses 64; Ninth Crusade 152; perception 63; Pope Urban call, response 68; rational causes 159–160; religious/political habits, reflection 64; Second Crusade 93; Seventh Crusade 145; Sixth Crusade 133–134; sources, re-evaluation 108; studies, context 108; Third Crusade 46, 117, 118; trauma 155
Curfürsten (Elector Princes), king election 43, 59, 70, 122–123
cursus publicus 31
Cyprus 81, 114, 118, 135, 145, 148, 150

Dagobert of Pisa 86, 87
Damascus 9, 15, 34, 38–40, 52–53, 79–80, 88, 91
Damaskenos, Johannes (John of Damascus) 52
Damasus I, Pope (death) 38
Damietta 133, 136–137, 141, 146–147
Dandolo, Enrico 124–125, 180
Danishmends 81, 95
Dar al-Ahad (Dar al-Sulh) (abode of reconciliation) 53
Dar al-Aman (abode of security) 53
Dar al-Dawa (abode of the invitation to Islam) 53
Dar al-Harb (abode of war) 40, 52
Dar al-Hudna (abode of the truce) 52–53
Dar al-Islam (abode of peace) 40, 52
Dar al-Kufr (abode of the infidel) 52–53
dehumanization, unconscious process 4–5, 112
départements d'outremer et territoires d'outre-mer (DOM-TOM) 117
Desiderius, Peter 74–75
Deutschland, endonym 2
Dhail Ta'rikh Dimashq (Continuation of the Chronicle of Damascus) (Hamza) 108
Dictatus Papae (Pope Gregorius VII) 60
Diocletianus, Emperor (impact) 17

Diyar Bakr (Diarbakir) 132
Docap (Duqaq ibn Tutush (prince of Damascus) 91
Dome of the Rock, *Templum Solomonis* (Crusader name) 104
Donatus Magnus (heretic) 25–26
Dukak Timuryaligh (Duqaq of the iron bow) 55–56

Eastern Roman Emperor: Alexios Komnenos 70, 71; Basil I 41; defeat 59
Eastern Roman Empire 21, 54, 69; "barbarian" invasion 23; strengthening 67–68
East, estrangement 129–130
East-West dialogue, evidence 65
East-West Schism 43
Eban, Abba 170
Edessa, County of 73–74, 77, 82, 87–89, 93, 96–97, 105, 117
Edward I (Edward Longshanks) of England 166, 167; alliance 152; Crusade 103
Egypt: Crusaders, sailing 136–137; Fatimids, entry 54; invasion 132; land-and-sea attack 153
Egyptian Mamluks, identification 7–8
Eickman, Patrick 163–164
eid ul-adha (Feast of the Sacrifice of Isma'il to Allah by Ibrahim) 80
Eighth Crusade 150
Einhard, battle of Roncevaux account *see* battle of Roncevaux Pass
eis tin polin (Istanbul) 21
"Elder House of Welf," founding 40–41
Eleanor of Aquitaine 93–94
Ellenblum, Ronnie 64–65
Emicho, Count, army (joining) 162
Emir Fakhr ad-Din ibn al-Shaykh, attack 146
emirs (princes) (commanders) 34, 53
endonym: ethononym division 2; human group psychology, relationship 3
entitlement ideology 1
Eracles de Colbert-Fontainebleau 115
Eracles de Lyon 114
Estienne (Étienne) de Blois 67, 90–91, 159
Estoire de la Guerre Sainte (Ambroise) 46, 48, 85, 121
Estoire d'Eracles (History of Heraclius) 114–115
Estonia 98
ethnic groups 37
ethnic tent 1

ethnocentrism 1–3, 6, 25, 33
ethononyms 2
Eudokia Angelina 129
Eugenius III (Bernardo dei Paganelli di Montemagno), Pope 93, 95, 98
Eugenius III, Pope; papal reign 93; Second Crusade preaching 98
Eugenius, Pope (arrival in France) 94
euphemisms 2
Euphrosyne Doukaina Kamatera 129
Eusebius Sophronius Hieronymus (Saint Jerome) 37–38
Eustache II of Boulogne, Count (Baudouin de Boulogne) (Baldwin of Boulogne) 70–71
Eustace III of Boulogne, Count 71, 78, 89
exonym 2–3
externalization ix, 1, 24, 48, 52, 59, 65
Extreme Unction 142
Ezzelino da Romano 88

Fathers of the Church (theologians), 52
Fatima az-Zahra 54
Fatimids 8, 15, 53–54, 57–59, 74, 78–79
Ferrand of Flanders, Count (King Philippe August of France conquest) 47
feudal lords, absolute authority 87
fideles Sancti Petri (faithful of Saint Peter) 57
Fidler, Richard 157
Fifth Crusade 132; European country involvement 133; failure 137–138, 141; history 132–133; leadership 137
Figueria, Guilhem 138
First Crusade 41, 49, 56, 63, 94; accounts 108; aftermath 81; analysis 157; collective trauma 159; initiation 68–69; leaders, identification 67; post-traumatic stress disorder 164; preaching 66
First Crusaders, Jerusalem massacre 156
Flanders, Robert de 159
Flandre, Count Baudouin de *see* Count Baudouin de Flandre
Flandres, Robert de (army, leading) 78
fnkhw (Egyptian name) 13
foederati (allies) 23, 31
Folkmar (knight), troop pillaging 69
Fornari, Franco 1; theory, confirmation 142
Fourth Crusade 114, 122; army, numbers 124, 127; blunders 125; joining, Republic of Genoa (disinterest) 124; leaders, papal letter 126; papal call 121; participation 123; plan 124; Pope Innocentius III ambition 123; tragedy 132
France: unification 44; upheavals 161
Francesco d'Assisi (Crusader arrival) 137
Franci (Franks) 41, 48, 85; exonym 30; people 20, 27, 30
Francia 40; disintegration 40–41, 48; empire, lands 33–34; expansion 27–28
Francia Media 40, 41
Francia Occidentalis [*Francia occidentalis* (West Francia)] 40, 48; German claim opposition 41
Francia Orientalis [*Francia orientalis* (East Francia)] 40; Burgundy, reunification 41; "Holy Roman Empire of the German Nation" 46
franj: animals, perception 112; battles 39; infidel, perception 54–55
Frankenland 46
Frankenreich (empire of the Frank) 46–47
"Frankish" Ardennes-Bouillon dynasty 78
Frankish army (ambush/defeat), Basques of Spain (impact) 83–84
Frankish kingdoms, reunification 41
"Frankish" letter 92
Frankish princes, personal rivalries 73
Frankish rulers, defeat 116
Franks: battle of Hattin 116; control, prevention 168–169; culture 111; jealousy, absence 109–110; legal procedure 110–111; march, description 115; misperception 79; *outre-mer* (beyond the sea) name 117; Romans/Germans, interaction 25; Saracens, contrast 77; Saracens, family ties 65; Saracens perception 107; self-naming 48; Zengi defeat 96
Fratres militiae Christi Livoniae, impact 99
Fredegarii chronicon (Chronicle of Fredegarius) (Latin manuscript): author question 33; psychological aspect 33
freemasons, Templar connection (speculation) 105
Friedrich, Emperor; approach 142–143; excommunication, Pope Gregorius IX decision 142
Friedrich II: Hohenstaufen dynasty 136; Holy Roman Emperor 141; *Imperator Romanorum* 137
Friedrich VI of Swabia, death 120
Froissart, Jean 159
Fürsten (princes) 43

Gabrieli, Francesco 107
Gagauz 26
Gaius Cornelius Tacitus (Roman historian) 16
Gaius Julius Caesar Octavianus Augustus (defeat) 16
Gaius Marius (battle win) 18
Gaius Suetonius Tranquillus 16
Galli (etymology) 18–19
Gallia, Julius Caesar invasion 45
Gallo-Roman language, adoption 46
Gallo-Roman population, Germanic immigrants (merger) 28
gallus (cock) 18, 22
Gambrivii (appellation) 20
ganana (ethnic name) 11
Gaston of Béarn 76
Gaugava River, Meinhard arrival 98
Gaul (Gallia) 32; Merovingian Frankish conquest 29–30
Gautier sans-avoir 69, 95
Gawhar as-Siqilli (the Sicilian) 54
Gaykhalt (Gaykhatu Khan), reign 9
Genghis Khan *see* Chinggis Khan
genocide: cause/encouragement 2; committing, preparing (social forces) 2
Genoese Crusade 88
gens Francorum (exonym) 30
Geoffrey de Villehardouin: chronicler 132; death 124
Geraudo institutori ac praeposito Hirosolimitani Xenodochii (papal bull) 104
German Crusades, arrival 98
Germania ("savage" tribal land) 19, 25; account 19–20
Germanic tribes, Roman perception 16–23
Germanic Visigoth, battle 28
Germans: niemci (exonym) 2; Romans/Franks, interaction 25
Germanus, name (usage) 25–26
Gerusalemme Liberata, La (Tasso) 77
Gesta Danorum (Deeds of the Danes) 45, 76
Gesta Francorum (Latin-language book) 57, 67
Gesta Tancredi (de Caen) 77
Getae (exonym) 22–23
Getic nations 23
Ghaznavid Empire (Turkic-Persian Muslim state) 58
Ghazni (capital) 58
Gibraltar *(jebel al-Tariq)* 15
God: concept 128–129; replacement 5

Godefroy of Bouillon (Godfrey of Bouillon) 71, 81; death 87; Latin Kingdom control 86–87; popularity 78
Godefroy of Saint-Omer of the Order of the Knights Templar, *Templiers* co-founder 104
Godefroy V of Lower Lorraine (Godefroy de Bouillon), agreement 69
Godfrey of Tuscany (death) 60
God the Father, myth 56
Göktürk (Göktürkler), conquest 6
Golden Bll, issuance 133
Golden Calf, sin 57
Golden Horde. *see Ulug Ulus*
Good/Bad struggle 134
Good mother, rescue 65
Gothi: migration 22; Thracian *Getae,* confusion 22–23
Gothica sors (Visigoths) 15
Gothic nations, presence 23
Gothic Thervingi, "barbarian" invasions 23
Gothic war, Visigoth battle 28
Goths 129; tribe, presence 23
goyim (gentiles), exonym 3
Graeci, Roman self-naming 2
Grailly, Jean de 167
Great Countess (Marchioness) Matilda of Tuscany 60; Rudolf kidnapping/marriage 61
Great Good Mother: longing 21; symbolization 68
Great Khanate, geography 11
Great Mosque, sermon 108–109
Great Saxon Revolt 60–62; Pope Gregory VII support 62
Great Schism (1054) 43, 58–59
Great Sea (Mediterranean), Canaanite existence 12–13
"Great Seljuk Empire," establishment 55
Great Wall of China: construction 6; overrunning 7
"Greek" Christians, "Latin" Christians murder 122
Greek Orthodox Christian population, exile 72
Gregorius de Turones (chronicles) 29
Gregorius VII, Pope 59–60; Benevento, impact 62; *Dictatus Papae* 60; Heinrich IV, power struggle 63; revenge 62
Gregorius IX, Pope 140; excommunication reason 142; provocation 143
Gregorius X, Pope 166

Gregorius, Pope (King Heinrich opposition) 88
Gregory VII, Pope: accession 60–61; deposition 61; Great Saxon Revolt 62
Gregory X, Pope 166
Gregory, Pope (Third Crusade call) 119
Greuthungi (steppe dwellers) 22
group purification 1
Guadalajara, *Andaluz* brook 16
Guillaume le conquérant (William the Conqueror), invasion 46
Guillaume II of Nevers, Count 81; regent election 97–98
Guillaume of Normandy 161
Guilscard of Apulia, Byzantines (feud) 62
Guiscard, Robert (of Apulia) 63, 71
Gunther of Pairis (Günther von Pairis) 124, 131

"Hagarenes" (Arabs, name) 51–52
Hahn, Philipp M. 105
Haimaz (homeland: *Heimat*) 17
Hainault, Ide de 162
Hakenkreuz (swastika) 4
Hamadan, sultanate creation 55
Hamas (Islamic group) 171
Hamm (settlement) 17
Hamza ibn Asad abu Ya'la ibn al-Qalanisi 80, 108
Hannibal: army 13; Carthage return 13; death 13
Harran, caliphate setup 53
Harun al-Rashid (caliph, reign) 53
Hassan-i-Sabah, Nizari Ismaili community establishment 79
hatred, cause/encouragement 2
Haute Cour (High Court), endorsement refusal 97
Hazor city-state, leadership 12
Heavenly Host, protection 70
Hebrew Bible: Canaanite Hebrew writing 14; genealogies, comparison 50–51; *Septuagint* Greek translation 51; *Vulgata* Latin version 37–38
Hebrews, Ionim self-naming 2
Hecataeus of Miletus (writings) 19
Heebøll-Holm, Thomas Kristian 162–164
Heim (home) 17
Heinrich der Finkler *(Heinrich der Vogler) (Henricus Auceps)* 44
Heinrich, Emperor (Henry II) 161

Heinrich IV 59–60; Bertha of Maurienne marriage 60; bribe 62; crowning 60; emperor, crowning 63; Great Saxon Revolt 60–62; Holy Roman Emperor 67; penance 62; Pope Gregorius VII, power struggle 63; refuge 61–62; Rome entry 62–63
Heinrich VI: Crusade 120; death 122; murder accusation 121
Hellenes, Greek self-naming 2
Henriques, Afonso (King Afonso I of Portugal) 94
Henry, Archbishop of Mainz (regency) 98
Henry of Burgundy, Theresa de León (marriage) 94
Heraclius, reign 115
heresy, components 134
Hermann of the *Cherusci* (Germanic tribe leader) 16
Herminones (coast tribe) 20
Herodotus (*Keltoi* location) 19
Herrenvolk (master people // master race) 4
Hijra 108–109
Hilal bin al-Muhassin al-Sabi 108
Hillenbrand, Carole 107–108
Himmler, Heinrich 5
Hisham III (Caliph of Córdoba) 53
Hispania: Germanic tribe invasion 20; identification 14–15
Historia constantinopolitana (Gunther of Pairis) 124
Historia Francorum qui ceperunt Hierusalem (d'Aguilers) 72–73, 83
Historia Hierosolymitanae expeditionis or Chronicon Hierosolymitanum de bello sacro (Albert of Aachen) 80
Historia rerum in partibus transmarinis gestarum (William of Tyre) 114–115
history, division 29
Hitler, Adolf 4
Hitti, Philip Khuri 109
Hizballah (Islamic group) 171
Hoffmann, Christoph 105
Hoffmann, Gottlieb W. 105
holy cities (sacred space) 68
Holy City: peaceful purchase 140; rescue 98; taking 76
Holy Lance (holy lance): discovery 73; miracle 73
Holy Land: appellation 21; Christians, Greek Orthodox Patriarch authority 86–87; Crusades 88; defense 87–88;

European Christian Crusader invasion 28; fortifications, creation 104; French/Norman Crusaders arrival 49; recovery 135; rescue 98; seaport access 118; Seljuk capture 59
Holy Roman Empire 100; fantasy 42; Magdeburg (capital) 44–45; translation 42–45
"Holy Roman Empire of the German Nation" 42
Holy See 21
"Holy Sepulcher", Church of the ix, 56–57, 65–68, 70, 74, 78, 98, 115, 121, 130, 143, 159, 165
Holy Sepulcher (Holy Sepulchre) 87; Jesus burial 165; liberation 74; rescue, goal 98; road, entry 66; sacred space 68
holy shrines (sacred space) 68
Holy Spirit, myth 56
holy war, waging 98
Honorius III, Pope 133; attack, absence 143–144; Cardinal Cencio), election 133; Crusade entry, reluctance 140–141; Fifth Crusade role 140; Holy Land recovery 135; machinations 137–138; papal legate 137
Horowitz, David 170
hospice of St. John 104
Hospitallers 103
House of Plantagenet (House of Anjou) 119
Hugh the Great 90
Hugo of San Severino 166
Hugues Capet (Duke of France) (Count of Paris), crowning 44
Hugues de Payens, *Ordre des Templiers* founding 104
Hugues le Grand (Duke of France) 44, 70
Hülegü Khan 9, 153; attack 8
human beings, group division (predisposition) 2
human groups, self-naming 2
human warfare, existence 1
Humphrey III of Toron (Latrun) 113–114
Hundred Years War 159
Hurlock, Kathryn 164–165
Husayn, surrender (refusal) 86

Iamnia (Yavneh) (Jabneh) 114
Ibelin, Hugues d' (Hugh of Ibelin), de Courtenay engagement 97

Iberia: Christian kingdoms 161–162; conquest 39, 160; Saracens/Charlemagne battle 85
Ibn al-Athir (Abu al-Hassan Ali ibn Muhammad 'izz al-Din ibn al-Athir al-Jazari) 55, 86, 108
Ibn al-Khashshab (impact) 109
Ibn al-Qalanisi 80, 96; instruction 108–109
Ibn Battuta (Abu Abdallah Muhammad ibn Abdallah al-Lawati) 10
Ibn Munqidh: medicine instruction 111–112; memoir 113
Ifriqiya 150, 166; Musa bin Nusair governance 38
Iftikhr al-Dawla 74
Ijssel River (Netherlands) 17
Ilghazi of Mardin (Seljuk ruler of Aleppo) 89
Ilkhan Aqaba (Abagha Khan) 152
Imad ad-Din Muhammad ibn Muhammad al-Katib al-Isfahani 113, 116
Imad ad-Din Zengi al-Malik al-Mansur (Victorious King), Abbasid caliph rule 96
Imazighen (Amazigh) (free men) 25
Immaculate Conception, myth 56
Imperator Augustus (Charlemagne crowning) 35–36
imperator Romanorum (*Imperator Romanorum*) 28, 31, 35, 42, 137; term, usage 44; title, assumption 43–44
imperial world-order, collapse 22
indeh (people) 17
indigenous North Africans, pride 25
Indo-Aryans, derivation 4
Indogermanen (Indo-Germans) 4
indulgences: granting 67; medieval Christian belief 66–67; receiving 66; seriousness 66–67
infidels, conversion 101–102
Ingaevones (coast tribe) 20
inglés, exonym 3
Innocentius III, Pope 123, 126; agreement, ratification 124; battle/alliances 136; death 133; Fourth Crusade 123; Livonian Knights agreement 100; machinations 137–138; marriage order 131; opposition 140–141; papal bull 132–133
Innocent, Pope (Crusade control) 134
inter-cultural influence 65
interfaith cooperation 158
internalization 24

Investiture Controversy, origin 61
investiture, usage 60
Ioannis Komnenos of Byzantium, Emperor (Latin kingdom expansion) 96
Iranian Samani dynasty 58
Iraq (gift of God) (garden of God) 53
Irene Serantapechaina, Empress (death) 35
"Iron Bridge" (attack) 91
Isaakios II Angelos (Byzantine emperor) 124, 126; Crusader restoration 127
"Ishmaelite Arabs" ("Arabized Arabs"), central/North Arabian location 51
"Ishmaelites" (Arabs, name) 51–52
Isidore of Seville 22
Islamic Jihad (Islamic group) 171
Istaevones (coast tribe) 20
Italian Crusades 88
Italy, military integration 161
iter (voyage) 57
Izz ad-Din Aybak, murder 147

Jadera (Jadres) 125
James II of Aragon 167
Jami al-Tawarikh (Rashid al-Din Fadlullah Hamadani) 9
Japan: inferiority complex, defense 5–6; Mongol invasions 5; superiority complex 5–6
Jauhar ar-Rumi (the Byzantine) 54
Jean de Brienne (Crusade) 88
jebel al-Tariq (Gibraltar) 15; Jerusalem (Al Quds): Fatimid capture 109; Frank, destination 57; "Latin" kingdom 86–92; Latin Kingdom, end 167–168; Latin Kingdom, "Frankish" rural settlement 64; Latin Kingdom, psychogeographical fantasy 76; Latin Kingdom, tribute demand 167; liberation 130; losses 49; peaceful conquest during the Sixth Crusade 140; recapture 145; restitution 143; siege 74; taking, Franks desire 79
Jesus Christ as God the Son, myth 56
Jesus Christ: birth/crucifixion 68; replacement 5; True Cross 137
Jesus Christ Ouor Lord, Jewish identification 101
Jewish Agency for Palestine 170
Jewish *Talmud*, burning 145
Jewish Zionists, losses (mourning) 49
Jews: debts, non-repayment 145; massacre 68–69; Rodolphe inspiration 95

jihad (holy war) poetry, translations 107
Jochi Khan, death 10
Johannes II Komnenos attack 96
Johannes II, Pope (crowning) 42
Johannes XIX, Pope (death) 44
John of England *see* King John of England
John of Parker 153
John the Baptist 56
John VII the Oxite, imprisonment 72
John XII, Pope (Charlemagne crowning) 35–36
Joinville, Jehan de 148
Jordanes 22
Josselin de Courtenay, Count: Crusade leadership 95–96; defeat/capture 97; Edessa capture, attempt 96–97
Josselin II of Edessa 95–96
Judas Maccabeus (The Hammer) 34
Julian the Apostate, *Salii* (Salian Franks) invitation 31
Julius Caesar: *Galli* perception 19; text 18
Jurchens, impact 6–7

Kabyles (indigenous North Africans) 25
Kálmán, Könyves (Coloman the Book Lover), Crusaded choices 69
kami (gods) 5
kamikaze (divine wind) 5
Karakorum (Kharkhorin) (Mongol capital), destruction 11
Karl der Grosse (Charlemagne), empire 46
karling (kerling) (descendant of Charles) 37
Karney Hittin (Hebrew for the Horns of Hattin) 115
Kedar, Benny 89
Keltai (Keltoi) 18–19
Kerak Castle 116; *Crac des Moabites* 113–114; Knights Hospitaller headquarters 103
Kerbogha. *see* Qiwam al-Dawla Kerbogha
Kerman, sultanate creation 55
Keykavus (Seljuk Turkish leader) 137
Khagan (Great Khan) (emperor), election 7
khalifa (successor) (replacement) (representative) 34
khalifat rasul Allah (successors to the messenger of Allah) 34
Khans (leaders) 6, 7
Khitan, rule 6
Khitans, impact 6–7

198 Index

Khorasani 26
Khübilai Khan 153; Khagan election 10
Khwarezmids, remnants 10
Kievan Rus: military campaigns 10; Mongol invasion 7
Kiev, sacking 10
kihnahhu (dye, synonym) 11
King Afonso I of Portugal 94–95
King Alfonso II of Asturias 85
King Alfonso VI of Castile 89
King Alfonso VI of León 94
King András of Hungary 135
King Baldwin IV (envoy) 113–114
King Baudaouin III of Jerusalem, death 97
King Baudaouin IV of Jerusalem, leprosy 114
King Baudaouin, reign 103
King Boiorix 18
King Charles d'Angjou 166–167; attacks 152
King Charles *le gros* (Charles the Fat), Frankish kingdom unification 41
King Clovis, Queen Clotilde marriage 38, 42–43
King Conrad (murder), Heinrich VI accusation 121
King Conrad III, cross (receiving) 93–94
King Conradin of Jerusalem and Sicily (Crusade) 88
King Corrado del Monferrato (King Conrad of Jerusalem) 114
Kingdom of Cyprus: creation 114; Holy Land authority claim 148
Kingdom of Heaven (film) 114
Kingdom of Hungary, Crusader fight 69–74
"Kingdom of Jerusalem" (setup) 48
Kingdom of Lower Burgundy 44
Kingdom of Upper Burgundy 44
King Foulques of Jerusalem 110; castle construction 114; Latin Kingdom extension 96
King Guy de Lusignan 114–116; life, sparing 117
King Henri of Cyprus (Henry II) 167
King Henry II of England 119; Crusade, leadership 120
King Hugues of Cyprus (Hugh III) 153
King Jean of Jerusalem 135; Damietta attack 136
King John of England, return 136
King Louis IX of France (Saint Louis): attack, hopelessness 147; Crusader force, annihilation 146–147; death 150; Jerusalem recapture 145; Paris return 148–149; Seventh Crusade 146
King Louis *le fainéant* (the idle) 44
King Louis *le Gros* 162–163
King Louis the Lion, death 134
King Louis VI *(Louis de gros)* 94
King Louis VII 93–94
King Louis VIII (Louis de Lion) 134; death, blame 138
King Manfred of Sicily 166
King Manfred von Hohenstaufen 150
King of Cyprus 135
King of Jerusalem (Baudouin de Boulogne) 87
King of Jerusalem, displacement 118
King of Naples, alliance 152
"King of the Franks," election 45–46
"King of the Latins of Jerusalem" title 87
King of the Romans, coronation 160
King Otto IV of Germany (defeat) 136; King Philippe Auguste of France 47
King Otto "the Great" of Germany, crowning 42
King Philippe Auguste of France, conquest 47, 136
King Philippe II of France, Crusade leadership 120
King Philippe le Bel of France 105; Pope Clement V, impact 104
King Philippe of France (war cessation) 119
King Richard of England, arrest 121
King Roderic 38
King Roger II of Sicily, Conrad enemy 97; marriage 88; offense 97–98
King Thuedobod (battle win) 18
King William II of England 71
King William II of Sicily 118
Kipchak Khanate 10
Kipchak Turks, regiment (impact) 147–148
kitab al i'tibar (Munqidh) 113
Kitab al-'itibar 110–111
Knights Hospitaller 103; control 118; Grand Master 168; order, Thom founding 104
Knights of Malta 103
Knights of Rhodes 103
Knights Templar 104; Grand Master 168
Köktürkler, conquest 6
Komnenos. *see* Alexios Komnenos
Komnenos, Johannes: Edessa, extension attempt 96; usurpation 127

Index   199

Kosovo, battle *see* battle of Kosovo
Kubla Khan (Coleridge) 153
Kurdis Muslim dynasty 132

LaCapra, Dominick 155, 158, 165
Lafranc of Cantebury (Lafranc du Bec) (Lafranco di Pavia) 161
La Hoz (cave) 16
Lake Baikal (Dada/Dadan/Tatan/Tantan) 7
Lake Trasimene (battle) 13
l'Allemagne, exonym 2
La Manche (English Channel), Duke of Normandy crossing 46
lamentation, *troubadour* tradition 138
Lanahlauts (Gothic name) 15
Landgrave Ludwig IV of Thuringia 142
"Land of Iran" (Iran), Ilkhanate name 8
"Land of the Rising Sun" (Japan) 5
Langobards (long beards) 81
language, importance 2
langue d'oc 27, 47–48
Languedoc, political control 134
langue d'oïl 27, 47–48, 68, 85; biography 57
Laodicaea, Frankish letter 91–92
large-group formation, language (importance) 2
large-group identities 158
large-group narcissism 1
large-scale organized warfare, dating 1
Late Bronze Age 12
Latin clergy, discussions 128–129
"Latin Crusaders," impact 122
"Latin Empire of Constantinople" establishment/creation 129, 132
Latin enemy siege engines, destruction 128
Latin Kingdom: defense 81–82; expansion 96; influence 105–106
Latin Kingdom of Jerusalem 119; Latinness 87; location 77
"Latin" kingdom, passage 97
Latin King of Jerusalem 143
Latin Patriarchate of Jerusalem, archdiocese divisions 86–87
"Latin Patriarch of Jerusalem": Guillaume de Tyr prevention 97; letter 90
Latin Rule, creation 104
Latin soldiery, impact 129
Le Crac des Chevaliers (Qala'at al-Hisn) 103
Leo I, Pope (papal authority) 21
Leo IX of Rome, Pope (conflict) 43

Leon (Christian kingdom) 47–48
Leopold of Austria (duke), 120–122, 133, 135–136
les Maures noirs 26
Lesser Genesis (Leptogenesis) 51
Lewis, Bernard 50
Lex Ripuaria, origin 30
Lex Salica (Salic law) 30
Liber Historiae Francorum (Book of the History of the Franks) 33
Light/Darkness struggle 134
light-skinned people, naming 26
lingua franca (language of the Franks) 47
Lisbon, Portuguese capture 99
Livonia: Bishop Berthold arrival 98; colonization, *Fratres militiae Christi Livoniae* (impact) 99
Livonian Crusade 99
Livonian Knights (Brothers of the Sword): agreement, Pope Innocentius III signing 100; incorporation 143
Livonian Order (Livonian Knights) 99
Lombardia 34
Lord of *Oultrejordain* (Trans-Jordan) 116
Lord of Oultre-Jordain, marriage 113
Lordship of Ireland 119
Lotario Cardinal de' Conti di Segni, election 122–123
Lothar (realm) 40
Louis d'Or 28
Louis IV of France ("Louis d'outre-mer") 117
Louis *le Batailleur* (Louis VI) 162
Louis VII of France *(Louis le jeune)* (roy des François), Crusade leadership 95
Lucius Nonius Asprenas (commander) 16
Ludolf of Tournai 76
Lusignan, Guy de *see* King Guy de Lusignan
Lusignan, Hugues de 81–82
Luther, Martin 67, 138
Lydus, Johannes 22

Maalouf, Amin 107, 113
ma'arakat bala ash-Shuhada (Battle of Court of The Martyrs) 34
Madden, Thomas 122
madinat as-salaam (city of peace) 53
Magdeburg (HRE capital) 44–45
Magna Carta, signing 136
Mahmoud Shah 58

Mahmud Ghazan Khan (Chinese Buddhist education) 9
major domus ("Mayors of the Palace") 32, 34, 38
Malaspina, Saba 150
Malecorne, Arnulf (of Chocques / of Rohes) 78
Malik-el-Adil of Egypt, truce 141
Malik Ghazi Danishmend (Danishmend Emir) (Ghazi Gümüştekin of Sivas), expedition preparation 81
mamluk ("one who is owned") 7–8, 78
Mamluks: military activities 152; rule 166
Mamluks of Egypt, alliance 8, 10
Manfred of Sicily (Crusade) 88
Mannus (Tuisco son) 20
Manuel Komnenos of Byzantium, Emperor 113–114
Manzikert, battle *see* Battle of Manzikert
Maragheh (Mongol Ilkhanate capital) 10
Marcellinus Comes 22
Marcus Aurelius Septimius Bassianus Antoninus Augustus Caracalla (Roman Empire ruler) 30
Marcus Porcius Cato (Cato Censorius) (Cato Sapiens) (Cato Priscus) (Cato Major) (Cato the Elder) 13
Mari ruins 11
Maris (appellation) 20
Marle, Thomas de 162; atrocities 163; escape 162
Martel, Charles 27, 37, 38
Martin IV, Pope (successor) 166
Martin of Pairis 131
Martin, Raymund 89
mashiakh (Messiah) 3
Masoretes (Tradition Bearers) 14
Masoretic text 51
mass killing, broadcasting (absence) 2
Mater Ecclesia 94
Matilda. *see* Great Countess (Marchioness) Matilda of Tuscany
Maure, denotation 27
mauros (*moro,* relationship) 26
Maximianus (co-emperor) 17
medieval Christians, indulgences (seriousness) 66–67
medieval *Khorasan* (region) 58
medieval Muslims, oral traditions 86
medieval war, atrocities 126
Mediolanum (Milan), Germanic tribe (settling) 81

Meinhard (Daugava River arrival) 98
Melqart (King of the City) (god of Tyre) 13
Melun, Guillaume de 69
Meng Tian, tenure 6
Mente, Boye Lafayette de 6
Meroveus 37
"Merovingian" Frankish dynasty 37
Mesopotamia (Between the Rivers) 53
Messinopolis, Geoffrey ownership 130
Michaelis Palaeologos, Emperor 167
Middle Bronze Age 12
Migration Period 29
Miles of Plancy 113–114
milites Christi (soldiers of Christ) 57
Mitchell, Piers 156
Modu Shany Mete Khan, unification efforts 6
Molay, Jacques de 105
Molinier, Auguste 73
Monferrato, Bonifacio del 123, 126, 130; envoys, travel 123–124; fleet 126
Monferrato, Maria del 141
Möngke Khan: death 8, 10, 11; Khagan of the Mongol Empire 148
Mongol autonomous region 11
Mongol Empire: geographic reach 7; inheritance 8; West Asian parts, Hülegü Khan inheritance 8
Mongol Ilkhanate of 8, 10
Mongols: alliance 148; expansion 148; identification 6; Papal mission 145
Mons Peregrinus, castle (building) 82
Monpeslier, Gormonda de 138
Montaigue, Roger de 162
Monteuil, Adhemar de (Adhemar du Puy) death 67; ghost, vision 74–75; negotiation 72
Monteverdi, Claudio 77
Montfort, Philippe de (Lord of Tyre) (assassination) 153
Moor, denotation 27
moral injury, defining 164
morality, disengagement 2
moral justification, seeking 2
Moretus, Johannes 31
Moros: denotation 27; invaders 26
Morphia of Melitene, Boudouin (marriage) 105–106
moshavot (colonies) 171
Moshe ben Naphtali *(Masorete)* (Tradition Bearer) 14
mourzouphlas, meaning 127

Moussais-la-Bataille (Vouneuil-sur-Vienne) 34
Mughal Empire of India, naming 11
Muhammad al-Mustansir 150–151
Muhyi ad-Din ibn Abd az-Zahir 113
Mu'in ad-Din Unur al-Atabeki (Yaranqash arrest) 96
Musa bin Nusair: Al-Walid displeasure 39; battles 39; fortunes 40; governance 38
Muslim Baghdad, sack 153
Muslim MondolIlkhanate of "Iran" (disintegration) 10
Muslims: Crusaders battles 27; defeat, nonacceptance 48–49
musta'arib (Arabized) 28
mutafarnij (Europeanized) 55
mutual inter-cultural influence 65
myth of origin 32, 51

Nablus, capture 78
Najm ad-Din Ilghazi ibn Artuq: expulsion/death 79, 89; Saracen army, attack 89
Nazi Germans, murders 4
Neapolis (Nablus), Council of 105–106
Neustria 33–34
Nevers, Guillaume de (escape) 81
New Crusaders 170
Nicaea, camp movement 90
Nicolaus IV, Pope (Girolamo Masci) 167
Nicomedia (Izmit, Turkey) 17
niemtsi (mute people) 3
Nihon (Nippon) (source of the Sun) 5
Niketas Akominatos Choniates 130–131
Ninth Crusade 152, 166
Nizar. see Abu Mansur al-Nizar
Nizari Isma'ili "Assassins" murders 8
Nizari Ismaili community, establishment 79
Normandie, Robert Curthose de 159
Normandy 40, 44–46, 71, 78, 119, 136, 161
Normans: colonial ambitions 68; conquest 160
Norsemen invasion 45
Northern Crusades: beginning, Pope Celestinus III (impact) 99–100; undertaking 100
Notsrim ("Nazarenes"), Christians (name) 52
Nova Roma 20–21; *Constantinopoils* (name change) 21
Novella, Guillem Augier 138
nuns, violation 129

Nuzi tablets 11

Odo (Eudes) (count of Paris), King of West Francia election 41, 45–46
Oedipal battle 140
Oedipal struggle 87–88
Oedipal theme 86
Ögedei Khan (Chinggis successor) 7
Oghuz Turks (Turkic tribe): member 57; migration 26
Ögödei Khan, succession 148
Old Testament, Septuaginin translation 3
Oliver of Cologne: Acre arrival 135; army leadership 133; Damietta attack 136; preaching 134–135
omikami (goddesses) 5
Onon River, nomads (presence) 6
Opus Maius (Bacon) 100
oral traditions, usage 86
Order of St. John 103
Order of the Knights of the Hospital of St. John of Jerusalem (Sovereign Military Hospitaller Order of St. John of Jerusalem) 103
Order *Thoroth* 15
Ordre des Hospitaliers (Knights Hospitaller) 103
Ordre des Templiers (Knights Templar) 104; Hugues de Payens (Grand Master) 104
organized human warfare, existence 1
origine actibusque Getarum, De (The Origin and Deeds of the Getae) (Jordane) 23
Orosius 22
Orthodox clerics, murder 129
Oster, David 22
Otto I (Holy Roman Emperor) 45
Otto IV of Germany, defeat *see* King Otto IV of Germany
Ottoman Turks, battle of Kosovo 49
Ottonian dynasty (Saxon dynasty) 43
Otto of Brunswick 126; papal support 123
Otto of Freising 97
Otto the Great (Holy Roman Emperor) 160
Oultre-Jordain (Trans-Jordan) 113–114
Outremer 166; remnants, attack 150
Outre-mer (beyond the sea), Franks (name) 117
Özbeg Khan (*Ulug Ulus* ruler) 10

pagan antisemitism, defense mechanism 4–5
"pagan" Baltic tribes, Christianity conversion 99–100
pagan idolaters, holy war 98
pagan race, faith (receiving) 101–102
Pairis *see* Gunther of Pairis
Palaeologos, Michaelis 166, 167
Palatium Cassiani 73
Palestine, Jewish settlement 171
Panegyrici Latini (Roman manuscript) 31
Papa (father) 140
Papacy, challenge 134–135
Papal Banner 70
Papal Curia, mediator 143
Paris, Mathieu de (Matthew of Paris) 148–149
Paris, Viking siege 45–46
Paschal Chronicle 22
Paschall II, Pope (papal recognition) 104
pastoureaux (shepherds) 156
paternal dictate, Heinrich IV reaction 60
Patriarch Michaelis Cerularius of Constantinople, conflict 43
Patriarch of Jerusalem, Extreme Unction 142
Pauperes commilitones Christi Templique Solomonici (The Poor Fellow-Soldiers of Christ and of the Temple of Solomon) 104
paupers, slavery sale 70
Payens, Hugues de (Grand Master) 104
peacemaking, efforts 158
Pégulhan, Aimery de 138
Pelagius of Albano (Pelagio Galvani), papal legate 137
penances, indulgence replacement 67
people's army, impact 69
People's Crusade (paupers Crusade) 69–70, 155–156, 159
peregrinatio (pilgrimage) 57
Persian Buyids (Buwayhids), political domination 58
Per Venerablem (papal decree) 123
Peter the Hermit 75
Petrarca, Francesco 159
Petrus Alfonsi 89
Peutinger, Conrad 31
Philip of Swabia: del Montferrato visit 126; excommunication, Pope Celestinus III decision 122
Philippe Auguste, control 136

Philippe of Ibelin 167
Philippe the First of France 70
Phillips, Jonathan 122
Phoenicia (Canaan name) 11–12
phoini (purple) dye 12–13
phoinix (phoenix) 13
Picquigny, Guermond de 163
Pier Damiani (Papal legate) 60
Pierre l'hermite 69–70, 95
Pietro Cardinal di Capuano (death) 124
pilgrimage, military leader journey 67
Pillars of Hercules (straits of Gibraltar) 23
Placentia (Piacenza), church council 65
Poitiers, Alphonse de 146
Poitou, Agnes de (death) 60
Polabian Slavs, Crusade 98
Ponte della Maddalena, Matilda commission 61
Post-Modern era 29
post-traumatic stress disorder 155, 164; diagnosis 165
prehistory 1
Prester John (Presbyter John), myth 148
primus inter pares (first among equals) 160
Prince Bohemond IV of Antioch 135
Prince Edward of England: army attack 152; rivalry, cessation 153–154
Prince of Achaea 132
Prince of Antioch 116; rule 113
Prince Roger of Salerno (death) 89
princes, absolute authority 87
Princes' Crusade (Barons' Crusade) 70
Principality of Antioch: founding 88; possession 73
Procopius of Caesarea 22
projection 23–24
Prophet Muhammad: death 34; emigration 108
Protestant Reformation, Luther initiation 67
Proto Indo-European language 14, 17, 19
Pseudepigrapha 51
psychic trauma 159
psychogeographical fantasy 65, 68, 76, 121
psychohistorical/psychogeographical fantasy 42
Pubio Fidei (Martin) 89
Publius Vergilius Maro (Virgil) 31
Puni (Punici) (Punicus), battle 13
punicus (exonym) 13
Punic wars, duration 13
"Pure Arabs," South Arabian tribes (migration) 51

pure race 46
Puy, Adhemar du 71, 159
Pytheas of Massalia (sailor) 19

Qalawun al-Alfi: army, attack 167; death 147
Qart Khadat (chief god) 13
Qashqai 26
Qatna (Amorite kingdom) 12
Qiwam al-Dawla Kerbogha (Kürboğa) 73
Qonqurtai (Mongol viceroy of Anatolia) 9
Queen Alix of France 123
Queen Clotilde of Burgundy, King Clovis marriage 38, 42–43
Queen Yolande-Isabella of Jerusalem, death 143–144
Queller, Donald 122
Quia maior papal bull (Innocentius III) 133
Quintilius Varu (Roman general) 16
Qur'an, genealogies 51

racism 1; cause/encouragement 2; tendency 3
Rahisum, trouble 11
Rashid al-Din Fadlullah Hamadani 9
Raymond of Aguilers 75
Raymond of Toulouse 159; religious/material motives 78, 81–83
Raymond III of Tripoli, Count 114
reconquista 48
Reconquista (process) 94
Reconquista (re-conquering) 161–162
Recueil des historiens des croisades 115
reges criniti (long-haired kinds) 32
Regnum Hierosolymitanum 76
Regnum Terrae Sanctae (Kingdom of the Holy Land) 76
relic of the True Cross 116, 156
religions, khan tolerance 9
rescue fantasies, persistence 93
Rex Francorum (Kings of the Franks) 35
Rex Germanorum (King of the Germans) 35
Rex Romanorum ("King of the Romans") 35, 135, 140–141; styling 95
rex Romanorum (King of the Romans) 31
Richard I of England, Cyprus conquest 118
Richard the Lionheart (*Richard Coeur-de-Lion* 118–121; Crusade 85
Ripuari ("savage" tribe) 29, 30
River Rhine ("Jordan River") 49
River Scheldt, *Franci* rule 31

Robert d'Artois 146
Robert de Normandie 45–46
Robert II of Flander, Count 71
Rodolphe (French monk), massacre inspiration 95
Roger II of Sicily *see* King Roger II of Sicily
Roger of Wendover (chronicler) 142
Roiaume de Jherusalem 76
Rolando, slaying 86
Rollo (Hrólf, Frankish Latin version) 45–46
Roma, Nazi murders 4
Roman Catholic Christian Church, split 43
Roman Emperor Basil I, Western Roman Emperor Louis II (alliance) 41
Roman empire, "barbarian" invasions 23
Roman Empire, indivisibility 17
Roman exonym, Germanic tribe adoption 20
Roman Gaul (Gallia), Frank invasion attempt 28
Roman Normandy, Norsemen invasion 45
Romanos Diogenes, defeat 59
Roman roads, building 45
Romans: allegiance, abrogation 62–63; forces (defeat), barbarians (impact) 16–17; Franks, interaction 25; Germans, interaction 16–23, 25
Roncesvalles, Rolando (slaying) 86
Roncevaux Pass *see* battle of Roncevaux Pass
Rossel, Reginald 153
Rothard of Metz 40–41
Rouran, power 6
Rowan, Jr., Spencer Ford 157–158
Ruanruan, power 6
Rudolf von Rheinfelden 60–61
Rumi (Jalal ad-Din Muhammad Rumi) (poet/scholar) 27
"Rum" (Anatolia), sultanate creation 55
Russia, Mongol invasion 7

Sacred Lance, bearing 72–73
sacred space (geographical/physical location) 68
Saif ad-Din Qutuz, death 147
Saint Augustine of Hippo (bishop) 25–26
Saint Bernard of Clairvaux 104
Saint Constantine 21
Saint-Gilles de Toulouse, Count Raymond 67, 71–73, 80; defeat, Seljuk Turks (impact) 82; "King of Jerusalem" crown, refusal 77–78

Saint-Maxence, Guernes de Pont de 57
Saint Helena 21
Saint Hippolytus, "Saracens" name usage 52
Saint-Jean d'Acre 118
Saint-Jean d'Acre (capital): capture/destruction 104; Mamluk conquest 87
Saint-Jean de Laon, abbey (land ownership) 163
Saint Jerome 18
Saint Louis, war (unhappiness) 145
Saint Peter, throne 21
"Saint Thomas the Martyr" (Thomas à Becket) 57
Saladin 39, 115; arrival 80; fortress 103
Salah ed-din Yusuf ibn Ayub (Ayyubi dynasty founder) 39
Salar 26
Saldana, Count of 85
Salian Frankish dynasty 32
Salian Franks 42–43; name, English change 29
Salii ("savage" tribe) 29, 30, 36
Salius (Dutch name corruption) 17
Salland (Dutch area) 17
saltus Teutoburgiensis (Teutoburg forest valley) 16
Samagar (Mongol general) 153
Samson Syndrome 5
Sancho, blinding/prison 85
Sanctum Romanum Imperium (Holy Roman Empire), birth 35
Sanskrit language, Greek/Latin (relationship) 14
Santa Maria Maggiore (Roman church) 61
saraceni (history) 50
Saracen Jerusalem, siege 74
Saracens 54–55; Ayyubids, fight 135; Charlemagne, battle 85; Christian Basques, connection (question) 85; Crusader notion 49; Egyptian Fatimid territory 87; evilness, perception 68; fanatical hatred 112; fight 94; Franks, contrast 77; Franks, family ties 65; history 50; name, interpretation (occurrence) 51–52; non-Greek-speaking "Barbarians" 51–52; princes, Seljuk Turkish emirs (relationship) 91; psychological repository 121; rule 103; struggle 130; vile race, perception 68; word, usage 84
Sarakenos, derivation 50

"savage" Germanic tribes, haircuts (absence) 32
"savage" tribes, migrations 29, 58
schismatics, impact 101
scholasticism, birth 161
Schwertbrüderorden (the Order of the Brothers of the Sword) 99
Scipio Aemilianus, attack 13
Second Council of Nicaea 35
Second Crusade 93; announcement 93–94; Crusader failure 99; European Christian king leadership 95; failure 119–120; kings of France/Germany, leadership 120; leadership 95; Pope Eugenius III preaching 98; success 99
Second Lateran Council, Bernard de Clairvaux attendance 95
Second Punic War 13
Second Temple, losses 49
Sefarad, vocalization 14
"Seljuk" (name, meaning) 55
Seljuk Sultanate of "Rum" 81, 136; alliance 133
Seljuk Turkish sultanate 109
Seljuk Turks 26–27; attack 74; conquest 155; title 93
semi-nomads, confederation 29
seneschal de Champagne 124
Sensodolo (Chems Eddaulah) 91
Sepharad, mystery 14–16
Septimania, Muslim armies (arrival) 39
Seventh Crusade 145, 156; King Louis IX (Saint Louis), impact 146; von Rubroeck, involvement 148
Shams al-Khilafa ("Sun of the Caliphate"), rebellion 79–80
Shari'a law, basis 111
sharqiyyin 50
Shiite Muslims, Fatimids (equivalence) 54
Shlomo ben Yitzhak (Yitzhaki) 14
Sibylla (Josselin grandchild) 97
Sicambri ("savage" tribe) 29, 33
Sicambria 33
Sicambrian Franks (name, English change) 29
Sidon, capture 88
Sidonius Apollinaris (chronicles) 29
Sinti, Nazi murders 4
sirventes far, D'un (Sirventes contra Roma) (Figueira) 138
Sixth Crusade 133–134, 138, 140; emperor, absence 142; truce 143

social forces, impact 2
Soltaniyeh (Mongol Ilkhanate capital) 10
Sovereign Military Order of the Temple of Jerusalem, founding 105
Spain: Charlemagne arrival 86; *Espamia (Aspamia) (Hispania)* 15; Muslims, Christians (attack) 161; Roman occupation 16; Umayyad conquest 53
Spanish, exonym 2–3
splitting 23–24; unconscious processes, operation 52
Stevenson, Robert Louis Balfour 24
Stevenson, William Henry 22
St. Peter's Day, Alfonsi baptism 89
Straits of Bosporus, Franks (crossing) 71
Strange Case of Dr. Jekyll and Mr. Hyde, The (Stevenson) 24
Süddeutsche Warte (Hoffmann) 105
Suevi (appellation) 20
suffragan dioceses 87
Suger, abbot and regent 97–98
Sui dynasty, reign 5
Sulayman al-Arabi of Barcelona, surrender (refusal) 86
Sulayman ibn Abd al-Malik 39; request, dismissal 40
Suleyman (Solomon) 39
Sultan Al-Kamil, attack 133
"Sultanate of Rum" 27, 54
sultans (rulers) 34
Sultan Salah ed-Din (Saladin) 113
Sunni Abbasid, contrast 54
Sunni Muslims, Shiite Fatimids (impact) 76
Sur la conquête de Constantinople (Villehardouin) 131
Swabians (Germanic tribe) 23
Syrian Greeks, Maccabean revolt 34
Syria, sultanate creation 55

Tabriz (Mongol Ilkhanate capital) 10
Tabula Peutingeriana (road map) 31
Tacitus, Cornelius 16, 19–20
tafarnaja (become Europeanized) 55
ta'ifa kingdoms 161–162
Talmud (rabbinic discussions) 50
Talmud, verses (indications) 3
Tanais River (Don River), Trojan migration 33
Tancred d'Hauteville 71, 73–74, 78, 80–82, 87; Prince of Galilee 76
Tanguts, defeat 7
Tantan, power 6

Taqi al-Din Ahmad ibn 'Ali ibn 'Abd al-Qadir ibn Muhammad al-Maqrizi 146
Tarifa 15
Tarif Abu-Zora (leader) 15
Tariq ibn Ziyyad: death 15, 38; fortunes 40; prison 39
Tarsus, Guillaume de Nevers escape 81
Tartares (designation corruption) 11
Tartarus (underworld), evocation 11
Tasso, Torquato 77
Tatari (invaders), Russian identification 7
Taurus Mountains 80
tawa'if (ta'ifa) (Muslim state/principality/emirate) 53
Tempelkirche (Temple Church) *(Deutscher Tempel) (Jerusalemsfreunde)* (Friends of Jerusalem), organization 105
Templars 103
Templars, internment 105
Temple of Solomon 76
Templier de Tyr (Templar of Tyre) 152
temporal domains, archbishop rule 70
Temüjin Chinggis Khan, leadership 148
Temüjin Khan, Mongol/Turkic tribes (unification) 7
Terman, David M. 4
Teutates (Celtic god) 18
Teutones (teutsch) 17
Teutones, defeat 18
Teutonic gods, temples (construction) 5
Teutonic Knights: Baltic Crusade 84; description 163; Grand Master, Crusade involvement 143; post-traumatic stress disorder 155
Teutonic Order 143
teutsch (endonym) 20
Teutsch-Land (endonym) 19
Theobaldo Cardinal Visconti 166
theodisk (Old German word) 17–18
Theodore Komnenos Doukas 135
Theodoros Sophianos, amity bond 112
Theophanes the Confessor 35
Theophylact Simocatta (historian) 22
Theophylaktos Simokattes (chronicler) 21–22
Theresa de León, Henry of Burgundy marriage 94
Thervingi (forest people) 22
Thibault of Champagne, Count 124
Third Crusade 46, 118; cessation 121; Heinrich representatives, impact 120; initiation 120; Pope Gregory call 119;

potency, diminishment 117; psycho-geographical fantasy 121
Third Punic War 13
Thom, Gerard (Hospitaller order, founding) 104
Thoros (Theodoros), son/heir adoption 74
Thracian *Getae, Gothi* (confusion) 22–23
Tiberias, vocalizers 14
Tiepolo, Lorenzi 167
Tiepolo, Nicolò 167
time: collapse (telescoping) 1; expansion 1
Tokuz-Oghuz group, clan confederacies 58
Tom, Gerard 104
Töregene Khatun, Regent of the Mongol Empire 148
Torre-Analuz (town) 16
Toulouse, Raymond de *see* Raymond of Toulouse
Tours-Poitiers. *see* battle of Tours-Poitiers
Toutatis (Celtic god) 18
"Tower of David" (Jerusalem) 78
Tractate *Nidah* 15
Trail of Tears 157
Transdanubian region, Gottschalk ravage 69
translatio imperii (transfer of the empire) 35
translation imperii (fantasy) 160
Transoxiana: Oghuz Turks migration 26; power expansion 58–59
trauma: modern notion 158–159; psychic trauma 159; psychological insights 158
Treadgold, Warren 122
Treaty of Saint-Clair-sur-Epte (911) 45–46
Trebia (battle) 13
Trembinski, Donna 158–159
Tripoli, fall 167
Troyes. Council of, Bernard attention 94
Troyes, Chrestien de 42
True Cross (Jesus Christ) 137
"True Cross" 115
True Cross, relic 116, 156
Tsar Kaloyan (Good John) 130; battles 131
Tuisco (earth-born god) 20
Tuisto (Celtic god) 18
Tungusic (language), link 6
Tunis, attack (cessation) 152
Turbessel, Josselin escape 96
Turkic Ghaznavids, Persianization 58
Turkic (language), link 6
Turkish Cypriots 26
Turkmens 26

Turkoman dynasty, Danishmends battle 95
Tyerman, Christopher 63–65
Tyr, Guillaume de (William of Tyre) 76, 80, 114; patriarch prevention 97
Tyre (purple cloth) 12

Ugarit (Ras Shamra), clay tablets (discovery) 12
Ulaanbaatar (Mongol capital) 11
Ulug Ulus (Golden Horde) (Great State) 8–11
Ulus Juchi (Batu Khan creation) 10
Umayyad Caliphate of Córdoba, collapse 53
Umayyads: caliphates, contrast 54; Damascus location 53
ummah (nation)
unconscious psychological processes (splitting/projection) 23–24
Untermenschen (subhuman) 4
Urban II, Pope (inflammatory speeches) 157
Urbanus II, Pope (Otho de Lagery) 65; church council 66; Crusade call, response 68; Gregory successor 63; indulgence, receiving 66
Usamah ibn Munqidh 109
Us and Them paradigm 24
Uyghurs, impact 6–7

vandal, barbarian (comparison) 23
Vandalicia (Arabic name corruption) 15
Vandalii (appellation) 20
Vandals 129; Germanic tribe, presence 23
van Rubroeck, Willem (William of Rubruck) 148
vásus (Sanskrit) 22
Vermandois, Adélaïde de 163
Vermandois, Henri de 163
Vermandois, Hugues de 159; Papal Banner 70–71
Vesi (good/noble people) 22
village liberation, destruction 2
Villaret, Guillaume de 168
Villehardouin, Geoffroy de 130; death 124
violent oppression, perpetrators 158
Virgil. *see* Publius Vergilius Maro
Virgin Mary: hymn 138; intercessor 94; miracles/visions/apparitions 164; myth 56
Visconti, Bernabò (Crusade) 88
Visigothi, invention 22
Visigoths: rule 15; tribe, presence 23

Vita Karoli Magni (Einhard) 84
Volga-Kama Bulgaria (Volga Bulgar Emirate) 7
Volkan, Vamik 157
Volkan, Vamik Djemal 1
Voltaire 35
von Braunschweig, Otto 122
von Freising, Otto 42
von Hohenstaufen, Friedrich 137, 140
von Jeroschin, Nicolaus 164
von Krosigk, Conrad 124
von Leiningen, Emich 69
von Pairis, Günther *see* Gunther of Pairis
von Rheinfelden, Rudolf (anti-king): election 60–61; murder 62
von Salza, Hermann 143
von Schwaben, Philip 122
Vryonis, Speridon "Speros" 129
"Vulgar Latin" dialects 47–48
Vulgar Latin dialects, speech 37
"Vulgar" vernaculars, usage (absence) 68

Waller, James 2
war, cause/encouragement 2
warfare: human warfare, existence 1; understanding, multidisciplinary approach 1–2
"War of the Sicilian Vespers" 166, 167
War on Terror 108
Waus, Godefroi de 153
Welf, Count (Hwelf of Metz), dynasty founding 40–41
Wendish Crusade *(Wendenkreuzzug)* 99, 160; authorization 98; German involvement 84
Wesi (good/noble people) 22
Western Anatolia, Lydian language 14
Western knights/soldiers (laboring), strategic reason (absence) 64

Western Roman Emperor Louis II, Roman Emperor Basil I (alliance) 41
Western Roman Empire, disintegration 54
West, estrangement 129–130
West Goths, Spain rule 22
White-skinned people, superiority 26
Wifflisburg (German alternate name) 33
Willem of Holland, Count: Crusade exit 137; Damietta attack 136
Willem of Holland (William the Crazy), impact 135–136
William the Conqueror (1027–1087) 46
Wisi (good/noble people) 22

xenophobia, cause/encouragement 345782
XII Panegyrici Latini (panegyric orations) 29
Xiongnu, decline 6

Yaghi-Siyan: death 71–72; escape 72; *Palatium Cassani* 73
Yamato-jidai (Hinomoto) (Source of the Sun) 55
Yamkhad (Amorite kingdom city) 12
Yaranqash, arrest 96
Yerushalmi, Yosef Hayimi 15
Yeshua of Nazareth, existence 56
yishuv (colonization) 171
York Rite of Freemasonry 105

Zara (Zadar), attack 124–126
Zaragoza, siege 86
Zarephath 15
Zengi, Atabeg: assassination 96; invasion/capture 96; Second Crusade failure 119–120
Zosimus (chronicles) 29

For Product Safety Concerns and Information please contact our EU
representative GPSR@taylorandfrancis.com
Taylor & Francis Verlag GmbH, Kaufingerstraße 24, 80331 München, Germany